Cruising Authority

Cruise Ship Reviews & Cruising Adventures,
Forecasts and Tips for Getting the Best Cruise Deals

Cruising Authority

Cruise Ship Reviews & Cruising Adventures, Forecasts and Tips for Getting the Best Cruise Deals

Barry M. Vaudrin

WITH A FORWARD BY
BRUCE NIERENBERG

BMV Publishing
2017

CRUISING authority

A CRUISING AUTHORITY BOOK
PUBLISHED BY BMV PUBLISHING

Copyright © 2017 by Barry M.Vaudrin

ISBN 978-0-578-19788-3

First Printing 2016
BMV Publishing (Self published)
To reach the author and publisher visit www.cruisetalkshow.com
Ordering information:
This book is printed by Lulu at www.lulu.com Visit their website and
search for the title of this book to make your order.

Foreward by Bruce Nierenberg

Cruising has become a mainstream vacation choice for the entire travel industry. From mass market products featuring ships that hold up to 5000+ passengers with all the bells and whistles today's technology can provide to expedition vessels holding less than 100 passengers traveling to the 4 corners of the world's oceans visiting places like Antarctica and the Amazon rivers of Peru and Brazil. Whether your thrill is seeing icebergs and penguins or rare birds and Piranhas in the Amazon or just an uninhabited, unspoiled island in the Caribbean, cruising offers a great way to see all the wonders of the world at a great value as well as in a safe and convenient environment. Only a handful of people had ever taken a cruise when I got into the business in 1973. Today that number has grown to millions a year, all over the world, and from all geographies. I have been blessed to be a part of the birth of this industry and watch it unfold right before my eyes.

Books like Barry Vaudrin has written can share with you his unique experiences as a member of the cruise industry for many years and add sage advice as to how to choose cruise vacations that are right for the individual traveler. I have known Barry for many years and I am sure you will enjoy following his personal travels and experiences and appreciate his advice on how to best have the cruise experience take you to your personal destinations that fit your lifestyle.

Bruce Nierenberg's Background and Experience

Bruce Nierenberg started his tourism career in the Airline industry in 1967 and brings over forty years' experience in the areas of cruise line and ferry company management, hotels and resorts, destination development, passenger shipping product development, and airline service. He has been a senior executive or owner of cruise line and ferry operations since 1974 and has been responsible for some of the most significant new product development in the cruise industry.

President & CEO of the Delta Queen Steamboat Company
President & CEO of Costa Cruise Lines
Founder and managing partner of Premier Cruise Lines ("The Big Red Boats")
CEO of Scandinavian World Cruises
Executive VP. Norwegian Caribbean Cruise lines and Norwegian Cruises

4

Preface

This is my third book. The first is called **Titanic Decision** and the second book is called **Cruise With A Purpose**. The first two books were very niche-oriented and were written for a very specific demographic, however; Cruising Authority is the culmination of eight years immersed in the podcasting and journalistic work with the talk show at my multi-media business called Cruising Authority. I can also say that this book has thirty years of experience with the cruise industry, which started when I opened a cruise-only travel business from my dorm room in college in 1985. At that time I started a business called the International Cruise Ship Connection, which later, in 1994, evolved into Global Cruise Centers. I sold thousands of cruises and made some money with Global Cruise Centers, but in 2007 I officially threw in the towel and closed down the business and instead went into the podcasting business with Cruising Authority. I was a one-man-show with Global Cruise Centers and found it difficult to compete with all the online mega agencies. This book, Cruising Authority, is designed to benefit anyone planning to book a cruise with all the valuable tips and advice from an Elite Cruise Counsellor – qualified expert in the cruise industry. Readers will also enjoy the stories included in these pages. Some of these stories have never been published or even talked about until now. Read how the author of this book once was a stow away on a cruise ship in 1984, or how the Author experienced first-hand the epic account of when the QE2 ran aground off of Martha's Vineyard. Now that QE2 is rotting away in Dubai, the exclusive story can be told about the grounding as experienced through the eyes and ears of the author of this book. In addition to the cruise tips and advice on getting the best deals on a cruise, read the cruise reviews of some of the most interesting cruise ships in the market today. Live vicariously through the author as he embarks on an exquisite Atlantic crossing aboard the Queen Mary 2, or learn about the very unique journeys available in Sweden aboard the Diana with Gota Kanal Steam Ship Company, one of the oldest vessels still in service today. There's something for everyone in this book. Read about the adventures of a Cruise Journalist as he travels the world's oceans and rivers. Discover what it must have been like to work onboard the cruise ships. Savor the intricacies of life at sea and the fascinating journey of the author as he fulfills his lifelong dreams and aspirations.

Best of all is the cruise advice and some projections of the cruise industry! There are also some great videos of the many cruise adventures in this book that can be found at the Cruising Authority website which is: www.cruisetalkshow.com   See for yourself the videos from a Queen Mary 2 trans-Atlantic crossing, several Alaska cruises, cruises to the Caribbean, river cruises, luxury cruises, and other very unique cruises around the world.

I'd like to offer a special note to Fox News and the morning show where "mornings are better with friends", as the author of this book and an expert in the cruise industry, it would be my sincere privilege to sit with the morning crew on the curvy couch to talk about cruises and this book. Of course I would also feel privileged to be a guest on any of the morning news shows, either local or national to talk cruises.

Acknowledgements & Thanks

I'd like to thank my wife Terri and my son Jacob as well as my entire family including my mother and father, for putting up with my continual dedication to pursuing my dreams and passion for the cruise industry. As a writer and a Cruise Journalist sometimes I have had to make sacrifices which caused us to struggle financially, and that has been frustrating to my immediate and extended family as well as myself. I have continued to reach for my dreams and have tried to orchestrate my career so that I can afford to comfortably support my family…this is my ultimate goal, to effectively support my family financially, provide for the needs of my wife and my son Jacob. I have been blessed to have had numerous opportunities to travel the world and take my family on exciting trips. A cyclical pattern has been that of feast or famine….the famine of which has not been pleasant, so as I strive to press forward, my goal is to minimize the famine element. I also want to express the commitment I have to my faith in Jesus Christ…a decision I made many years ago. I know that through the good times and through the valleys, Jesus has been there for me and I don't want to take that for granted. This is my third book, and as with my other written material, I pour myself into what I write. My previous books were very niche-oriented, while this book is written to appeal to nearly everyone and will have a broader audience. With this book I'm thrilled to be able to share some of my adventures and offer many years of knowledge and experience when it comes to tips and suggestions on how to cruise like a professional.

In Memory of Mr. John Maxtone-Graham

My passion for the trans-Atlantic era was enhanced by the books written by John Maxtone-Graham like "The Only Way To Cross", and "Liners To The Sun", and "Crossing and Cruising", among many others. I loved his books and his writing style. John was among the first big interviews I conducted for my podcast, Cruising Authority, and that interview catapulted my talkshow into the forefront of popular podcast culture within the cruise industry. John Maxtone-Graham was always incredibly gracious as to even invite me into his home in New York to interview him on video. Visiting John and Mary's home was like going to ocean liner Mecca with so many fabulous collectible items from the liners and cruise ships. John said he simply couldn't accept anymore ocean liner gifts from people and collectors around the world, because there simply was no more room in his home to display anymore items. I visited the home of Mary and John Maxtone-Graham twice, and both times I was so honored that he would give me the time to speak with him and interview him. This past year, 2015, we lost a great maritime author and historian and a regular speaker on cruise ships, John Maxtone-Graham, at the age of 85, to respiratory failure. My sincere condolence to his wife Mary and his children.

Table of Contents

Introduction to Cruise Stories

The cruise vacation industry has grown from it's infancy in the 70's, and has matured to the point where cruise lines have amassed fleets of giant vessels far beyond what anyone from the 70's could have imagined. When Norwegian Cruise Lines introduced the SS Norway, at roughly 70,000 tons in 1980, many cruise industry executives thought the ship was too big, but the SS Norway proved everyone wrong, thus was the beginning of the mega ships. Today, with ships like the Oasis of the Seas at 240,000 tons, I wonder if the size of cruise ships have reached a peak. Time will tell, but I am not as optimistic as many of my colleagues. I think, in America, we have just begun to see very challenging economic times where Americans will begin to rethink what they do during their vacations. If you've always wanted to take that cruise vacation, now is the time, before the economy takes a nosedive. I will also try and present a plan for those considering a cruise, and how to get the best deals during these tough times. Yes, I think we are heading towards more challenging economic times, however, I don't want this book to be about gloom and doom, rather I'd like to offer hope, and encouragement.

This book is very personal because through these words I hope to pour my life-long passion into these pages. How is it that a kid from the Midwest can become fascinated with ocean liners and cruise ships? I think my story is unique, and this journey I have taken since I first set foot onboard the Queen Mary in Long Beach in 1977, to when I lived out most of my wildest dreams and aspirations of crossing the Atlantic by ocean liner, and even working on the cruise ships; you are about to take this journey with me through the pages of this book. I hope to pass on to you some interesting stories, and take you with me on some of my adventures on cruise ships. I also hope to offer valuable tips, and commentary on how to save money the next time you plan a cruise vacation, and how to maximize your cruise experience by the years of knowledge gained from making over three hundred voyages. Another fascinating journey, is when I started a little podcast called Cruising Authority in 2007. This podcast blossomed into an incredible opportunity to travel the world and share many of these travels with my wife, Terri. When I worked on the ships in 1989 – 1992 there was something missing from these adventures in exotic locations throughout the Caribbean, and that one missing element was a traveling companion to share these experiences with. It is truly wonderful and rewarding to bring my wife into my most captivating dreams and aspirations. Cruising Authority has grown from a simple podcast with various interviews conducted over the phone with interesting guests, to producing videos and multi-media content. As I have dreamed over the years about how far I can go with my ideas for Cruising Authority, there is still exciting room for continued growth and expansion. Someone once said to me "Reach for your Dreams – Aim High", these words were told to me by astronaut James Irwin, who was one of only twelve men to walk on the Moon.

Another gleam of advice was from Evangelist Lowell Lundstrom, when he said; "If your dream isn't big enough to scare you, then dream bigger". I hope my story in the pages of this book will encourage you, give you some nuggets of information that will be helpful to you, maybe inspire you and even make you laugh. I don't know many people who have had lofty dreams and made those dreams a reality. It's not my desire to put myself on a pedestal for making my dreams come true, rather, I hope to say, it's possible! Through determination, and a no-quitting attitude, I reached for my dreams and now you get to read about the many fun and adventurous experiences I've had over the years. It is my sincere desire for people all around the world to read this book before, during or after their cruise. Maybe one day as I'm strolling on deck, I'll see a cruise passenger leisurely resting on a deck chair with this book in their hands.

Through Cruising Authority, you may soon be able to turn on the television and see a cruise-related documentary directed by Barry Vaudrin. I hope to make this a reality soon, within the next couple of years. I've also been working on a concept for The Cruise Channel, where historical programs about ocean liners of the past and cruise ships today will be available for people to watch as a cable television station.

I still recall the early years of this passion I have for ocean liners. It began in 1977 when I was about 13 years old after our family visited the Queen Mary in Long Beach, California. While other boys were fascinated with cars, sports, airplanes, at age 15 I was passionate about ocean liners and read everything I could about the trans-Atlantic era. The Queen Mary was the focal point of my obsession, but soon I discovered other ships that were equally fascinating, like the SS United States. From what I read the ss United States, at the time, was still laid-up (mothballed) in Norfolk, Virginia. I wrote a letter to Newport News Shipbuilders to inquire about the SS United States and they responded by saying the ship was recently purchased by a Seattle-based investor, Richard Hadley. So I wrote to Richard Hadley and received a letter back from a woman (Maureen) who was involved with the project to return the ship to service as a cruise ship plying the Hawaiian Islands. I began corresponding with Maureen at United States Cruises and one day received an astounding invitation. My family and me were invited to Norfolk, Virginia to be personally escorted aboard the SS United States for a grand all-day tour of this amazing superliner.

Maureen, from United States Cruises, worked directly with prospective interior designers, and it was during this special visit to the SS United States, that a small group of people from the office in Seattle and a few potential designers, as well as my family, spent nearly the entire day aboard the ship exploring every nook & cranny. It was a hot day in August of 1979 that we explored the SS United States. The ship was like a time capsule, as if the crew and passengers just abandoned ship one day in 1969. All of this grand ship's original fixtures, furniture, décor was in-tact and it seemed like a few days of cleaning and she would be ready to sail. The giant propeller shaft was still greased, the piano in the First-Class lounge was still

somewhat in-tune. There were forks, knives, and spoons in the waiter's stations, the beds just needed some fresh linen, the indoor pool could have been filled with water, and I think if we added some eager passengers we could have a voyage. Her interiors were amazingly preserved from her fifties look and feel, but the exterior of the ship was another story. The proud super liner SS United States needed to have the flaking, peeling paint on her hull removed, and with a bit of sandblasting, some primer and a fresh paint-job, her powerful engines fired-up, the grand liner would be ready to take-on the Atlantic again.

I recall that moment when I had my first glimpse of the liner from the entrance to the shipyard…I could see those massive funnels with faded red paint and the faded blue top. It really is an amazing experience to see first-hand such a historical vessel after having read about the ship and studied many black & white photos…the reality of the ship as it loomed before me was surreal. Her funnels really were massive, and even resting still against the pier she looked super powerful. Still-camera's loaded with film, and 8mm movie camera in-hand, we were ready to board the ship and see all the wonders the SS United States had to reveal. Since 1969 the Big U had been docked here at this lonely pier with only a few security staff to guard access to the ship. The security guard looked at us as if we were VIPs, because for 10 years very few people were allowed access to the ship, so we felt privileged and honored to walk across the gangway and board the SS United States. Even my family, my mom & dad and younger brother, who are not ocean liner enthusiasts, felt that this was a very special opportunity, and I believe they were fascinated and honored to explore the ship. At the time I was not as learned about the details of the SS United States as I was of the Queen Mary. I knew she held the Blue Ribbon for the fastest trans-Atlantic crossing of three days, ten hours and forty minutes, and that she was 990 feet long with a 105 foot beam. I knew some of the statistics about her power-plant and the fact that she was designed by William Francis Gibbs. I remembered that there was no wood aboard the ship except for the butcher's block, pianos and the bilge keels. I guess I knew more about the ship than the average person on the street, but wasn't very familiar with her interior layout or the lounges. At 14 years old, I was soaking it all in as we toured every lounge and even explored the crew areas.

After our visit aboard the ship our group met at a restaurant for dinner where we had a surprise guest join us…his name was Nicholas Bachko and he was the Supervisor of Construction during the time when the SS United States was built in 1950. Mr Bachko was on the design team and worked closely with Gibbs during the ships construction. Interestingly enough, Mr. Bachko spent most of his time talking with me and discussing details of the ship's unique design features. We talked about where stabilizers would be added when the ship was restored to service as a cruise ship. I surprised Mr. Bachko with my knowledge of the ship at the ripe age of only 15 years…so much so that he stayed in-touch with me over the years and he even sent me some great collectibles from the ship. Mr Bachko was on the ship during her amazing trials before she was handed over from the shipyard to United States Lines, and he revealed to me that the Big U managed an incredible top speed pushing 48 knots.

One of the most intriguing facts about the SS United States was her secret engines which were the most powerful ever installed on a passenger vessel. While the Big U was in service her engines were a military secret and civilians were never allowed to see the secret engine room much less take pictures of her engineering machinery. There were few photos of her engines and boilers, and photos of her in dry dock were also kept away from the public. Her designer was very secretive about what made the SS United States so fast. It was only recently after the ship had been laid-up in mothballs that her secrets were revealed. Some of her secrets that were finally revealed include the high-pressure her boilers were able to reach, her horse power of 240,000shp was never before and never again seen on a passenger vessel, her top recorded speed on trials was over 42 knots and she sported two five-bladed propellers and two four-bladed propellers. The SS United States basically had the same powerful engines as on military vessels and non-nuclear aircraft carriers. Additionally, she could remain afloat and even powered if one of her engine rooms were breached and flooded. These are a few of the secrets that came out after the ship was retired in 1969. During our visit to the ship, I was very surprised when our

guides took us to see the engine room, and even more surprised to learn we were among the first civilians to photograph the powerplant aboard the SS United States.Seven years later I made another journey to Newport News to visit the SS United States, but this time I explored the ship alone, and much of her interior fittings had already been removed. I don't recall how I was able to arrange this visit, other than I got permission from the current owner to purchase items onboard. On this visit, there were piles of aluminum cabinets, drawers and stateroom fittings stacked-up along the pier. She still looked magnificent! On this visit to the ship in 1986, much of her furniture was gone, but the lounges and much of her décor was still in-place. Sold at auction, most of her furniture and some of her fittings were gone, there were piles of lifejackets, chairs and aluminum vases throughout the ship and in some places there were papers and debris scattered all over the floors. The messes around the ship were the result of scavengers seeking for anything of value, memorabilia, items that could be sold or saved. For me, that day, I had the ship nearly to myself, except for the security guard at the entrance to the ship. Once again I explored everywhere onboard and even went places I only wished I could have explored during my first visit in 1979. The bridge was a sad place to see, because all of her engine telegraphs, navigation equipment and wheel were removed, leaving only stumps on the flooring where they were once bolted to the deck. I managed to get up into the mast, I even walked around the top of the massive forward funnel and took some great photos! The item I wish I brought with me was a flashlight, which would have allowed me to explore some areas that had no lights. I did find some wonderful items to purchase that I treasure to this day. I have a lifejacket that says SS United States on it, a log book found on the bridge, one of those aluminum vases, and something really unique…a wooden oven scrapper. The significance of the wooden oven-scrapper comes from the fact that wood was extremely rare on this ship. Gibbs, the ships designer, was eccentric about not having ANY wood onboard his ship. One time the band leader had his wooden directing baton taken away and replaced with an aluminum version. The original coat hangers in the staterooms were made of wood to the dismay of Gibbs who angrily had them removed and replaced with aluminum ones. After Gibb's death, some of the anti-wood requirements must have been loosened a bit. For hours I wandered around the ghost ship, peering into staterooms, crew areas, storage compartments, boiler rooms and lounges.

Since my last visit to the ship in 1986, the SS United States was towed across the Atlantic to the Baltic Sea where all of her interiors were completely gutted. The ship has also changed owners a couple of times and was finally returned again to North America where she is currently tied-up at a lonely pier in Philadelphia. The current owner is Norwegian Cruise Lines, with great aspirations of one day restoring the SS United States as an American-flagged cruise ship. Her future is still uncertain, and many liner enthusiasts are convinced she will end up as scrap, as horrible as that would be. Why would that be horrible? The SS United States is a part of our maritime history. There was a time when she was the pride of all Americans. American ingenuity, talents, and creativity went into constructing a vessel that was the epitome of strength, speed, efficiency and pride. The SS United States carried famous actors, politicians, presidents, and dignitaries from around the world, as well as the common traveler. Scrap the Big U and a piece of history will be lost, but restore the vessel either as a museum or active cruise ship and further generations will be able to appreciate the heritage this vessel carries with her. Unfortunately in business, people don't care for heritage, only profit. The ss United States doesn't have nearly the efficiency or capacity of a modern cruise ship, and it would cost an astronomical amount of money to restore her to active service. She would have to be re-engined, because her fuel-oil guzzling engines are massively inefficient compared to today's modern ships, and today's cruise passengers demand balconies, which are on every new cruise ship. The fate of the SS United States is a conundrum and her future is looking bleak. Regardless of this magnificent liner's ultimate fate, I feel very fortunate to have had the opportunity to explore and photograph every nook & cranny on two occasions. Seeing this great ship first-hand has also deepened my passion and appreciation for ocean liner history.

Update: SS United States may once again go to sea as a luxury cruise ship, after being purchased by Crystal Cruises, which plans to invest $800 million into the conversion of the historic vessel. The SS United States may cruise again in 2018. The ship will be fitted with balconies, which is a necessity on modern cruise ships. *(Yet another update...this refit has been scrapped)*

Before my first assignment working on a *major* cruise ship (Summer 1984)

In the summer of 1984 after I had completed high school, and a little college, I applied for a job working on a Mississippi river cruise boat with a company called the Paddleford Packet Boat Company located in St Paul, Minnesota. I lived in Minnesota, so there were few opportunities to find a job working on boats. The boat was called the Viking Explorer and carried about forty passengers on overnight excursions from St Paul to as far south as Florida. I was hired as a crew member, and I worked on the boat for only a few days preparing the vessel for a seven-night cruise down the Mississippi. I chipped paint, cleaned the decks, but a day or so before the boat was to take on passengers, I was let go and told that I would not work out as a member of the crew. Interestingly enough I was told that I shouldn't pursue working on cruise boats, and that I wasn't cut out for that type of work. I suppose you could say that I was disappointed, but I didn't let that incident kill my dream to one day work on a cruise ship. I read somewhere that the Viking Explorer was sold in the 1990's and repositioned in Alaska.

My First Cruise Gig was the Nordic Prince (June 1989)

To give some perspective on the cruise lines and ships I worked on and the dates, the following information may be of interest. I attended college starting in 1985 through 1991, but in June 1989 I took a break from college and accepted a job as Cruise Staff with Royal Caribbean aboard the Nordic Prince, cruising from New York to Bermuda. I can't express enough how excited I was to step across the gangway and onto the Nordic Prince. I was immediately greeted by the staff who helped me with my stuff and showed me to my cabin. A member of the cruise staff, Paul, told me we were to be roommates, so he helped me with my luggage and told me to get into my uniform whites with the Royal Caribbean blue blazer. I quickly put some of my things away in the very tiny cabin, and got dressed for the departure of Nordic Prince from New York. I think I was running on adrenaline, because I was so thrilled to be there and to finally depart from New York on a cruise ship, the Nordic Prince. We departed from the same docks that the old ocean liners use to dock. While we were leaving, we gathered in one of the lounges for the weekly meeting with the Cruise Director. I did get to go out on deck after the meeting to see the Nordic Prince pass the Statue of Liberty and go under the Verrazano Bridge. My first cruise contract was finally happening and I couldn't wait to get to Bermuda because I had never been there. We spent a couple days at sea enroute to Bermuda, and I must say it was a thrill to be cruising in the Atlantic. The little Nordic Prince was a fine ship, and one thing I had to get use to was the movement, as we cruised the Atlantic Ocean. Nordic Prince pitched and swayed a bit, and as some passengers got a little seasick, I was thoroughly enjoying the movement. It was especially pleasant sleeping at night to the sway of the ship, and watching the reflections dance on my ceiling… reflections from the ocean just outside my porthole. We docked right down town Bermuda for three days! During this time in port I was given the job of escorting a group of passengers to a show one evening. It was on-the-job training for me as I also met with the Cruise Director to let him know what kind of magic I had to perform during the crew show. I also learned a few dance moves and was immediately put in one of the crew skits as Sergeant Major in the popular skit, "If I were Not Upon The Seas". I had to quickly learn the ropes as a member of the Cruise Staff, which was pretty demanding but fun. One day at sea, I was told to make my way to the Crew Purser to get paid, and received my first payday. I couldn't believe I was actually getting paid for this! My first pay was $225 in cash, which was only a few days into my first contract.

Second Contract was on the Song of America
(July – November 1989)

I worked on the Nordic Prince for a few weeks then I was told I will be transferred to a different ship in early July. A past staff member was returning from vacation, so I was transferred to the Song of America, where I would remain for the duration of my contract which was about six months. The itinerary of the Song of America was the Western Caribbean, which I had an absolute blast getting to know these Caribbean ports of Jamaica, Grand Cayman, Cozumel and Labadee. I enjoyed the staff I worked with as well, and truly enjoyed working on the Song of America, which was a prototype to a new class of cruise ship for Royal Caribbean, that lead to the design of the Sovereign of the Seas. The basic concept was to have the majority of staterooms forward and the lounges and dining rooms were midship to aft. In the months I worked on the Song of America, I learned a lot about the politics onboard and gained a more in-depth understanding of the lifestyle onboard as a member of the Cruise Staff. This contract was a great opportunity for me to polish my magic act, in fact, while working this contract I ordered a new illusion from Abbott's Magic Catalogue, a levitation that became my trademark. It was so fun to perform in the Can Can Lounge several times a week to a great audience! When you're a performer on a cruise ship you become famous to all the passengers who get to know you by name and compliment you on your performances in the corridors and on deck. I have fond memories of shipboard romances, exciting adventures in the ports and fine-tuning my magic act. One of my favorite excursions on this itinerary was the trip to Tulum to see the ancient Mayan Ruins, and to swim in XelHa. I would usually volunteer to escort about two hundred

passengers a week on the Tulum tour, so I had plenty of times to explore the ruins and swim at the incredible waters of XelHa, and it was a bit of a much-needed break from life on the Song of America. Some other adventures I had were to rent horses in Ocho Rios, Jamaica and ride on the beaches.

Third & Fourth Contract MV Empress & Pacific Star
(July – November 1991)

I had recently took a job as a Cruise Sales Agent at a travel agency in Orange County, California, and then was offered a position working on the new MV Empress as Assistant Cruise Director cruising out of La Paz, Mexico to the Mexican Riviera. The Empress was originally built as the Empress of Australia in 1964 as a car ferry and passenger ship. While working for Starlite Cruises, I started working on the Empress in the Mexican Riviera, and at the end of my contract I also worked briefly on the Pacific Star which did day cruises from San Diego to Ensenada, Mexico. It was on the Pacific Star that I was the relief Cruise Director, which I enjoyed immensely. Back on the Empress, however; I spent a few months as Assistant Cruise Director and Shore Excursions Manager. My primary role was as Assistant Cruise Director. I enjoyed the Mexican Riviera because this was the itinerary that The Love Boat did each week. It was great to see the ports of Acapulco, Mazatlan, Puerto Vallarta, Manzanillo, and Cabo San lucas. I had many adventures when I signed-on to the MV Empress, and I was taking a position with a cruise line that was brand new, so few people even knew about Starlite Cruises. The Cruise Director's name was Franco, a high-tempered, emotionally passionate man from Cuba. This passion, however; was volatile, and on more than one occasion, I was worried he was going to jump off the stage and pick a fight with me, which nearly happened on one sail away party. Here's what happened...we were having a dance party where passengers dancing on the dance floor were

eliminated if the music stopped and they didn't have a partner. It was a lite-hearted, fun game, however; the MV Empress was a small ship and would often react to the ocean swells, pitching from bow to stern and rolling from side to side. Franco was on the stage hosting the party and the dance game. His instructions for the staff which included me, was to keep the passengers in the center of the dance floor...a tough challenge considering the ship's swaying side to side, as you can imagine the passengers couldn't stay in the middle of the dance floor if they tried. Franco glared at me with his angry eyes and motioned for me to keep the passengers in the middle of the dance floor,

and I simply shrugged my shoulders, because there was literally no way I could enforce his demand. With rage in his eyes, Franco jumped off the stage and started to come my way right through the middle of the dancing passengers, and started yelling and swearing at me for not keeping the passengers under control. I don't recall what stopped him, but he did not reach me, and I think he realized what he was doing and changed his behavior. Franco was also the type of person that created tension and division among the different departments onboard, for example, the Hotel / Purser department, and the Food & Beverage department had many issues with the Entertainment department, mostly because of the Cruise Director. The MV Empress hosted many travel agents from southern California, and I am convinced that the tension and frustration with the many departments onboard, created an atmosphere that was not happy, and that translated to the passengers. The Empress quickly developed a reputation among the travel agent community, of being an undesirable and unhappy ship. It really is amazing how important a happy staff on a cruise ship can make or break the overall passenger experience. You can have great hardware, a cruise ship with great amenities, etc. and if the crew are poorly trained, not happy, or they do not provide a happy environment, that can be reflected in unhappy passengers who may never book with that cruise line again. Eventually, Franco was fired because he was trying to lure an underage female to his cabin, which resulted in a serious situation. After Franco departed the ship, immediately there was a wave of relief among the entire crew onboard the MV Empress, however; the damage to the ship's reputation was done and irreversible, bookings dropped and the ship was eventually removed from the Mexican Riviera and leased to a company in Singapore that offered a casino cruise experience. When the Empress was removed from service in the Mexican Riviera, I was temporarily place on the Pacific Star, which did day cruises out of San Diego to Ensenada, Mexico. It was during this time I was Cruise Director, while the full-time Cruise Director had some time off. The day cruises on the Pacific Star had a very unique passenger demographic which was not the most favorable to entertainers, because more often than not, a majority of passengers would get so drunk they would sometimes throw food and trash at the performers.

This particular demographic of passengers might not typically be seen on mainstream cruise lines for the three or four night market, these were party animals.

I had many wonderful experiences on the MV Empress, particularly in the ports like Cabo San Lucas, Puerto Vallarta, Mazatlan, Manzanillo and Acapulco. One of the perks working as Shore Excursions Manager, I was able to benefit from extra income through under-the-table cash from some of the specific shops in the ports that we would send passengers to each week. It was almost like a little side business, the way it was many years ago with Cruise Directors before the cruise lines started to regulate all revenue-producing options. One of my favorite excursions in Puerto Vallarta was a visit to Chico's Paradise up in the jungle. I would often bring friends with me on the hour-long drive up to Chico's Paradise and we would have lunch there, and then maybe rent a couple horses for a ride into the jungle. There's some interesting terrain up there where the river runs through the little village. I had fun with an old wooden bridge that allowed us to cross over to a huge rock island. Years ago, that old bridge had no hand rails, and it was very primitive, however; today there are hand rails for protection and the bridge was modified and modernized. Chico's Paradise is still a great place to visit, so I recommend taking that trip and consider it an adventure. Manzanillo was an interesting port where our ship docked in a very industrial area, which seemed like an oil refinery. The place to visit in this port was Las Hadas that was very similar to a resort you might find in Santorini, Greece with it's white buildings and amazing beach-front vistas. The movie "10" was filmed at this resort, starring Bo Derek and Dudley Moore, with Bo Derek famously running along the beach in slow motion with her hair in braids. In Acapulco, the tourist place to visit was the cliff divers, which was always very exciting. I recall organizing a very elaborate first date with a young woman who worked on the MV Empress as a bar waitress. I told the Captain that I had a date and he purposely took the Empress into port a little quicker than usual, so I would have more time to get all the passengers off the ship and away on their tours and excursions, so I could take this young woman on a date. I arranged for a limo to take us to the cliff divers, then off to a restaurant perched high up on a hill with a spectacular view of the Acapulco bay. This was supposed to be the best restaurant in all of Acapulco. My date and I had a wonderful dinner, then the limo driver took us to the entrance to the beach, so I could have a romantic walk with my date along the beach with a full moon and our ship glistening off in the distance. It truly was one of the most story-book-like perfectly romantic dates I had ever been on up until that time. In Mazatlan, I enjoyed riding the open-air cabs called Pulmonias, that were similar to a golf cart that was reasonably priced. The fresh fish restaurants right on the beach in the Golden Zone was a favorite place to eat. Finally, Cabo San Lucas had an extraordinary beach called "Lover's Beach" that was mostly accessed by boat, however; if you were truly adventurous, you could climb around the rocks on the Pacific-side and find your way to "Lover's Beach". It is near "Lover's Beach" where the famous rock Arch of Cabo San Lucas is located. This famous El Arco, is at the very tip of the Baja Peninsula, where the Pacific Ocean and the Baja Gulf meet.

I truly enjoyed my contract working on the MV Empress, especially after Franco was fired, because the work atmosphere was so much more enjoyable after he was gone. Unfortunately the damage was already done to the ship's reputation, and she was sent off to Singapore to work as a casino ship. The MV Empress was renamed Royal Pacific, and one night she was hit by a fishing trawler and sank within about 15 minutes. When the Empress ceased operation to the Mexican Riviera and sent to Singapore, I was eventually laid-off.

Fifth Contract MV Zenith (March – June 1992)

I had some time unemployed, if I can recall, I did some work on the side as a portrait photographer in southern California. I wanted to get another gig on a cruise ship again, so I put out my resume and an updated video showing me as a Cruise Director doing my thing on stage. I was hired by Celebrity Cruises to work on a brand new ship that was still in the shipyard in Germany. I was so excited when I got my sign-on info and airline ticket to Germany to meet up with the MV Zenith in Emden, Germany. The Zenith was the second ship constructed with that particular Horizon design. The Horizon was the first sister ship in the two-ship series. Both the Horizon and the Zenith were very similar, with a very modern design. I was impressed with the Zenith and her structural design and solid construction. Germany makes great cars and now, I'm convinced they make great ships too. There was also a vast difference in how this ship was run by it's Greek captain. When I worked on the Empress with the Greek captain and crew, I was not impressed with the seemingly sloppy seamanship. The Greek officers on the Empress would talk big, but I was not impressed with some of their attitudes, where they put-off this impression that they were the greatest sailors in the world, and God's gift to women. It must be a cultural issue, but one experience left me questioning this Greek culture when the captain would grab the rear-end of our ship's Hostess even while she stood next to her husband. What do you do, as a female Hostess, when the man with the most authority on the ship grabs her rear? It boggled my mind the arrogance of this man to do such a thing. Well, getting back to the Zenith, I was very impressed with the Captain of the Zenith....he ran a tight ship. The entire Cruise Staff had to stand in line at attention, while the Captain did an inspection of the uniforms, I had never seen this done before. Actually, I saw pictures of captains and Pursers in the old days of the trans-Atlantic liners do inspections like this, so I had a great appreciation for the Captain of the Zenith who seemed to command perfection.

Having been a Cruise Director, Assistant Cruise Director, and Shore Excursions Manager, I was hired aboard the Zenith as Entertainment Staff with the understanding that I could quickly be promoted to Assistant Cruise Director and even Cruise Director, however; I was new to Celebrity Cruises, and treated by my fellow staff members as a complete newbie to life at sea on a cruise ship. The delivery of the Zenith was in Ft Lauderdale, yet in Southampton, Boston, Philadelphia, New York and Cape Canaveral, Zenith

made stops to introduce travel agents and the media to the new ship. We had a very interesting experience in Philadelphia, a story worth telling. Nearly the entire Entertainment Staff went into the city for dinner at a restaurant / bar. The staff was having a wonderful time and there may have been a few too many drinks by some of the staff. I noticed it was getting late and we should return to the Zenith. I had no money on me and was dependent on my fellow staff members to help pay for taxi transportation back to the ship. I was not a drinker, so I had no alcohol, and I was getting worried about getting to the ship in time. I made several statements suggesting we get a cab and get back to the ship, but I was scoffed at and teased for being a prude. The scheduled departure for the Zenith was 10:00pm and it was only about 8:30pm. I was told to

relax, and that I didn't know what I was talking about, since we had the Assistant Cruise Director with us and he knew what he was doing, and he was in charge. Finally, after a few more drinks, we all departed in taxi cabs back to the ship. We arrived at the Zenith at about 9:00pm, just as the lines were dropped and the ship was already underway. We all watched in horror that the Zenith was leaving without us; next stop was New York. The women in our group cried and the men lit cigarettes, and all we could do was watch and wave as our ship departed without us. As the only sober one among us, I went to search for the ship's Port Agent. Whenever a ship docks in a port there is always an Agent that oversees the operation until the ship departs. I found the agent and told him of our circumstance. For some reason, the Captain of the Zenith decided to leave an hour early from Philadelphia, in actuality, we were there in time, technically; yet that was no consolation for the fact that nearly the entire Entertainment Staff was stuck in Philadelphia as our ship

disappeared into the darkness. I spoke to the Ship's Port Agent and I suggested that we meet up with the Harbor Pilot, as he leaves the ship while still underway. The Harbor Pilot is always on the Bridge of the ships to guide them out of their port, by law there must be a Harbor Pilot. The Ship's Agent was able to reach the Harbor Pilot Boat before it departed to retrieve the Harbor Pilot....so we made arrangements to ride out with the Harbor Pilot Boat to board the Zenith as the Harbor Pilot exits the Zenith. The Harbor Pilot Boat Captain radioed ahead to the Zenith and asked the Zenith's Captain if he was agreeable to allowing the Entertainment Staff to board the ship during the departure of the Harbor Pilot. The Zenith Captain was agreeable, so we all had the unique opportunity to climb the ladder that was hanging out of the ship's embarkation door, and one-by-one we climbed up into the Zenith. Interestingly enough, the entire Entertainment Staff was given a letter of reprimand for missing the ship, and we had to pay about $400 to the Harbor Pilot Boat Captain for transporting us out to the Zenith, even though he was already going there anyway. It was an adventure, that was for sure, but we were all very glad to be back onboard the Zenith where we belong.

The Zenith would alternate on an Eastern and Western Caribbean itinerary, for example, one week the ship would do an Eastern Itinerary from Ft Lauderdale, then the next week she would do a Western Caribbean itinerary. Both itineraries had their good points, yet I preferred the Western Caribbean itinerary because I enjoyed going to Tulum from Playa Del Carmen, and I enjoyed Grand Cayman. A fond memory I have of cruising the Eastern Caribbean was visiting St Thomas, where Zenith happened to be in port the same time SS Norway was anchored just outside of St Thomas. I would often jump on Little Norway 1 or Little Norway 2 and take the tender to the SS Norway for a visit. Back in 1992, security was not as tight as it is today, and they didn't have the same modern security procedures seen today where passenger and crew boarding passes are computerized. Several visits to the SS Norway, I brought friends that I worked with on the Zenith, and I gave them the tour of this fabulous ocean liner treasure. Every chance I had to visit the SS Norway, I took that opportunity, because she truly was a treasure, and I was saddened by her boiler explosion and eventual scrapping on the beach of Alang, India. It was difficult to look at the images of this great ship being taken apart piece-by-piece, because she had such an illustrious history as the SS France and again when she was reborn as the SS Norway. I was fortunate to have cruised on the SS Norway in 1990 with a buddy. I had to be very careful, however; while working on the Zenith that I didn't make too big of a deal on my time off visiting other cruise ships with other cruise lines, because some of those I worked with didn't understand my passion for the cruise industry, and they didn't understand why I would work for the Celebrity Cruises brand, and then make such efforts to visit cruise ships within a different brand like Norwegian Cruise Line, Holland America Line, Princess Cruises, and some others. I suppose as a member of the Staff on a Celebrity Cruises vessel, I should be entirely loyal to that cruise brand only. There was only one time where someone said something, because I went to look at the Song of America with Royal Caribbean in Montego Bay, Jamaica, which was a ship I worked on a few years earlier. I didn't even get to board the Song of America, I just went over to the pier to look up at the ship. This was an example where politics on the Zenith were particularly thick and uncomfortable. Even after several months of working on the Zenith, I was still considered a newbie, and I watched as a young guy among our Entertainment Staff was promoted to Assistant Cruise Director on the Horizon, even though I was more experienced and should have probably been considered for that promotion. Interestingly enough, I had heard that this young guy didn't work out too well over on the Horizon. This was a very difficult political environment to work in, on the Zenith, with the particular arrangement of Staff. Had I stuck around onboard the Zenith for a few more months, it looks like I could have seen a promotion, because I heard from my former crew mates that there was a turnaround in Staff shortly after I had left. This leads me to the next section of this chapter of where I went after I left the Zenith.

Years before I got my job on the Zenith, I had worked very hard to apply for a position with Cunard Line aboard the Queen Elizabeth 2, which was my dream to one day work on that famous ocean liner.   Finally, after many resumes sent, and many phone calls, faxes, post cards, and even an interview, I called my voice mail system back home in southern California, and heard the message that there was a position open aboard the QE2 as Stage Manager, and I was offered the position if I was available. Words can hardly describe the incredible jump for joy I experienced when I heard this voice message. I couldn't call the Cunard hiring person at that very moment after hearing the message, so I made a ship-to-shore phone call while at sea aboard the Zenith, and told the hiring Director at Cunard Line that I will accept the position.   I was told an airline ticket would be mailed to me, and sure enough I received that airline ticket which was from Miami to England, where I would meet up with QE2 in Southampton.   When I told some of my fellow Staff members that I was going to work on QE2 as Stage Manager, I think some of them were impressed; others were confused as to how I could get a gig like that. One member of our Zenith Staff, Amanda, was the ship's Hostess, and she had worked aboard the QE2 as a Dancer for I think twelve years before coming to Celebrity Cruises. When a month or so ago, that young guy was promoted to Assistant Cruise Director on the Horizon, there was a big party for him put on by the Cruise Director, with a cake and gifts, however; when I gave my notice that I was signing-off the Zenith and going to work on QE2, only my roommate, Anthony, and one other Staff buddy congratulated me, and there really was no party, a testament to the lousy politics onboard the Zenith.

Sixth Contract Queen Elizabeth 2 (June – August 1992)

It was the realization of a childhood dream to drag my steamer trunk and luggage onto the crew gangway of the QE2 in Southampton, England. It was like a I was dreaming, and I remember that day with great fondness, when I sign-on to work as Stage Manager aboard the Queen Elizabeth 2. Interestingly enough, the person who greeted me at the gangway was Andrew Graham, an Australian gentleman I worked with on my first cruise ship contract aboard the Nordic Prince. I was issued a tiny one-person passenger stateroom or cabin, then after that first week, I was given a more permanent cabin on Deck Five, which was a little bigger than the first, but not by much. I didn't care how small the cabin was, I was living and working aboard the QE2! Years ago, when I first began my interest in ocean liners, I read books like The Only Way to Cross by John Maxtone-Graham, also the Sway of the Grand Saloon, and many other book about life at sea on the trans-Atlantic liners. Back then, I couldn't possibly conceive of the possibility of working aboard the QE2 because years ago, the Entertainment Staff was mostly from England, and it was not possible for an American citizen to work aboard the QE2. Cunard Line changed owners at some point and the ship's crew and staff were opened-up to an international mix. A couple years earlier, I crossed the Atlantic aboard QE2 as a passenger from Southampton to New York after traveling around Europe on a Euro-Pass. This time I didn't have to leave the ship, I was now officially a card-carrying crewmember, and my address was the Queen Elizabeth 2. Every day was a thrill to me. I found that the politics onboard QE2 were a little less challenging than what I had experienced on the Zenith. On QE2, I was treated with respect. The only challenge was that most of the Entertainment staff had been working on the QE2 for many years, and they developed somewhat of a family environment, so I knew it would take many months and even years to truly become part of this family. I did feel like an outsider most of the time. I didn't care, however; because I was living and working aboard the famous QE2. I recall on several occasions when I was asked to run some errands, which included navigating the depths of the QE2's lower decks to retrieve champagne from the ship's store. Even a mundane task like that was a thrill. I was hired as Stage Manager, and although I didn't have the experience to operate the sound system, so I was a quick study to learn it as quickly as possible, however; I seemed just fine with mastering the electronic stage lighting system which, for the early nineties, was state-of-the-art. My main post was in the Grand Lounge where the Broadway-style production shows took place. For one of the shows, for example; here were hundreds of lighting queues with all sorts of moods and settings. All the light queues could be programed into the system, and then simply monitor it during the show just in-case some light queues were not in sync with the activity on the show floor. There were several major production shows in our singers, dancers and musicians repertoire. The QE2 orchestra was a live band that played the charts using a click-track. It was a complex set-up, which also included spotlight operators taking instructions from me via a headset. As a Stage Manager, when I wasn't running the light systems for a production show, I would be responsible for setting up microphones and sound systems in other areas of the ship, like in the Card Room where sometimes smaller classes or lecturers needed some sort of audio visual assistance. I would also be involved with setting up bingo in the Grand Lounge and other presentations that required microphones, lighting or music tracks. The QE2 Orchestra would also set up to play in the Queen's Lounge where passengers could use the dance floor with their best mamba, samba or waltz. A fascinating event to watch on QE2 was when we celebrated the 4th of July in New York harbor. Cunard pulled out all the stops and had an incredible orchestra in the Grand Lounge with a famous conductor…I forget the name, I suppose I could look it up in my daily programs that I kept. It seems like every week on QE2 there were celebrities onboard. I saw Neil Diamond, George Kennedy, The Cure, Suzanne Somers, John Maxtone-Graham, and many others. What a thrill it was to meet such fascinating people. A story I like to tell, is one day in New York, prior to a trans-Atlantic crossing, I was walking through the ship and at a bar aft, in the magradome area, I saw these guys hanging out that looked like punk rockers with makeup. I mentioned that I saw these guys to my co-worker Carlos, and he said to me, "Don't you know who that is"? I said "no". He said, "that's the CURE". I said "the cure for what?" I had no idea who The CURE was, but I guessed that my brother Paul would know who they are so I walked over to these guys and struck-up a conversation. I took a picture with them specifically for my brother, Paul, because I knew he would appreciate who these guys were. Sure enough my brother still talks about how his brother met The Cure. Every morning, I felt like I had to pinch myself to make sure I wasn't dreaming because I thoroughly enjoyed my experience on the QE2. I recall during a trans-Atlantic crossing, one time, when QE2 had a pretty strong cross-wind that caused the ship to list to port pretty heavy, so passengers and crew had to deal with walking at a serious slant for several hours before the winds finally calmed down. Seeing the QE2 in many different weather conditions was fascinating to me. One thing that I recall, after all these years, was how the QE2 had some of the same smells that some areas of the original Queen Mary has in Long Beach, California as a static hotel ship. I also noticed the creeks and growns of

QE2 as she handled different seas. QE2 was without question an ocean liner, so much different than a cruise ship. The difference could really be experienced when QE2 was at speed pounding at 30 knots across the Atlantic, you could feel the energy of QE2 during these times when she was at her cruising speed. Cruise ships just don't go that fast, so QE2 was certainly unique. I wrote a whole chapter in this book about my experience on QE2, when she ran aground in Martha's Vineyard, so don't miss that chapter.

This concludes my experiences working on the cruise ships. After my last ship contract, on QE2, I never worked on ships again as a member of the crew. People often ask me do I miss working on the ships? My answer is usually, sometimes, but now I have a family and working on the ships is not practical.

The CURE in the Queens Lounge

My experience as a business owner

Before I worked on cruise ships, and while I was in college, in 1985, I started a cruise-only retail agency called International Cruise Ship Connection, and I sold cruises from my dorm room. In 1985 there were not many "cruise-only" agencies, however; there were plenty of brick and mortar travel agencies. There was a difference between a cruise-only agency and a regular travel agency...a cruise agency exclusively sells cruises, while a travel agency sells everything from hotel rooms, airline tickets, rental cars, and resorts. The reason why so many agencies wanted to sell more cruises, was because that's where the higher commissions were. I sold a few cruises during college, but not enough to really pay the bills while in college. Over the years while I was in college, when I was working on the cruise ships, and after my last cruise contract on QE2 in 1992, I worked in a few agencies to sell cruises, but that didn't work out too well. In 1993, I finally decided to take on another cruise job working with Port Promotions International which was a business built by Porthole founder and Chief Editor Bill Panoff. I made a trip to Florida for an interview to work on a cruise ship out of Aruba as a Port Lecturer. Unfortunately, that position I was hired for, evaporated and I ended up moving back to Minneapolis. It was in Minneapolis that I took on a cruise-selling job with a Uniglobe agency. At this Uniglobe franchise agency, I developed a cruise retail concept partnering with several Uniglobe agencies in Minneapolis, similar to a consortium, called Global Cruise Centers. One thing lead to another, and I decided to pull away from Uniglobe and go into business again for myself selling cruises through Global Cruise Centers. I registered as a cruise agency back in 1985 with CLIA, Cruise Lines International Association, and had

continued registering year after year for about 17 years, so I have 17 years of CLIA badges, and I became a Master Cruise Counselor. I poured everything I had into developing the Global Cruise Centers brand. I registered the "mark" or the Global Cruise Centers name and logo with the U.S. Patent and Trademark Office. I had some high points as a business owner, particularly when I put together several large group cruise events. There was a cruise group that stood out as one of my most accomplished and successful sales experiences of my career in 1999, when I promoted a cruise event with 225 passengers on a cruise to the Western Caribbean aboard the Sea Breeze with Premier Cruises. The most rewarding elements to running a cruise agency was putting groups together, and helping people get the vacation of a lifetime. I put thousands of people on cruises and enjoyed my business, yet it became increasingly challenging to compete with several large charter companies in Minneapolis, and then after September 11th, 2001 business decreased even more. The cruise industry rebounded better than most travel companies after September 11th, 2001, because a cruise vacation was a safe vacation option. Some who planned vacations to Europe, canceled and booked cruises because it was a safer alternative. Then another game changer was the internet. As the internet grew, mega travel and cruise agencies started to establish their mark, like Travelocity, Orbitz, and some others. The last group I booked was in 2006 and shortly after that I closed Global Cruise Centers because it became too difficult for me, a one-man-show, to operate the business and compete with the internet agencies. It was shortly after my final group booking that I ceased operation, but then I was introduced to something new.

The Beginning of Cruising Authority the Talk Show

I received a call from a friend of mine in college that asked me a peculiar question....he asked me if he could interview me on his talk show. My friend, Jeff Roney, had a podcast and he seemed to think that I had an interesting life of adventures, so he wanted to talk with me about some of those adventures on his podcast. This was my first introduction to the word "podcast", so I was intrigued. I agreed to be on Jeff's podcast talk show, and enjoyed the experience. I also saw how that might be fun to put together my own talkshow and interview interesting people in the cruise industry. My first talkshow episode was September 10th, 2007 when I interviewed a friend of mine who worked on ships, Vance Snyder. Vance and I went to high school together and I helped him get a job on cruise ships in 1996, where he worked on the Big Red Boat, with Premier Cruises. I discovered that it wasn't too difficult to produce these podcasts, so I scheduled more episodes. I thought to myself, who would I want to talk to within the cruise industry? One man, author, that I admired since I was a kid was John Maxtone-Graham, so I got in-touch with him and scheduled a phone interview. This interview was a huge success, and it single-

CRUISING authority

handedly launch Cruising Authority to become a big hit with ocean liner and cruise ship fans. In 2007, there were no other cruise-related podcasts out there, so my talkshow gained momentum through cruise message boards and word of mouth. I watched as the number of clicks to listen to my show went from 10 clicks a week to over 850 clicks per week. Eventually, at it's peak in 2011, Cruising Authority featured at www.cruisetalkshow.com and also available on iTunes was getting 7,500 – 8,000 clicks per week. Each week I scheduled fascinating guests, and then in May of 2008, I produced the first "Virtual Cruise Experience" aboard the Liberty of the Seas. The Five-Episode series recorded aboard the Liberty of the Seas was immensely popular because listeners could experience vicariously, an audio cruise vacation in the form of a podcast. I interviewed the Captain, the Cruise Director, the Hotel Director, and many crew members and some passengers. What does the pool deck on a sea-day sound like? What do passengers hear in the distance while visiting Labadee? It was a virtual audio experience that no one had ever done, so it was a home-run for Cruising Authority! Interestingly enough, all of the episodes ever recorded

are still on-line and can still be heard at any time. For this cruise on the Liberty of the Seas, I went out and purchased a digital recorder so that I could conduct interviews on-the-go. I used this digital recorder until it broke during an Alaska cruise. I had to go into Juneau and find an electronics store to buy a replacement recorder. When I returned home from that Alaska cruise, my next big gig was to China, so I splurged and bought a state-of-the-art recorder called an Olympus LS10 that had two microphones on top with two black foamy things that made the device look like a mickey mouse gadget. The Olympus LS10 is like having a recording studio in my palm. Combine the Olympus LS10 with the Apple MacBookPro and the audio editing software, Logic Express, I was able to produce some pretty fancy and professional-sounding shows. This leads me to the next chapter in my gig with Cruising Authority where I became a Cruise Journalist.

The Fabulous Story and Adventures of a Cruise Journalist

My first "gig" as a Cruise Journalist was in June of 2009 on a cruise to Alaska aboard the Regent Seven Seas Mariner. April 2009, I had a special guest on my talkshow, Tim Rubacky, the Director of Corporate Communications at Prestige Cruise Holdings. We talked about Regent Seven Seas Cruises and particularly their Alaska itineraries onboard the Regent Seven Seas Mariner. He was telling me that the line was more "kid-friendly" than many people may realize. He suggested that I cruise Alaska on the ship, and so off-air, we talked about the possibility of booking passage for the upcoming Alaska cruise season and one email lead to another and my family was booked on the Regent Seven Seas Mariner for June of 2009, a few months away. The total cost was 100% covered as an industry courtesy and a trade for exposure on Cruising Authority the talkshow. The general idea is that if I cruise on the Regent Seven Seas Mariner with my family, I will report back to my audience with Cruising Authority and this will be a great PR resource for Prestige Cruise Holdings. You can read the complete overview of this cruise experience in a later chapter in this book. I was new to this experience of being offered fabulous trips that are completely complimentary. We were placed in a suite on the Seven Seas Mariner, and our entire family enjoyed the experience immensely. What's not to like? This was a five-star luxury cruise ship and all of our excursions were also complimentary which is normal for regular passengers too. I had the great opportunity to take my family on a dog sledding adventure they will never forget. We flew in a helicopter in Juneau up onto a mountain glacier and went dog sledding for about two miles. Of course the dining onboard the Seven Seas Mariner was fabulous! For my talkshow, I interviewed the Captain, the Cruise Director, and Hotel Director. I wrote an article about the cruise experience, which you'll see later in this book, and I produced video segments too. When talking with people about this experience, for example; it is customary not to brag that we got a free cruise, but it certainly is an amazing perk of being a Journalist, and many wonder how in the world can

an ordinary person receive such amazing perks. The answer is simply that as a Journalist, I have something to offer in exchange for what the cruise line gives to me, which is word-of-mouth exposure to our existing audience, and the various media I produce as a result of the cruise. Like most companies that rely on excellent public relations, and positive exposure to potential customers, sending someone with my knowledge and experience in the industry has media value, which is how they can justify the expense.

My second "gig" as a Cruise Journalist happened while I was on a cruise aboard the Norwegian Pearl where I was being presented by Cruise Holidays as the official podcast / talkshow of Cruise Holidays and the many franchise owners around the U.S. While onboard this special annual cruise event for franchise owners, there was a tradeshow put together by Cruise Holidays to present the many cruise lines that are preferred companies of Cruise Holidays. Many cruise line reps were represented from Carnival

Cruise Lines, Royal Caribbean and Viking River Cruises. While visiting the private island of Norwegian Cruise Lines, I met the Director of Sales for Viking River Cruises, Michael Wiersema, and asked him about their China Yangtze River cruises. He started to tell me how Viking River Cruises was unique and offered an excellent experience in China, and then suggested that he should send me on one of their trips on the Yantze River. The purpose for Mr. Wiersema, to send me on their Yangtze cruise was to generate exposure to our Cruising Authority audience. I took him up on his offer, and in August of 2009, my wife and I flew to China to embark on the Viking River Cruises experience on the Yangtze River. You can read the complete overview of our Yangtze River cruise aboard the Viking Century Sun. This China trip was epic in scale for us, and I came through with what I promised to Michael Wiersema to produce videos, audio podcasts, a written review and professional photography. Here's where it gets interesting. The cost of this entire trip to China was 100% covered for my wife and I basically as an industry courtesy and a trade for exposure on Cruising Authority. To acquire such lavish complimentary trips is not easy, and does require a return on investment to the cruise line, which in our case, is positive media exposure to our Cruising Authority audience. Six years later, today in 2015, I continue to receive emails from people considering a Yangtze River cruise with Viking River Cruises, and as a result of the media I produced for Cruising Authority, there have been at least ten couples that have booked a Viking River Cruise in China. Viking River Cruises certainly received a return on their investment because the media I produced resulted in numerous bookings worth tens of thousands of dollars.

As a result of the first two experiences as a Cruise Journalist, I eventually learned how to better maximize these complimentary cruise opportunities. If I were to make a living as a Cruise Journalist, I had to somehow learn to generate an income with this "gig". Sure, it's incredible to be offered fabulous complimentary trips around the world, but free trips do not pay the bills. I had to learn how to leverage these complimentary trips and cruises, and offer further exposure to other companies and various products by offering product-placement or sponsorship opportunities for cruise-related companies. I started to sell banner ads on our Cruising Authority website and produce mini-commercials of various products and services offered to the

cruise / travel consumer. I contacted cruise retailers, travel insurance companies, luggage companies, limo companies, airlines, hotels, shore excursion companies, any type of business that a cruise passenger may encounter. I started out with cruise retail agencies as sponsors and grew from there to fascinating companies that have unique cruise / travel related products. In many cases, I negotiated a trade, for example; limo companies. I have had the great privilege of traveling the world with my wife and my family using private cars and sometimes stretched limousine service as transportation from the airport to the ship etc. My sales pitch to these limo companies is to offer advertising space on our website related to a particular project as a trade. The limo company gets exposure and I get a ride in style to where I need to be. Both the limo company and Cruising Authority benefit from the trade. I enjoy trades, however; I need to pay the bills, so I must continually seek sponsorships and advertisers to be featured with my programing and trips. This is where people looking into what I do from the outside do not understand, in that I work extremely hard to put all the pieces together for a successful trip and sponsorship program. This type of work takes someone who has extensive experience with the cruise industry, someone who is also a seasoned sales and marketing professional, someone who has the writing skills, the photography skills, the videographer skills, the video editing skills, and the ability to be an on-camera Host. It takes a multi-talented individual who can see a project from beginning to end, create the scripts, write the articles and publish a multi-media project onto a website. I'm not trying to toot my horn, but there are few people who have all of these skills wrapped-up into one person. I have great aspiration for growth and further development as a Cruise Journalist, in-fact I have been working on the structure of creating a Cruise Channel for television similar to the Travel Channel. There are only a handful of "Cruise Journalists" that write or produce content exclusively about the cruise industry, and I know most of them. Some Cruise Journalists specialize in river cruises while others specialize in luxury cruises. I have reported on the luxury segment, the river cruise segments and mainstream cruise lines, and I find them all very enjoyable to work with. I feel like I am in my element when I'm on a cruise ship at sea. Talking about things to come....I am also working on a documentary made for television. I am in-touch with a Hollywood producer who sees my vision for a particular story, and I hope to see this project pull together within the next year or so. To be in this position, you can see that I have a tremendous-level of passion for what I do, and if I could direct my future, I'd work on cruise-related projects full-time as a career, as long as I can support my family and pay the bills.

Cruise-related Media Empire

If I look out past today, past tomorrow, after this book is published, I can imagine developing a media-business that's focus is entirely on the cruise industry, where I would train people to become journalists that produce content for Cruising Authority or whatever brand I happen to develop. There truly is not a business out there currently that follows the model I have in my head. Some organizations come close, but I do believe I have a valid, potentially large vision for a media empire that employs various writers, videographers, television producers, photographers, and journalists to create high-quality media for the consumer.

Chapter One – **Short History of the Cruise Industry**

"Carnival Cruise Lines bought Costa Cruise Lines in 1997....We built vessels with an economy of scale with a boutique-style ambiance."

Maurice Zarmati
President & CEO of Costa Cruise Lines (2008-2013)

What is it about stepping across the threshold from solid land onto the teak deck of a large floating structure that seems to cool the senses, churn-up feelings of adventure and romance, and magnify the urge to kick-back on a deckchair with a good book? Those were the days, in the late seventies and early eighties, when I set aside reality, and made numerous journey's to Miami for short visits aboard these lovely white cruise ships. At an early age, I developed a unique passion for cruise ships, but unfortunately, as a young man, living in my parent's house, I could not afford on my own to go on a cruise and my folks, although well-traveled, were not about to take a cruise as a family vacation. I would, however, make my way to Miami on an occasional weekend trip to visit the cruise ships, but this only teased and fueled my desire to one day go to sea on one of these ships. To me it was like stepping into a fantasy world even as a visitor on these early cruise ships, and it was so hard to leave the ship, knowing all these passengers were going to live-out what I only dreamed of doing. The idea of "the voyage" and cruising to exotic destinations, and being on a ship at sea was so intriguing to me. I still recall the many times I would fly into Miami, rent a car, and immediately make my way to where the cruise ships docked. I loved the humidity in the air, and driving over that bridge seeing cruise ship row with several ships docked. I remember the haze in the air with the cruise ships in the distance, and I could hardly wait to park the rental car and get on the ship. My home was Minnesota, so seeing these big cruise ships lined-up was so exciting for me. The ships were bigger-than-life from my point of view, and I would just be giddy as I made my way into the cruise terminal to register as a visitor and go aboard to look around. In these days it was rather easy to obtain a visitor's pass and go aboard the ships for a look around. Of course, I always enjoyed the free lunch usually served onboard for the passengers that were boarding the ship that day to begin their week-long vacation. The atmosphere was always festive, and all these lucky passengers were also giddy with anticipation as they familiarized themselves with their ship and home for the next seven days or more.

It seemed I was always a visitor and never an actual passenger. Sometimes I would explore one ship then move on down the line to the next ship, and the next...I would often visit three ships in one day. What I found interesting was even though I would go from one cruise ship and one cruise line to another, there was always that same festive feeling of anticipation onboard. Now, back then in the late 70's and early 80's, most of the ships were around the same size, about 20 - 30 thousand tons. I think what really made my ship visits special was the fact that some of these cruise ships were real ships, older ships or liners converted for cruising. The moment I stepped aboard I felt I was on a ship. I can still recall that familiar smell mixed in with the humidity and the air-conditioning onboard the ship, with hints of fresh paint, sea air and fresh luggage stacked in the corridors, I knew I was in my element and those smells were invigorating for me. It was ships like the Mardi Gras or the Festivale, the Emerald Seas, and even the newer Nordic Prince that were really fun to explore and those ships had such an interesting charm. My interest in ships started with ocean liners, which is why the older ships were so appealing to me...but that's another story.

I would spend hours on a ship exploring the public rooms, hanging out by the pool and the lido area where the food was, I took many pictures and sometimes I met with friends in Miami and brought them aboard with me for a tour. I really couldn't get enough of these ships and wished that someday I could be a passenger. After a full day of hanging out on the ships, I would usually jump in my rental car and head out across the channel and towards the beach where I would watch the ships leave the port of Miami and cruise out into the sunset, off on another voyage full of eager passengers. You can't help but wave at the ships as they pass by. There truly was something romantic and exciting about seeing these ships that were bigger-than-life cruise by and out to sea. The longing inside me to one day stand on the deck of one of those ships as a passenger was tremendous and I brought that feeling all the way home with me back to Minneapolis and back to reality.

The history of the cruise vacation industry starts back when ocean liners were the only way to get across the Atlantic or the Pacific oceans. Occasionally liners, or ships of state, deviated from their usual routes to visit warm and exotic ports of call. These liners weren't really designed for such excursions to the warmer climates because many didn't have air-conditioning, and it would get hot onboard these big floating steel boxes.

The great liners had their heyday and then the jet airplanes started to carry more passengers than the ships and the shipping companies struggled to maintain business. Some of the strategies by the big shipping lines was to send their vessels on more cruises. Finally, the ships could no longer compete with the jets, and the ships were either scrapped, redeployed or made into cruise ships. The cruise industry as we know it today started in the 60's where a few companies gambled with old remodeled ships, and some entrepreneurs even built new ones. The cruise industry made it's home port out of Miami, primarily, and the ships that ported there were called the "white ships". The base of cruisers was mostly the elderly and their parents, which created somewhat of a stigma that cruising is for older people. A cruise was indeed a luxury and the elderly seemed to be the only people who could afford this type of vacation.

Life onboard the ships in the early days was mostly about warm-climate cruising, exotic islands and destinations, and great food. It was a simpler life onboard during these early years, with many fun activities but nothing like we see today on the big 100,000+ ton ships with huge show lounges, water parks, rock-climbing walls and multiple dining venues. There were a couple of "game changers" that forever transformed the cruise industry.

The first significant "game changer" for the cruise industry was a little TV show called The Love Boat. I'm not sure where the cruise industry would be today or if we would even have such an industry if it wasn't for The Love Boat TV series, which was very popular for middle America. Each week The Love Boat would have movie stars and famous personalities on the show, which brought humor, romance and adventure into our households. I can recall watching The Love Boat and then Fantasy Island every Saturday night. There were two TV shows my father wasn't too happy about me watching, one was The Love Boat and the other was Three's Company, however; I usually managed to watch The Love Boat, because I loved ships and of course the Love Boat was about a crew onboard a cruise ship called the Pacific Princess. This story of how The Love Boat started is quite fascinating. It all started with a woman who happened to get a job working as a Cruise Director on some ships plying the Pacific to Alaska and Mexico in the late 60's, and her name was Jeraldine Saunders. In a nutshell, Jeraldine wrote letters back to her mother about her fascinating adventures working on cruise ships, and her mother suggested she write a book, which she eventually did. Jeraldine's book was called The Love Boats and it made a big splash with television producers who thought it might make an interesting movie for television. A Pilot was made which didn't go over too well, then another pilot with different actors was made and it became a hit. The Love Boat television series lasted for about ten seasons and, it's my opinion that this TV show significantly impacted the success of the cruise business. There were funny stories I heard from talking with Gavin MacLeod, who played the captain on the TV show. Gavin said some passengers were determined to find Meril Stubbing, Julie McCoy, or the Doctor Adam Bricker, and some were disappointed when they were not there on the ship. One passenger in particular insisted on meeting Captain Stubbing and when she was told that he is only a television actor and not a real captain, she was so disappointed that she asked to get off the ship in the first port. I'm still amazed at how a little TV show was instrumental in the development of a multi-Billion Dollar industry.

The second major "game changer" that impacted the evolution of the cruise industry was when an entrepreneurial man with a vision, Mr. Knut Kloster, purchased an ocean liner for conversion into the first mega cruise ship. The SS France was, at the time, the most expensive ocean liner ever constructed for the French Line in 1960 and made her maiden voyage to New York in February of 1962. The SS France was built to withstand the rigors of the north Atlantic even at her cruising speed of 28 knots. She was the longest ocean liner ever built and boasted the finest dining at sea. Unfortunately, the trans-Atlantic trade was dwindling, and even massive subsidies from the French government couldn't afford to maintain the costs of the SS France, and in 1974, she was decommissioned and laid-up in mothballs in a lonely backwater of Le Harve. In 1979, Knut Kloster purchased the SS France and had her towed to Bremerhaven, Germany to be transformed into a cruise ship. The SS Norway was built as an ocean liner for the Atlantic, and not necessarily for the sunshine of the Caribbean, so this transformation opened-up her decks so passengers could enjoy sunning and swimming while cruising the Caribbean.

Executives in the cruise industry with the major cruise lines, watched with great curiosity, the success of the SS Norway. It turned out that the SS Norway had a unique, economies of scale unseen in the cruise industry with the smaller vessels. The massive SS Norway was enormously profitable, and this caused executives throughout the cruise industry to take notice and consider building larger more modern cruise ships. The first cruise line to construct a larger vessel than the SS Norway was Royal Caribbean Cruise Lines, when they launched in 1988 the Sovereign of the Seas at 73,192 gross tons, about 3,000 tons larger than the SS Norway. In 1990, however; the SS Norway underwent a conversion, which brought her tonnage to 76,000 tons, granting her the prize of once again being the largest cruise ship. In 1996, the size-race was on, when Carnival Cruise Lines introduced the Carnival Destiny into the cruise market, the first passenger vessel in history to exceed 100,000 tons.

Chapter 2 - Author's *Stowaway on a Cruise Ship* Story

"In the beginning of Carnival Cruise Lines we realized we weren't in the cruise business we were in the vacation business".

Bob Dickinson
Retired President & CEO of Carnival Cruise Lines
(1972 - 2007)

The following story was written in my journal while I was in college in 1985. It is a story of how I managed to be a stowaway aboard a cruise ship in 1984. I felt that it was important to write down the experience so I didn't forget the details. I want to preface this story by saying that times were very different in 1984, and my little scheme would not work on today's cruise ships because of the high-tech, computerized identification of passengers and crew coming and going across the gangway from the cruise ships in the ports. I also want to say that I was young and adventurous, but today I also recognize that what I did was wrong and I want to make the statement that, "yes, I shouldn't have done this", and I chalk-it up to being young and a little devious. So needless to say, I wouldn't suggest that anyone attempt this today, mostly because times have changed, and the ships do have a brig to put people in before turning them over to the authorities. The ship I stowed away on was at the time called the Caribe I, but was later renamed the Regal Empress and given a new and more appropriate funnel. The Regal Empress was finally sold for scrap and sent to Alang, India to be beached in July of 2009.

My father was an airline pilot, so I had the great privilege of flying nearly anywhere I wanted to go on a pass, which was nearly free passage. While I was in high school, I would often fly to Miami on my own, rent a car and visit my high school friends in Miami who worked in a bookstore. I had a place to stay while in Miami, and I usually scheduled my visits on weekends when most of the cruise ships were in port. Upon scheduling and planning for a unique trip, unlike previous excursions to Miami, I sat in my bedroom at home in Bloomington, Minnesota and designed a scheme that I'm certain would work. I was going to stow away on a cruise ship. I was able to create the perfect plan based on the many visits to Miami in the past and knowing the cruise ships the way I did. After I had successfully boarded the ships in Miami, it was part of my plan to obtain a cabin key from each ship that I went on. I had discovered that passengers used the key from their cabin as a pass to re-board the ship while they were in the different ports of call. Before I arrived in Miami, using the deck plans from brochures, I plotted out which cabins would least likely be booked, based on their location within the ship. I picked the cabins, which were on the lowest passenger deck, with no porthole, and the cabins, which were the furthest forward and aft. While the ships are in port taking on new passengers, all of the cabin doors are left open, and there were usually several cabin keys left on the nightstand. This is how I was able to obtain the cabin keys, which were my ticket to board the ships when I later flew to St Thomas.

It's in my blood to seek adventure, and travel to new and exciting places. The island of St Thomas seemed very exotic compared to the cold winter

days in Minnesota. I looked forward to exploring this tropical paradise with great anticipation, however; my priority was to see if I could pull-off this little adventure of stowing away on a cruise ship. I wanted desperately to experience what it was like to be at sea on a cruise ship. Every time I went to Miami to go aboard the ships and look around, it only teased my desire to experience the ship at sea. I wanted to see how these big ships react in the ocean, and feel the crisp ocean breezes. I had read so much about ocean liners and cruise ships, that I could almost feel what it would be like as the ship moved beneath my feet, caused by the force of the ocean against the hull. When I finally arrived in St Thomas, I was amazed at how beautiful this place was. I stayed in St Thomas for two days with some friends from my high school who work there as missionaries.

With a rented moped, I explored the island, and soaked-in the warmth of this tropical environment. I noticed that the native people of St Thomas were very friendly. While I was exploring part of the island on foot, I needed a ride to the nearest hotel, so I put out my finger and pointed up, and within minutes, a taxi driver stopped and picked me up. This taxi driver already had passengers in the back seat, and when I offered to give him some money for the ride, to my surprise, he refused to take my money. It can be dangerous driving a moped in St Thomas because the natives drive on the left-side of the road which can make driving in St Thomas confusing.

After exploring St Thomas, I decided to swing by the cruise ship terminal to see which ships were in port that day. To my surprise, the Caribe I was docked, which was one of the ships that I was able to get a room key from, while I was in Miami. Fortunately, the Caribe I was one of the ships that was sailing to San Juan, which is where I wanted to go next. I was so excited to see the Caribe I , that I rushed back to where I was staying, grabbed my bags, and I went directly to the pier where the Caribe I was docked. This was the magic moment when I would see if my plan would work. I walked up to the gangway, and I flashed the security guard the key that I had obtained while visiting the ship in Miami a few days earlier. As I expected, the guard didn't even flinch, and I walked aboard the ship. My next plan was to see if the cabin that I got the key from was being used. Fortunately, no one was using that particular cabin, so I stowed my bags in the closet, and I went off the ship again to return the moped that I had rented. I also went to find the person who I was staying with, and let him know that I was leaving. My friend, Dave Erickson, was at work, but because of the unique circumstances, he was able to leave work for a short time, so I gave him a tour of the cruise ship. I gave my friend a tour of the ship, then I said goodbye to him, and boarded the Caribe I.

I went up on deck to watch the ship sail away from St Thomas, wondering if I will have any difficulties going ashore in San Juan. As the engines started to finally rumble into motion, and the lines to the pier were dropped, I felt exhilarated, watching the ocean churn while the propellers started to spin into action. I watched the beautiful island of St Thomas disappear behind us ever so slightly as the Caribe I steamed it's way towards San Juan. The gentle movement of the ship below me was soothing, compelling me to reflect back to the days of the trans-Atlantic liners. I thoroughly explored the vessel, and I tried to experience all that the ship had to offer, without disclosing my identity as a stowaway. Instead of eating in the dining room, I ate up on deck at the buffet. I even had an opportunity to see the bridge and meet the Captain.

Somehow I had to get in-touch with my friends in Puerto Rico, because they were not expecting me to arrive on a cruise ship. The only solution was to call them "ship-to-shore", and tell them to meet me at the cruise ship terminal. When the Caribe I finally pulled up to the pier in Puerto Rico, I was standing on deck, watching the docking procedures. My friends were waiting for me on the pier waving frantically to get my attention. I felt a sense of pride as I realized that my scheme was successful. Not only did I accomplish something practical by traveling from St Thomas to Puerto Rico for free, but I also fulfilled one of my dreams of going on a cruise, even though it was only about a twelve-hour trip.

Dreams were a big part of my life. I have always been the type of person who thinks big, and aspires to accomplish all that I can. My next big adventure was to go to college and get a degree in Business, even though my academic counselors felt that I was not a person who would be successful as a college student, considering the struggles that I've had in school. My goal was to get into a career doing something that I enjoy, rather than getting stuck with a job that doesn't allow me to utilize my creative abilities, and interests.

Chapter 3 - Purpose and need for a vacation - Cruise Therapy

"The family is the hottest growing market in the cruise industry today".

Carolyn Spencer Brown
Editor in Chief at Cruise Critic

I've heard people say the words, "I've never been on a cruise but I'd like to try it someday", and my response is usually, "What's holding you back?". Oh, there are reasons why people have not been on a cruise, which is, in my opinion, the best therapy for all sorts of problems. Just the thought of a cruise vacation, in my mind, resonates images of fine dining, being treated like royalty, and the soothing luxury of being at sea on a quest for relaxation, or adventure. Then again, I have many images stored in my head of endless days and nights on a cruise ship, because I use to work on the ships. It's a strange phenomenon, when you have been working on a ship for several months, you sometimes find yourself counting the days for when you will have shore-leave, and yet, when you have been on shore-leave you often find yourself missing the ship. A cruise ship is a unique world, an environment that is exciting, always changing, and always in-motion, figuratively speaking. It is this world of cruising that I'm continually drawn to, and for me...it's therapy.

Question: *Who would be prescribed a dose of Cruise Therapy?*
I have indeed heard, depending on the patient, that doctors have been known to prescribe for their patients a vacation. I wrote out a prescription for myself one time when I was in desperate need for sun, fun, adventure and peace of mind. My self-diagnosis lead me to booking a cruise to the western Caribbean on a five-night get-away. People in all walks of life and all sorts of work environments are plagued with ailments that require time away from their everyday routine. If you are suffering from the "blaahs", or you need a break, Cruise Therapy is highly recommended. Is your job stressful? You need to loosen the tension and spend some quality time with a deck chair in the sun. Perhaps you have gone through surgery recently, or you have completed a round of cancer treatment....ask your doctor first, but a cruise can be a very relaxing, restful experience. Business people, executives, lawyers, doctors, managers, entrepreneurs, homemakers, assembly workers, construction workers, pastors, teachers, the list of those who could use Cruise Therapy is epidemic.

Why Cruise Therapy?

What is it about a cruise that is so wonderful to be considered "therapy"? To understand this question you need to know four basic elements that make a cruise vacation experience unique. The four elements are: the ship, the crew, the ocean, and the passengers. First, when you step aboard a cruise ship, you are entering a fascinating world of comfort, fine dining, and a sophisticated, self-contained, micro-city created to move across the oceans from port to port. The ship is a magical place that offers all the comforts of a fine resort, and when at sea, one can walk the decks and feel the heartbeat and the magic of the vessel come alive! In the past, ships have been known to almost express a personality through all the subtle movements, creaks, shutters, and the way the vessel below your feet seems to gently move upon the ocean. The movement of the ship at sea can cause you to use muscles you didn't know you had, but once you acquire your "sealegs", which doesn't take long, you'll find it a refreshing experience. At night, the gentle movement of the ship will softly lull you to sleep. The ship is the first element.

Designers can build the most fantastic ships with all the luxuries known to man, but without a good crew, a ship is just a building that floats. The soul of a ship is it's crew, and their sole purpose is to comfort, dine, relax, entertain, and to serve the ship's passengers. Today's cruise lines employ crew, staff and officers from all over the world, so a cruise is like living in a utopian society...a virtual united nations, a microcosm of the world, and yet a place where everyone works in harmony, for the sole purpose of pleasing the lucky passengers. Every week cruise passengers leave the ship after a wonderful cruise vacation, having bonded with their waiter, who may be from Italy, France, or Jamaica. Passengers will get home from their cruise wishing they could pack in their suite case their friendly cabin steward who turned down their beds every night and even made cute little creatures out of the towels from the bathroom. Perhaps their steward was from Haiti, Indonesia, or Brazil. The crew is the second element.

For thousands of years men and women have gone to sea in ships. There is a lure to the ocean that is difficult to put into words. Cities, kings, presidents, and nations come and go over the centuries, but the ocean remains ever constant, a massive, unpredictable, ominous force. For centuries, man has been building ships to travel across the oceans of the world, but even the most experienced, modern captains have a humble, healthy respect for the sea. The ocean is so vast and mysterious, adding to the unique mix of elements we've discussed already. Anyone wanting to be close to mother nature or God's creation, can marvel for hours at the beauty of the ocean from the decks of a cruise ship. Nearly every evening in the Caribbean, there is a spectacular sunset, where the Sun meets the Sea. The ocean can be a soothing source of solace for the weary traveling man or woman, in fact I'm convinced that the ocean air has healing qualities. The Ocean is the third element.

You can have a wonderfully designed ship, and a fabulous crew at sea, but the key element that completes the formula for the perfect therapeutic vacation is the mix of passengers onboard. You can't get it at a resort, a hotel, or on an airplane, but on a cruise ship there is a unique camaraderie among the passengers who share a common goal of enjoying all the luxuries a cruise ship has to offer. If you are looking for love, the chances are pretty good that you'll meet some wonderful people. If you want to make some great friends, I have heard story after story of how couples have gone on a cruise not knowing anyone, and during the cruise they make a few really good friends, and end up keeping in touch even after the trip. It's so easy to meet people on a cruise ship. At the dinner table you may have your regular table mates night after night. Then there are the buffets where you will meet more people. The Cruise Director will often host some optional "mixer" games that force people to get to know each other. Then there's the passenger's talent show, the masquerade party, the singles parties, shore excursions, the sing alongs….there are endless ways to meet new friends and really bond with people. The passengers are the fourth element.

With all four elements in place you have the ingredients for a magical experience that will transport you to a fulfilling, relaxing, entertaining, adventurous, and maybe even a romantic vacation! You could even throw in a "fifth" element…the interesting ports that cruise ships visit. Statistics show that over 90% of the first-time cruisers say they will cruise again someday. Fewer than 3% of the traveling public in America have been on a cruise, which means that a huge percentage of vacationers have never experienced the joy and wonder of a cruise vacation. Typically, with married couples, it's the woman who desires to go on a cruise, and it's the men who don't want to leave the ship, and are so eager to book the next cruise. Cruise Therapy really does have a positive effect on people.

Janice from Oregon was just involved in a messy divorce that crumbled her world. She needed to get away and regroup her thoughts and feelings. A friend of hers suggested a cruise. Desperately needing to change her surroundings, Janice booked a last-minute cruise aboard the Carnival Triumph to the Western Caribbean. She went by herself using the share program for singles that Carnival offered. She was issued a roommate on sailing day who was also traveling solo. Janice just wanted to have fun and meet some new people. With 2,000 passengers onboard the Carnival Triumph during that sailing, Janice had some wonderful opportunities to meet some really fun people. After her cruise, Janice was feeling much better about herself and her situation. During the cruise, and because of all the distractions, and the new people she had met, Janice acquired a new sense of hope that she could once again be happy. For Janice, her cruise aboard the Carnival Triumph could be considered "Cruise Therapy".

Anyone who has experienced the terrifying reality of cancer will tell you that they develop a stronger sense and longing for "life". Even the simplest experience of watching a bird eat from a feeder near the window can evoke emotions of thankfulness, and joy. Charley from California had a cancerous mass in his chest which the doctors used a new kind of chemotherapy on. It took many visits to the hospital for chemotherapy and an operation to remove the cancerous mass, but after four months of treatments, the doctors gave Charley a clean bill of health with the wonderful news that they had destroyed all the cancerous cells. Of course the doctors said that there is no guarantee that the cancerous cells will not reappear, but they are very positive that Charley will live a full healthy life. Of course during the treatments Charley gained a new sense of passion for his life, so to celebrate his recovery, Charley and his wife Maggie went on a cruise aboard the Maasdam. Every night during the cruise, Charley and Maggie danced till their feet were sore and laughed at the comedian till their stomachs ached. During each day was a whirlwind of culinary extravagance and both Charley and Maggie made sure that they were on deck each evening to watch the sunset. Charley loved to fill his lungs with the invigorating ocean air as he often stood with his wife Maggie on deck for hours just enjoying the big blue ocean waves. Charley gained a new appreciation for living life to it's fullest aboard the Maasdam, and he discovered a new sparkle in Maggie's eyes. For Charley, his cruise aboard the Maasdam was without a doubt "Cruise Therapy".

Todd and his wife Julie live in Chicago. Todd is a successful day trader with a large investment firm and he is responsible for several million dollars from a number of clients. Each client's portfolio has it's daily challenges, and he seems to work constantly on maintaining those high-profile portfolios. Stress is a factor in Todd's lifestyle, that is beginning to take it's toll. His wife, Julie, works out of the home as a photographer, and she also paints portraits. Todd's career keeps him so busy, that the Chicago couple has drifted into a routine that is pulling them apart. The bottom line is that the two need to spend more time together. Todd needs to schedule his work so that he can come home to his wife and enjoy a nice dinner and maybe even watch some TV. Todd is over-worked, stressed out, and never seems to plan quality time with his wife. Todd and Julie made an appointment with a counselor, who prescribed that the two try and experiment with some new time management principles, and take some time off from their busy careers, and go on a vacation together with no cell phones, email, or stock quotes. Julie suggested a cruise, but Todd was apprehensive. All Todd could think of is no phones, being in the middle of the ocean with no faxes, emails, or stock updates. Wanting desperately to strengthen his marriage he books a cruise aboard the Zenith, round-trip from New York to Bermuda. As the Zenith passes the statue of Liberty and heads out to sea towards Bermuda, Todd and Julie watch on deck as the lights from the New York skyline fade into the distance. Buzzing through Todd's mind is the fact that Wall Street is also fading into the distance, while Julie is hopeful that the two will be able to spend some quality time together. That night the Chicago couple enjoys a wonderful dinner like they've never had before, and then an entertaining, high-energy production show, before calling it a night. The next morning Todd is a little nervous, but the moment he walks out on deck and sees that beautiful blue ocean all around him, that nervousness begins to slip away. With four days at sea and the three days playing on the pink sandy beaches of Bermuda, both Todd and Julie develop a new, more clear, relaxed perspective on their lives back home. The two agree that they need to plan their weeks so they can spend more time together. They realize that their relationship is far more important than their work. During the cruise they met another couple from the Chicago area, whom they are for sure going to keep in-touch with when they return home. For Todd and Julie from Chicago, their cruise to Bermuda aboard the Zenith was indeed, "Cruise therapy".

Listen, when you really think about it, just about everyone has moments in their life when a little "cruise therapy" would come in handy. Considering all the best reasons for people to go on a cruise, like; to meet new people, create a change of pace, explore new places, be treated like royalty, or heck, even go for a little romance, there are a few vacations that offer the sensations of a cruise. I would like to take this opportunity to write out a prescription for you. Take this prescription to your favorite cruise agent to be filled. Plan a CRUISE for your next vacation...and just think of it as therapy.

Chapter 4 - *Luxury Cruise vs Luxury Resort*

"I'm always excited and challenged by the blank piece of paper...nothing will leave my drawing board until I'm completely satisfied."

Joseph Farcus
Architect for Carnival Cruise Lines

Gerry Miller of Wisconsin has worked hard throughout his career as a small business owner, and after selling his business to settle down and enjoy a more leisurely lifestyle with his wife Lynn, of 46 years, the time has come to shower his bride with a season of luxury, travel and adventure. You may know someone like the Millers who are healthy and active and on the hunt for the perfect getaway. The hunting begins on the internet, with making a list of places to see, things to do and a schedule of fine dining, spa pampering, and a virtual bucket list of how to spend quality time together. Their friends have shared stories of world travel destinations and experiences, and there are piles of travel books and magazines on the nightstand next to their bed. The choices are numerous, giving the Millers a challenge as they have narrowed their search down to two basic plans, a luxury ocean cruise and a luxury all-inclusive land resort.

In the early eighties, when the cruise industry was gaining momentum, cruise sellers were comparing the value of a cruise vacation to land-based resorts, and the scale seemed to usually tip towards the cruise as the best value. Today, that rivalry continues between cruise and resorts, however; both sides have sweetened the pot offering fantastic amenities and luxuries including butler services, celebrity chefs, and exotic spas. The two basic dynamics between a luxury cruise and a luxury resort are whether the vacationer desires a voyage with multiple stops in fascinating ports or to remain in one carefree location and simply absorb the local surroundings. Cruise ships, like Royal Caribbean's Oasis of the Seas, with a passenger capacity of over six thousand and a crew of over two thousand, has become so massive that they are in many cases larger than land-based resorts and have more to offer, including full-scale Broadway production shows, and a Central Park area with real trees, plants and flowers. These giant new ships are evident that cruise ships are no longer "like" a resort, rather they have become full-fledged, self-contained floating resorts, and they give the land-based resort a run for the money.

The Millers chose to cruise from England to Norway and Germany for ten nights aboard the Queen Mary 2 in May, then in October they would stay at Couples Tower Isle in Jamaica for a week. The Jamaican resort was Gerry's idea. The two trips are very different, however; the Millers had very specific reasons for what they wanted out of their vacations. Lynn's parents were from Norway so she had often dreamed of visiting Norway one day. Gerry wanted nothing less than first class, and booked the Queen's Grill aboard the QM2, so his bride could see Norway in Style. Gerry and Lynn boarded the Queen Mary 2 with the great anticipation of fine dining in the Queens Grill, with luxurious accommodations in their 506 square foot Queens Suite with butler service. Gerry was heard saying, "This ship is like a palace making us feel like royalty".

The Millers had a unique opportunity to taste the differences and similarities of cruising and the land resort experience. Over the past twenty years cruising and resorts have both adjusted to the times and the ever-evolving demands of the vacationer. To find a true all-inclusive cruise vacation is challenging because cruise lines have fine-tuned the art of up-selling onboard amenities like private cabanas, spa facilities, drink packages, specialized dining venues, and shore excursions. Many cruise lines and resorts are bringing in celebrity chefs like Todd English onboard the Queen Mary 2, and Stefan Spath at the Couples Tower Isle in Jamaica. Regarding the restaurant bearing his name aboard the QM2, Chef Todd English explains, "Because of where the Queen Mary 2 goes and the great reputation and celebrity status of the ship itself, I think the clientele is a little more diverse than what you might find at a resort setting". Todd Continues by saying that, "The only drawback to having a restaurant on the ship is I cannot use a wood-burning oven…I like that smoke which adds to the flavor of the food." The upscale and luxury cruise lines often build into their pricing a wider range of included amenities and services. Crystal Cruises, for example; has experimented with offering a $1,000 per person ship-board credit. Regent Seven Seas Cruises offers complimentary wine and excursions. The expectations of today's Luxury vacationer are a more all-inclusive mind-set. Just like with the cruise industry, resorts have varying levels of all-inclusive offerings, and it's usually the higher-priced luxury resorts that are truly all-inclusive.

When you look closely at cruise vs. resort there is a completely different psychology associated with the two options. People simply have different perspectives of what they want out of their vacation. Some choose to do as little as possible, sit near the beach in a hammock, sip a fruity drink day after day, and that's it, while others prefer more available options. The spa services on luxury cruises and at resorts can be very competitive as well. Most of the cruise lines bring-on outside concessions to operate their spas, like onboard the Queen Mary 2, for example, Cunard has invited Canyon Ranch Spa to provide their signature spa services.   John Roseby, the Managing Director of the Canyon Ranch Spa at Sea Division has worked on both the Queen Mary 2 and at the land-based Canyon Ranch properties. Mr Roseby mentioned that; "The ship is a perfect way to introduce guests to the Canyon Ranch high standards of excellence that comes from all our services. It is, however; difficult to capture the true essence and feel of the 'real' Canyon Ranch that integrates the health and wellness experience as a result of the direct link to our wellness department of doctors and nurses at the land-based properties."   John continues by saying; "The whole experience on board the QM2 is geared to our exceptional spa services with links to our Canyon Ranch menu served in the dining room… all are there to serve as a taste of the expectations to come from the resorts." A significant benefit the land-based resorts have is space, whereas on a ship, space is a premium and every square foot of decking is calculated to produce revenue.

In October, the Millers headed off to Ocho Rios, Jamaica and stayed at the Couples Tower Isle all-inclusive resort, which Gerry discovered at the All Inclusive Outlet, an agency that specializes in luxury resorts. It was Gerry's dream of the perfect getaway, a quiet, peaceful, island paradise. Their room was very spacious and opened-up to a spectacular view of the beach. Different from their QM2 cruise, the Couples resort had a serene, relaxed, unhurried atmosphere.   They enjoyed the cuisine of Chef Stefan who created unique foods based on local island fruits and ingredients. Chef Stefan Spath said; "One of the most amazing things when I came to Jamaica; I couldn't believe how wonderful our produce in Jamaica tastes… It's really all about good food and good flavors". When you ask the Millers how the two luxury vacation experiences compare, one on the stately Queen Mary 2 cruising the Norwegian coast and the other at a Couples resort in Jamaica, you'll get a smile from both Gerry and Lynn as they look at each other and tell you that both trips were too short.

Chapter 5 - *Games on Cruise Ships*

First published in the Cruise Watch News Letter in August of 1996
Slightly modified and updated

"A head hunter in 1999 asked me if I'd be interested in the cruise industry, and I said absolutely not, I have no interest at all...it took me half an hour once I arrived at the Royal Caribbean office what a fool I had been to initially say no to the interview, and how lucky I was that he had called me back."

Dan Hanrahan
President of Celebrity Cruises (1999 – 2012)

From the very beginning when ships carried passengers to faraway places either to simply visit or to colonize, the people on these long voyages at sea found ways to amuse themselves with various games and activities. Some of these games included gambling, which has been a favorite past time of sailors for centuries, and various forms of shuffleboard on the deck. In the early days of long trans-Atlantic crossings by sail ship, the often weary passengers would find ways to entertain each other by singing songs, telling stories, boxing, gambling, dancing, eating, and of course romance. Often times these passengers would be at sea for a month at a time, tired from the constant movement of the ship, it was important to remain active and healthy to avoid becoming ill. Once a person became ill on a long voyage, it was very difficult to recover, and sometimes these passengers would never arrive at their destination, only to be buried at sea.

In the early days of the trans-Atlantic steamships, the entertainment and various activities onboard were less of a survival plan, and more of a way for passengers to get to know one another and to have fun. Some liners that happened to cross the equator would traditionally have a ceremony where Poseidon, the ocean god, could initiate some of the more willing passengers with water. It was all in fun, and even today the ceremony often will take place on cruise ships, navy vessels and even cargo ships. Rather than a voyage to endure, ocean liners became a very comfortable and relaxing place to be while being transported across the ocean. The larger and more luxurious these ocean liners became, ship designers began to create more advanced and sophisticated forms of entertainment for their passengers. Ocean liner passengers, in the trans-Atlantic era were on a voyage to get from point "A" to point "B", and played games to keep from being bored during the long days at sea, similar to why movies are shown on long flights on airplanes. In contrast, passengers aboard our modern cruise ships choose to take an ocean cruise and participate in the many activities offered, as a way to enjoy a vacation and get away from their daily routine.

Rather than a form of transportation, the passenger ships today have become floating resorts, which cater to virtually every whim passengers may desire for enjoyment. Some of the traditional games like bingo, horse racing, pool games, shuffleboard, and even the mileage tote, have survived as activities for the cruise passenger to enjoy. In contrast to the trans-Atlantic era where the games were organized to distract passengers from the long days at sea, in today's passenger ship industry, the act of cruising has become the distraction from every-day life. After participating in horse racing, bingo, and pool games a hundred times, seasoned cruisers tend to enjoy the simplicity of a good book from a deck chair, the exhilaration of the sea air, along with a great view of the ocean passing by.

On many of today's cruise ships, there are more games and activities scheduled that any one passenger could possibly engage in during a seven-day cruise. On some cruise lines there is a heavy focus of high-energy activities and the games are promoted throughout the day in the daily program and over the loud speakers. Other cruise lines may tend to be subtler in promoting the various activities. As an example, on Carnival's ships you may hear an announcement, in a very up-beat and excited voice, over the PA system that says; "Ladies and gentleman, may I have your attention please. At this time in the Atlantis Lounge, you do not want to miss our biggest ever, grand jackpot super duper bingo, where you could win thousands of dollars! Cards are being sold for five dollars each and the game will begin in just five minutes!" During the game, the MC may have a lot of funny jokes as he or she calls out the numbers to a high-energy group of bingo players all eager to win the BIG jackpot. In contrast, aboard the Queen Mary 2 for example; there will be no announcement, other than a notice in the daily program, that bingo will be played in the Queens Lounge at 12:00pm. The cruise staffer will roll out the big electronic bingo board, and in a very reserved tone, he or she will begin calling out the bingo numbers. The game is played with a more relaxed tone rather than a high-energy atmosphere. Both cruise lines may offer the same games for their passengers but have completely different energy-level and style.

Some of the more wild games of the modern cruise ships may be a high-energy scavenger hunt with perhaps ten different teams all scrambling to find the item the Cruise Director has called out. The first teams to bring the selected item up onto the stage will win points. In the warm Caribbean sun, there's no better form of entertainment than a game of joust, where two players slide out over the pool on a slippery beam with a bag of balloons to strike their opponent with. The object of this game is to knock your opponent off the beam and into the pool. Horse racing on deck is another traditional activity that is a favorite with many passengers. Cruise passengers have an opportunity to make a bet on which ever horse they think will win the race, and the horses are moved along a track based on the roll of a dice. The masquerade parade is also a fun activity that is reminiscent from the days of the trans-Atlantic liners.

The distractions and forms of entertainment on today's modern cruise ships are truly amazing! Since this article was first published in 1996, the cruise industry has evolved dramatically. Who would have ever thought that you could go on a cruise in the Caribbean and slip on some ice skates and skate on an ice rink, or climb a rock wall, surf on a simulated surfing device, plunge through a giant water slide, climb a rope course, zipline eight stories above the deck, bowl with your friends in a bowling alley, or jump into a simulated sky-diving machine? The average cruise ships today are much larger than was imagined back in 1996. Ships like the Oasis of the Seas at over 225,000 tons (five-times larger than Titanic of 1912) with it's own neighborhoods is mind-boggling.

Whether you choose to cross on the QM2 or cruise on one of the ships of Carnival Cruise Line, there will be many games and activities for you to enjoy, however; if you just want to relax and curl up with a good book, that's ok too. The energy-level may vary from ship to ship, and it is your Cruise Expert's job to let you know what to expect on whichever ship you decide to cruise on.

Chapter 6 - *Behind the Scenes Aboard the QE2 – Grounding Accident 1992*

"The Queen Mary 2 was built in France, and it is interesting that Cunard and the French Line have similar funnel colors....here at Cunard we privately laugh among our colleagues that the French shipyard may have picked-up the wrong paint-pot to color the QM2's funnel".

Carol Marlow
President and Managing Director, Cunard Line - 2005-2009

The moon glistened upon a glass smooth ocean, with a huge ship sparkling in the distance, moving gracefully to her final destination, having just finished a seven day cruise to Canada. Mysterious and ominous, hundreds of portholes and an upper deck ablaze with iridescent lights reflect on the

water like a distant palace. Soon, the size of the vessel is more apparent, and a distinctive silhouette with a glowing red and black funnel crowning the top of the vessel, fills the night sky. It is clear to see that this ship has a magical appeal as it majestically moves through the ocean. Looking like an oasis of light at sea, this magnificent ship radiates excitement, mystery, power, and romance known only to the few privileged individuals who have sailed in her. The ship's wake, an almost imperceptible engine noise, and big band music playing in one of the ship's many lounges, is all that can be heard as she passes near the shores of Cuttyhunk Island.

Unaware of any danger ahead, at twenty-three knots, the ship looms closer to a mis-charted ledge, thirty-four feet below the surface of the ocean. Disturbed from her usual tranquility, suddenly, this great ship hasted a desperate cry of pain to her commander, as she violently began to shudder. For thirty seconds of tearing, puncturing and scraping, the hull of the most famous ocean liner in the world, the Queen Elizabeth 2, runs aground and is badly damaged.

The stately vessel came to a parsimonious halt at about ten o'clock in the evening, August 7th, 1992. Dismayed and shameful, she began to take on water, which flooded several fresh-water tanks, and one of her empty fuel tanks. The water-tight bulkheads below the waterline were shut immediately, sealing off the various compartments throughout the length of the ship. Moments after the bridge called for "all stop", concerned engineers rushed aft through a smoke-filled passenger corridor, and went to deck six down a crew access near "D" stairwell elevators. Ocean water began to spew out of an over-flood valve into the crew stairwell on Deck Six, just as the engineers made their way towards the engine room. Deep in the bowels of the grounded ship, crew members began to initiate emergency procedures, praying that the QE2 would maintain her structural integrity. A ship's officer stood on the after deck of QE2 with a flashlight pointed towards the ocean water below, perhaps looking for signs of fuel oild leaking from the damaged hull. After it was determined that the ship's hull was compromised, yet there was no danger of sinking, commands from the bridge were to try and wiggle the ship off of the ledge, by using forward and reverse thrust from variable-pitched propellers. Passengers throughout the various public rooms were curious as to what had happened, but continued to socialize as usual without alarm. The QE2's broad hull rising from the oceans for more than twenty years, has maintained a timeless strength and majesty, and yet with this moment of despair and uncertainty, she seemed to resonate an untimely end of a dream.

To me, the Queen Elizabeth 2 is more than simply the last of the great trans-Atlantic liners, or even more than the world's most famous cruise ship. Prestige, glamour and sophistication are characteristics which surround this great vessel, but once again, to me, the QE2 is much more. Since I was a child, I had aspirations of someday being a part of, and experiencing, this unique society enclosed within the confines of the Queen Elizabeth 2. For years my passion was to someday cross the ocean aboard the QE2, walk her decks in mid-Atlantic, and soak in the daily routine of life aboard this legendary ship. For several years I worked on various cruise ships in the entertainment department. I saw much of the Caribbean, and most of the Mexican Riviera, as Assistant Cruise Director, Shore Excursions Manager, Entertainer, and even Cruise Director. The fast-paced lifestyle on the cruise ships was fascinating and exhilarating, challenging me to perfect my management skills. In the back of my mind, however; while I was gaining more experience, it was my goal to someday acquire a position aboard the Queen Elizabeth 2. To my delight, I was privileged to see my life-long passion come true, as I dragged my steamer trunk aboard the QE2's gangway in Southampton, June 14th, 1992, to sign-on as a member of the crew. I saw my wildest passion come true, and then suddenly, on August 7th, it began to wither away, as if I were waking up from a great dream.

I was standing in my crew cabin on Deck Five, forward, preparing to continue my duties, which was to socialize with passengers, and dance with the ladies in the Grand Lounge, or the Queen's Room. As I made one last adjustment to my bow-tie, suddenly, the ship started to shake. At first, as I sat on my bed, I thought the propellers were put into reverse, or that there was a problem with one of the engines. When the shuddering continued, I realized that there was a more serious problem because I could feel that the ship had hit something. I heard sounds like gravel and rocks brushing against the hull below. While the shaking continued, I quickly ran into the corridor to try and determine what was happening. As the ship finally settled after about thirty seconds, I rushed forward, and down to Decks Six and Seven, towards the bottom of the ship, to try and see if there were any signs of damage. All that I could see was that the water-tight bulkheads were shut. As I made my way aft on Deck Five, I saw the worried engineers rushing down the crew access to Deck Six, past an over-flood valve which was gushing ocean water into the crew deck. At this time, I felt it was important for me to be up in the lounges to see the passenger's reaction to this unexpected incident. Fortunately, the passengers were calm, socializing as usual. A woman that I had visited with during the cruise, came to me, and was a little shaken up. At this time I knew that the ship was damaged, and yet there was no danger, so I tried to assure the woman that everything would be all right, ,and that there was nothing to worry about. The big band was playing a waltz, so I escorted her onto the dance floor for a dance.

Throughout the evening, after the accident, passengers continued to enjoy the various activities and shows aboard QE2. A few minutes after the ship ran aground, the Staff Captain made an announcement stating that: "The heavy vibrations felt, was a phenomenon caused by the vessel's propellers passing over a shallow shoal". This statement, although false, seemed to assure passengers that there were no problems. All one had to do, however; was to look outside to see that QE2 was not moving. Struggling to move the QE2's hulk off of the ledge, the massive variable-pitched propellers violently churned up the ocean, making a wake that moved off into the darkness, aft of the QE2. The wash from her propellers was diverted from side to side as the rudder moved back and forth, and yet the ship was not moving. Shortly after the propellers stopped churning, Captain

Robin Woodall made an announcement stating that: "The ship has struck and underwater object, and that due to the request of the Coast Guard, we must anchor, and wait for further instructions." Rumors buzzed throughout the ship, and passengers, as well as crew, waited eagerly for further announcements. How badly was the ship damaged? Will her passengers have to be evacuated? Will QE2 ever make it to New York? I remember feeling excited, being a part of this unfortunate situation, and yet sad, thinking that my contract aboard QE2 could possibly end sooner than I had anticipated. The Captain made one last announcement at about 1:00am, while passengers enjoyed stimulating conversation at the mid-night buffet in the Columbia Dining Room. "The hull has been damaged, but neither the ship or her passengers are in any danger. Arrangements are being made to transport passengers ashore in the morning, and the QE2's arrival into New York will be delayed." I couldn't help but think that the whole world will know about this drama tomorrow morning. From living aboard the Queen Elizabeth 2 for about two months, I have that where ever this ship goes, she makes the headlines. Earlier in the cruise, for example; at St John, over one million people came out to see the QE2, making front page news.

Before retiring to my cabin, I went for a walk along the QE2's Boat Deck. A helicopter was flying overhead and there were several leisure boats, as well as the Coast Guard, curiously surveying the QE2 as she sat motionless in the water. Considering my fascination with the history of the great liners, I compared the feel of QE2 running aground, and how eye-witnesses aboard the Titanic over seventy years ago described the grinding sounds when their ship hit the iceberg. Based on what I have read about the Titanic disaster, I think the vibrations and shuddering of QE2, while she was hitting bottom, was much more pronounced than the subtle grinding sounds of Titanic scraping the iceberg. As I stood on the Boat Deck and looked off into the blackness of night, I also began to reflect on how much I enjoyed being at sea in mid-Atlantic aboard this great ship. Before retiring for the evening, I felt as though my adventures aboard the QE2 were about to end, however; I prayed that I would be able to stay with the ship for as long as possible.

I signed-on as a Stage Manager responsible for running the sound and lights for the various production shows. Never in my wildest dreams could I have imagined that someday I would have the opportunity to live and work aboard the Queen Elizabeth 2. I felt very "at home" aboard QE2. Sometimes, when I was off duty, I would take a walk out on deck, and soak in the vigorous, yet refreshing ocean air. The crisp ocean breezes of the Atlantic would often penetrate my imagination, bringing me back to another era of the great liners, steaming their way across this vast ocean. I couldn't help but notice the similarities between the old Queen Mary, sitting in Long Beach, California, and the Queen Elizabeth 2. Some of the smells in the woodwork, the unique size, the powerful stature, and the images of ship-wide, regal luxury, permeated both ships. Although no longer a steam ship, the QE2 continues with an impressive array of diesel-electric engines that push her through the ocean at about thirty knots. Unlike many fancy new cruise ships that have been built recently, offering a multitude of activities, lavish shows, spectacular mid-night buffets, and exotic ports of call, the Queen Elizabeth 2, during her trans-Atlantic crossings, has a very relaxed atmosphere. Many QE2 passengers are very independent , and prefer the unobtrusive atmosphere available in many of the ship's lounges. Although the Queen Elizabeth 2 does have many activities indigenous to cruise ships, there is a unique and comfortable, subdued feeling of bliss that transcends the contemporary cruise experience.

The next morning after the unfortunate grounding, I met with the Cruise Director, and several other staff members for breakfast in a special room just outside the Mauretania dining room. We discussed the details of how

we were going to get all of the passengers ashore. Apparently, the QE2 drifted off the ledge that she has skidded across last night, and was at anchor amidst a flotilla of smaller crafts. Snuggled against the QE2's hull was a zodiac, with special Coast Guard divers, preparing to examine the ship's damaged bottom. Several crew members in the social department carried a radio to communicate with other staff, as well as to take commands from the Bridge. While the divers were examining the hull, with our radios, some of us could listen in on what they were saying. It was compelling to be one of the first to hear the extent of the damage to the hull. On the radio, one of the divers exclaimed: "...my God, this is bad....there's a big rock pushed up into the hull...we can't discuss this over the radio".

The evacuation of passengers from the QE2 started around noon, with about six hundred passengers loading onto a local ferry, and the remaining passengers were brought ashore by the QE2's own tenders. When the first boat carrying passengers arrived at the pier in Newport, Rhode Island, hundreds of press people with cameras swarmed the dock to capture a glimpse of the shipwrecked QE2 passengers. I was on the first boat, and it was a challenge to tactfully try and push press people out of the way so QE2 passengers could get off the ferry, and guided towards their buses for transport back to New York. Camera crews were quite forceful, so it was a difficult task trying to maintain an orderly debarkation. After the first load of passengers were landed ashore, the next boat did not arrive until about 7:00pm that evening. Unfortunately, it was a very long, hard day for QE2 passengers as they were forced to wait around either on the ship, or on the train, which was chartered by Cunard Line to transport passengers to New York. The last boatload of tired passengers did not reach the dock until about midnight.

When the landing crew that I was with finally returned to the QE2, I remember feeling wore out. Although very inconvenient for the passengers, I felt that the operation went fairly smooth, and the crew acted in a professional manner. August 9th, while the Queen Elizabeth 2 slowly cruised towards Boston, it was determined that the ship will be put into dry-dock, and most of the nonessential crew will be sent home. Because of the grounding, I was informed that my contract as Stage Manager would officially end about a month early, as soon as QE2 arrived in Boston. That last day aboard the Queen Elizabeth 2 was a very pensive time for me. As I stood out on deck and watched the two large tugs and a Coast Guard cutter, follow the QE2 while she slowly made her way towards Boston, I remember feeling very sad, and yet optimistic about the future. I made some great friends aboard this ship, and every day I felt my passion for being at sea grow, as QE2 gracefully moved through the ocean.

Although a British ship, the Queen Elizabeth 2 was a fascinating microcosm of a society, set apart from either side of the Atlantic. This ship is a special place that continues to transcend cultural change, and tradition, whether she is in Hong Kong, Australia, or in mid-Atlantic. The society aboard QE2 is like a small town, with the Captain as the Mayor, overseeing a community that has a shopping mall, barber shop, print shop, movie theater, a church, as well as an assortment of fine restaurants. Completely self-contained, this floating community has it's permanent residents (the crew), and each week a fresh assembly of visitors, who take advantage of all the amenities this quaint mini-city has to offer. This city, however; has a flare which is unique in that it encompasses a wide variety of cultures from all over the world who join together for the purpose of catering to, and pampering it's visitors with the finest pleasures the World has to offer. This unique society also moves from place-to-place, circumnavigating the oceans of the World. I was always amazed when I could sit in the theater and watch a current movie, and then after the show, I would leave the plush interior of the ship and make my way out on deck to see nothing but ocean all around. It seemed strange to board the ship in new York on day, for example; and be a part of this fantastic society, and then a few days later I could leave my room , walk across the gangway, onto another continent thousands of miles from where I first started.

When I was a young boy, I longed for the day that I would be able to walk across the decks of the QE2, and then when I was in college, I made every effort to visit the ship whenever I had the chance. Enroute to Boston, standing thirteen stories above the sea, just below QE2's giant red and black smoke stack, I reminisced about my experience aboard this great ship, and how special this place was to me. One of my favorite places to visit aboard the QE2 was the Bridge. I remember one time, an officer sighted a large sailing ship off in the distance, with full rigged sails billowing, and her bow rising and falling with the relatively choppy seas. It was a magnificent sight watching this four-masted old rigger challenging the sea, and obviously enjoying the element which it was built, as the massive Queen Elizabeth 2 slipped through the ocean at thirty knots, seemingly unaffected by the winds and swells the mighty Atlantic had to offer. I commandeered the nearest set of binoculars to catch a glimpse of this passionate sight, when suddenly, I felt an ominous presence behind me. Captain Robin Woodal, a very tall man, was standing behind me, waiting for me to let him use his binoculars. The Captain, a very accommodating, gentle man, smiled as I handed him his binoculars. For years I had studied the structural design of the Queen Mary as a hobby, and after living aboard the QE2, I noticed that this ship did not have expansion joints built into her length, as the two older Queens did. The expansion joints were designed to allow these huge vessels to sort of bend and twist with the ocean to alleviate any stress that might occur from rough seas. I asked Captain Woodall about this one time and he responded by acknowledging that my observations were very keen, and he that it was a mistake that QE2 was not built with expansion joints as her older sisters had. Other than the lack of expansion joints, however; Queen Elizabeth 2, I was told, is perhaps one of the strongest, and most successful hulls ever built into a liner. One other memorable experience worth noting, was when I met a young man of about fourteen, traveling across the Atlantic with his father. This boy reminded me of how enamored I was about ships when I was his age. It was such a privilege to give him a tour of QE2, and see his excitement for this fantastic ship. He was thrilled when I took him up to see the dog kennels which, by the way, had some resident dogs being fed and pampered by a crew member.

The Queen Elizabeth 2 has been in traumatic situations in the past. Before the ship was past over to Cunard Line from the shipyard, there were numerous problems with turbines, plumbing and wiring. In the seventies, there was a bomb threat that required bomb specialists to parashoot into the sea near QE2 while she was stopped. No bomb was found and QE2 continued on her way. Once again her turbines failed her at sea, and a ship called the Sea Venture (now the Pacific Princess) had to rescue all of QE2's passengers in mid-ocean using tenders. Just like her predecessors the Queens, Mary and Elizabeth, were used during World War II, the QE2 was also used as a troopship during the Falkland Islands incident. Her exterior and interior have gone through continuous changes through out her twenty-four years as a luxury liner, evolving into the ultimate expression of a modern liner / cruise ship. Penthouse suites have been added through the years, replacing a wind-protected deck space. The QE2 went from being a steam ship to generating thrust using diesel-electric engines in coordination with sophisticated variable-pitched propellers. Her original funnel, changed from white and black to red and black, a symbol of recognition and power, and was also replaced with a larger, more appropriate design. A bow anchor was removed, and a new elaborate magrodome structure was added, as well as two large tenders. Her hull experienced various shades of black, and even an awful pebble-grey color, which didn't last long. The ship's interior has undergone numerous changes in her dining rooms, lounges and shops. The Queen Elizabeth 2 is at her optimum design and sophistication for the nineties, which will easily bring her to the year two thousand. After minor repairs in Boston, following her grounding in August of '92, she was sent to Germany, and ten million dollars later, her damaged bottom was restored. Apparently there were gouges, scrapes, holes, and even a large crack in the hull, parallel to her beam, caused by the grounding.

My colleagues within the social department were all very interesting people, whom I enjoyed working with. Many of the people in this staff had worked together aboard QE2 for many years. The Cruise Director had at one time considered being a minister, and he enjoyed painting. The Debuty Cruise Director loved Star Trek, and enjoyed a good joke. The Social Directress has worked aboard the QE2 at least since 1983, and she enjoyed interviewing the many celebrities that would frequently travel across the Atlantic. Some of the celebrities that I saw during my brief experience aboard Queen Elizabeth 2 included: actress Susan Sommers, actor George Kennedy, writer John Maxtone-Graham, a rock group called The Cure, singer Neil Diamond, author Tom Clancy, and fianally movie critic Roger Ebert. I worked in coordination with Carlos, who was an expert sound technician from San Juan, Puerto Rico. The two of us were responsible for all of the technical equipment, like the sound and lights related to the shows in the Grand Lounge, as well as slide projectors and screens, video recorders for movies in the conference room, and microphones for the Theater Bar, and the Queen's Room. At sea, a typical day of work for me aboard the QE2, would start at 10:00am in the Cruise Director's office, where I would be assigned various duties for the day. After meeting with the Cruise Director, Carlos and I would usually go to the Grand Lounge and set up the microphones and stage for either a Steiner's beauty demonstration, a lecture, a dance class, or bingo. Through out the day I would be busy making sure that the proper equipment was set up in the various lounges, and then at night, it was show time. My specific job during the shows was to run the computerized lighting system, and by using headphones, I would direct the two spot light operators. In a typical show there might be over one hundred different light queues, which change the mood on the stage during a performance, from soft lighting for a ballet, to bright chase lights for up-beat music and action. We would usually do two shows a night depending on the passenger load, and there would be dance music before and after the shows.

I loved my job aboard the QE2 and even though I was only aboard her for about two months, I wouldn't trade the experience for anything. After the grounding, when I was sent home, I felt it was a good time for me to leave the ships, and develop a career on land. I enjoyed working on cruise ships for the past two years, and I had many adventures in the Caribbean, the Mexican Riviera, and even in the Fjords of Norway. I was fascinated by the unique culture aboard the QE2, which was in many ways different from other cruise ships. Today the Queen Elizabeth 2 continues to cross the Atlantic regularly and she also makes her annual world cruise, where cabins range in price from thirty-thousand to three-hundred thousand dollars for the eighty day circumnavigation of the globe. Passengers can still experience the romance of a traditional trans-Atlantic voyage and soak in the luxuries of a completely refurbished ocean liner with all of the most modern conveniences and services. I will always remember and cherish the voyages I had aboard the QE2, where I had the privilege to live out one of my wildest dreams. I will particularly remember the moment when the most famous cruise ship, or ocean liner in the world ran aground just outside of Martha's Vineyard. It is my sincere hope that this great nostalgic ship, the Queen Elizabeth 2, will continue to spur the imagination and emotions of future generations, and that her hull will grace the oceans of the world for many years to come.

Chapter 7 – *Trends the Cruise Lines Might Follow*

"In 1975 we started the first regularly scheduled Western Caribbean itinerary with the MS Southward and today that is still the dominant itinerary".

Bruce Nierenberg
Executive Vice President, Norwegian Caribbean Lines 1973 – 1979

As I write this, January 17th, 2014, another growth spurt in the cruise industry is being constructed in shipyards all around the world. Usually planned many years in advance, modern cruise ships are quickly expanding all areas of the ships, from dinning venues, sports, entertainment, amenities, spas and even loft suites. Royal Caribbean International built two massive giants, the Oasis of the Seas and her sister the Allure of the Seas, the largest, most expensive cruise ships ever conceived, but if that were not enough, another giant Oasis-class ship is being constructed that will be called Harmony of the Seas. In addition to the new Oasis-class ship, Royal Caribbean International is building yet another series of vessels with a completely new hull design, and futuristic new high-tech bells and whistles, including a giant boom-crane that lifts about ten passengers in a glass-capsule hundreds of feet in the air above the ship for a unique bird's-eye perspective. The list of high-tech gadgetry on this new "Quantum of the Seas" includes a sky-diving simulation chamber, bumper cars, basketball court, and a high-tech virtual scenery wall that changes the mood and look in the lounge. Norwegian Cruise Line has made a big splash with branded entertainment like, Blue Man Group, Second City, Legends in Concert, Nickelodeon, and a host of other brands. The use of private-labeling beverages, proprietary bars and celebrity chefs attaching their name to onboard dinning venues has increased. The trends also lead to maximize economies of scale by constructing very large vessels. MSC Cruises has a new category of futuristic cruise ships that offer maximum balcony staterooms, and a terrace pool area at the stern that brings passengers closer to the sea, and a towering superstructure with passenger staterooms. Most of the major cruise brands are building exciting new ships with fascinating features that are sure to create a "Wow-factor". The water parks on ships are growing, because passengers with families appreciate the hours of fun by the pools, especially the kids. Norwegian Cruise Lines and Carnival Cruise Lines are constructing huge fun-parks on their ships that include elaborate waterslides, rope-climbing balancing structures, and even a fascinating Skyride pod that is propelled by human effort hanging under a steel track kind of like a rollercoaster or monorail ride. It's like these cruise lines are building amusement parks on the top deck areas. Technological advances allow passengers to stay more connected with their family and friends at home, with faster internet speeds. Cruise lines are tapping into the power of social media. Royal Caribbean now has a special satellite in space that beams a superfast internet connection just like at home or your office so passengers can enjoy the internet and social media without missing a beat.

Carnival Vista's Skyride device invented by Scott Olson from Winona, Minnesota   Photo Credit: Tom Stieghorst

Chapter 8 – *Author's Forecast for the Cruise Industry*

This is a fascinating exercise that is purely imaginative, and to speculate what is new to come in the industry might be fun, so let's roll-up our sleeves and see what the cruise industry and cruise ships might look like in five years, maybe even ten years into the future. If we continue to follow current trends, in the year 2019 there will be more cruise ships in service, older vessels will be sold-off to bargain markets, and the range of dinning, entertainment and activities will continue to impress vacationers. Aside from the potential novelty-cruise ships with the name Titanic 2, where passengers can live the experience of the original 1912 ocean liner without the unfortunate accident with an iceberg, we can expect other novelty cruise experiences to become available. Perhaps new itinerary options will be discovered or engineered, taking passengers and vacationers to new places. What about ten years into the future? The year is 2024, and if we assume the trends continue to move in a positive direction, the sky is the limit when it comes to technologically advanced vacation experiences. New technologies will only enhance the experience even further. Ships may not be larger, rather, cruise ships of the future will explore new possibilities of permanent habitation on large ocean-going cities. What makes a cruise ship unique in 2024 is the ability to transport vacationers into hermetically sealed and sterile environments. People will book a cruise for the enhancement of their health, away from large land-based cities and into pure environments that promote advanced health spas and floating medical treatment centers. The very nature of a cruise ship is to create a fantasy environment and take passengers to places usually only found in their dreams. There is a science to building cruise ships to be profitable, and the term is "economies of scale". Generally speaking, the larger ships tend to have a higher profit per passenger based on the "economies of scale" formula, for which the major cruise lines continue to perfect with each newbuild. Yes, the future could be bright and exciting at sea, however; what would happen if the economy took a dramatic change. What if North America falls behind in the world economy? The one thing that makes a cruise ship or a cruise line unique and somewhat shielded from dramatic economic change is that they, (the ships) are mobile and can be repositioned to whatever markets around the world happen to be more wealthy or economically stable. The cruise lines have the luxury of mobility to follow the ever-changing demographics. What if there was a major catastrophic event that dramatically changes the economy, governments, allies, enemies, and living conditions around the world? What if hundreds of millions of people around the world expire from disease, disaster, or some unforeseen trauma, and the dynamics of life on land change? Areas over land may become uninhabitable, and an option will be to possibly move the more fortunate individuals with wealth or power out to sea where the air is filtered by the expanse of the oceans. It is this element of mobility that will secure the use of these giant cruise ships far into the future. I can see more automation to be seen on future cruise ships, mostly related to passenger amenities. The Quantum of the Seas with Royal Caribbean has integrated robotics for the entertainment of passengers, like a robot bar tender that can make nearly any drink you can imagine. A robotic bar tender seems more like a gimmick rather than an efficient, better way to mix a drink, however; in one of the show lounges Two 70, there are six amazing computer screens mounted to robotic arms that dramatically add a fascinating dimension to the production shows where live entertainers, musicians, lighting, projection screens and trap doors that performers pop out of all work together to create the most high-tech visual experience I have ever seen. Perhaps on future cruise ships, there will be more use of robotics for entertainment or even in the production of fine dining or other service aspects of the passenger experience.

In the future, high-tech ocean-going passenger vessels may take on more unique roles in offering an experience that on land may not be appealing, for example; ships designed to heal passengers from all sorts of ailments. These futuristic ships would be an alternative to hospitals that treat cancer, or a floating drug and alcohol treatment center. People with mental problems, drug abuse issues, even plastic surgery or corrective surgeries could happen on these ships with extensive rehabilitation services and environments. When you think about it, no one looks forward to going to a hospital for any treatments or surgeries, so what if patients had the alternative to board a sophisticated and specialized ship with the most technologically advanced surgeries and treatments, all designed to make the experience more comfortable. The sea already has healing and soothing properties; maybe some cruise ships would be designed to offer healing rehabilitating services?

Futuristic cruise ships will also become more technologically efficient and safe for the environment. The Quantum of the Seas has a fascinating high-tech system that allows the giant ship to cruise through the sea on a bed of air bubbles. This system has special portals that emit bubbles under and along the length of the hull allowing the ship to gain an extra knot or two of speed, while also saving on fuel costs. Specialized paint on the hull also makes the hull more slippery when cruising, also saving fuel costs and making the ship more environmentally safe. The future and technological leaps in hardware may allow the ships to harness power-sources we haven't thought of or invented yet. Even today we have a few cruise ships that have giant sails to harness the wind. The more cost-efficient futuristic ships are built, cruise lines can be more profitable and the cost per passenger can go down. In the future, passengers will shift from the simplicity of embarking on a vacation, to embarking on life-altering experiences that go beyond a simple vacation. The quality of life at sea on a futuristic cruise ship will offer experiences that are necessary to enhance the human experience.

Further yet, future ships may be constructed with non-combustion engines with zero emissions, I personally think the technology exists but if this type of power was unveiled, it would destroy the petroleum, fuel, gas, coal-burning industry world-wide. If this zero-emissions, FREE, unlimited power, trans-dimensional energy source was revealed to the world, we would see the end of poverty, the end of carbon fuel-based engines, the end of starvation, the world would change nearly overnight with a new purpose and a completely new lifestyle and quality of life world-wide. That being said, giant ships would take to the sea offering vastly different experiences that would be available to more people. A paradigm shift would take place where people and companies, that once had great power, would have to seek new ways to conduct business. This may be somewhat prophetic in nature, but the landscape of this world and humanity itself will go through a massive shake-up greater than anything this world has ever experienced previously, and what emerges on the other side of this shift will be a very different environment.

* Expert Tips and Advice Introduction

I want to introduce this section. There are so many tips to cruising I could offer. I thought of as many relevant tips and nuggets of advice that I thought might be helpful. In fact, I use to sell cruises and I have talked with hundreds of prospective cruisers with this advice, so I am very pleased to share it here with you wrapped in the cover of this book. If you were sitting right here in front of me asking for advice, these are some of the tips I would share with you.

Chapter 9 - *Where to find the best deals and what to look for*
Tips for booking a cruise for less money

In today's economy most people seek out the best possible deals to save money, and receive the best value. One of the mis-conceptions of cruising is that it's too expensive, however; when you make a chart that compares a land-based vacation verses a cruise vacation, you'll see that the best value is a cruise. Think of the tips in this article as GOLD, because I'm about to give you some nuggets of information that could save you hundreds, maybe thousands of dollars when you plan your next cruise vacation.

The very first tip is to contact a "cruise-only" agency that exclusively books cruises. Too often, I have had people tell me they booked their cruise directly with the cruise line, because they think they are cutting out the "middle-man" and saving money....these poor people think they're getting a great deal, when in fact they could get more bang for their buck if they go through a well-established cruise-only travel business. Let me break this down so it's easy to understand. The cruise line will certainly sell you a stateroom on a cruise of your choice and you might fall for the illusion that this is the right choice to save money. If you choose any cruise-only agency, you might find that they offer the same pricing that was quoted to you by contacting the cruise line directly, but here is the catch. The cruise–only travel agency is given special perks based on the volume they sell with any particular cruise line, so they are often able to offer something over and above the quoted cruise price. When you book through a cruise-only agency, you will not pay any extra fees, you'll get the best rate offered by the cruise line, but more importantly, you may be able to get special upgrades, discounts, onboard-credits, and extra amenities the cruise line only offers their top-producing travel agencies. The cost of the cruise might be the same, but when you book through a cruise-only agency, you may be able to receive discounts and amenities only offered to top producing agencies....that's money in your pocket!

There are a few other ways to save money when you plan your next cruise vacation. If you're flexible with the dates of your vacation, ask your cruise-only agency if there are any re-positioning cruises you can book into. These re-positioning cruises are often discounted at very appealing rates.

Ask your cruise-only agent if you can get a "guaranteed" category stateroom. A "guaranteed" stateroom means that you pay for a specific category, but because it's a "guaranteed" booking, you could get that particular category or better based on availability. It's like rolling the dice, but the chances you are upgraded to a higher category are pretty good.

Enroll in a cruise line's loyalty program. When you enroll into a cruise line's loyalty program you can often receive discounts and upgrades only offered to those enrolled in the cruise line's loyalty plan.

If you plan your cruise around an off-season cruise itinerary, you may be able to save money. Peek cruise dates are usually Christmas and New Year's cruises. These cruises often add a supplemental fee, so be aware of this fact. Christmas and New Year's cruises almost always sell out, so there are rarely any discounts to be found during these cruise dates. What's interesting is that the cruise before Christmas and after New Year's is often discounted.

If you implement some of these ideas when booking your next cruise, you will save money and get the best possible bang for your bucks!

Chapter 10 - *Note to first-time cruise-buyers – Packing for a cruise:* Cruise like a pro, not the usual tourist, by using the following packing tips.

Whether you're a seasoned cruiser or you're going on your first cruise, there are some unique things to pack so that you have the best possible cruise experience, and you're prepared for nearly anything during your vacation. The last thing you want to do is be unprepared for your vacation.

Tip Number One – Avoid packing all your luggage the night before.
Try not to scramble late into the night before your departure trying to pack. Plan ahead a few days and make a general list of things you may want to bring, including: clothing, camera gear, batteries, extra memory cards for your camera, hats, medications, bathing suits, etc. Wash your clothes and start to pack perhaps two nights prior to your departure, because if you wait till the last minute, the night before, you may not get the sleep you need for the rigors of traveling the next day.

Tip Number Two – Get plenty of sleep the night before your departure.
If you wait to pack the night before your departure, you may find yourself packing late into the night as you try not to forget to pack certain items. It's not uncommon to board early morning flights to get to your cruise port, and the hustle and bustle of travel can truly wear you out, particularly if you didn't get enough sleep the night before. When you board the ship for the first time, it's a very exciting moment, you may have somewhat of an adrenaline rush, but your body can only take so much before you collapse out of sheer exhaustion.

Tip Number Three – Consider buying Space Bags
You've probably seen them advertised on television. These Space Bags are truly a handy way to pack your luggage efficiently. Basically you put your shirts, pants, underwear, socks in their separate Space Bag, and roll out the air, which ultimately allows you to pack more items in your luggage with extra room to spare. Also, if your luggage, by some crazy accident, gets dropped in water, your clothes won't get wet.

Tip Number Four – Don't pack too much stuff
Travelers often pack way too much stuff into their luggage and overestimate how much clothes and stuff you'll need on your cruise. Additionally, you're going to want to leave some space in your luggage, prior to your cruise,

because it never fails that dirty clothes, bathing suites, souvenirs, will cause your luggage to be over-stuffed on your return home.

Tip Number Five - Consider using LuggageForward.com
A great new trend is to offer travelers a break from lugging their heavy luggage to and from the airport and spending time in baggage-claim. These companies will pick up your luggage at your home or office several days prior to your cruise departure. These companies will deliver your luggage directly to your ship or hotel, so you don't have to battle dragging your heavy luggage around. It's a great service, where you hand-over your luggage to a courier and the next time you see your luggage is in front of your stateroom on the ship. Check them out and you'll see that the pricing is reasonable and it will give you a peace of mind knowing that the airline won't lose your luggage.

Tip Number Six – Purchase luggage with four wheels
More and more travelers are discovering luggage with four wheels. It is such a convenient, and great way to move your luggage around when you have four wheels on the bottom of your luggage. You may also want to consider luggage with hardened sides to protect the contents in your luggage. An excellent brand to consider is Victorinox; they make excellent luggage pieces.

Tip Number Seven – Mark your luggage so you can easily identify your bags
Today, it is surprising how many people have similar or identical luggage and it can be confusing sometimes in baggage-claim trying to identify your luggage. The simplest way to mark your luggage is to tie a colorful cloth to the handle, so you can quickly identify which bag is yours at the pier or in baggage-claim.

Tip Number Eight – Pack heavier items at the bottom of your luggage
While you are packing, place heavier items on the bottom when the bag is upright. Place certain items inside the shoes you pack in your luggage so you are efficiently using every possible space in your luggage.

Tip Number Nine - Place electronic items or cords inside zip-lock bags
Zip-lock bags are a great way to organize, protect, and store certain loose items, cords, and electronics. You may also want to bring a couple large zip-lock bags to put some of your dirty / smelly clothes, and wet swim suits.

This way you will protect the rest of your luggage contents from smelly or wet items.

Tip Number Ten – A few unique items to pack
A highlighter marker would be very helpful to mark up your daily program that is delivered every day to your stateroom. With this marker, you can highlight the activities you want to go to. An extension cord and possibly a power-strip to plug in and charge all your electronic items, can be very useful. Most cruise ship staterooms have only a couple electric outlets. Earplugs might be helpful too if you are a light sleeper. The movement of the ship can sometimes generate sounds you may not be use to, like drawers or doors bumping due to the movement of the ship. Your neighbors or people in the corridors might make more noise than you prefer, so it's good to be prepared just in-case.

Chapter 11 - *More First-time Cruise Tips (seven)*

Tip Number One: Choose a cruise with more days at sea

In my opinion, most first-time cruisers make the mistake of choosing cruise itineraries with way too many port visits. The whole purpose of taking a cruise vacation is to enjoy the ship in it's element, which is being at sea. When the ships are docked in a port each day, passengers enjoy less time at sea, which is what the ships were built for. When a ship is in-port, in the hot sun, most of the entertainment on the ship is shut down, and most of the passengers, like cattle, make their way into the port, many on shore excursions. Shore excursions are great, but it can be very tiring if you are booked for an excursion nearly every day in a different port. Many passengers return to the ship hot, sun-burn, sandy, and tired, only to turn around and do it again the next day. That's not a relaxing vacation. So try to choose a cruise with fewer port visits and more days at sea, because it's during these days at sea when a cruise ship comes alive. Passengers can enjoy being at sea, all the activities, the sea air, and the great cruise ship entertainment.

Tip Number Two: Plan your cruise with a cruise-only agency
I am amazed at how many people think they are getting a better deal by booking their cruise directly with the cruise line. This simply is not true. When you're ready to plan you first cruise, locate a cruise-only travel agency and find a cruise-only travel agent that you can work with. A cruise-only travel agent can give unbiased cruise advice based on which cruise line would best fit your personality and expectations for the best cruise vacation. Each cruise line and each ship has it's own personality and attracts a certain demographic, so it's important for first-time cruisers to be place on the right ship and cruise the first time. All too often, I hear of negative first-time passenger's experiences that could have been avoided if they had been placed on a cruise and cruise line that is tailored for that particular passenger. It does NOT cost anything extra to plan your cruise through a professional cruise-only travel expert, and you'll get the best possible advice based on your personal requirements for the perfect vacation. Here are a couple of great cruise-only agencies to consider: Cruises Only, The Cruise Web, iCruise.

Tip Number Three: What type of stateroom should you consider?
Cruise ships have numerous different categories to choose from. There are inside staterooms which have no porthole or window, then you could choose

a stateroom with a porthole or window, finally, you could luxuriate in a stateroom with it's own verandah. First-time cruisers tend to skimp on the cost of their first cruise because they want to get the best deal and save money in-case they discover they may not enjoy their first cruise experience. This is not the best logic, in-fact the best choice is to book a stateroom based on your preferences for the perfect vacation rather than price. Most people who book an inside stateroom for their first cruise realize after the fact, that for a few more dollars they could get a room with a view or a verandah. Yes, a private verandah is a luxury, but most ships today have more private verandah's than inside staterooms, and there are some great deals out there which include a balcony. Don't be one of those passengers who regret not upgrading to a verandah. Go for it! It will be worth it.

Tip Number Four: Try to vacation with friends
If it's possible for you to plan a vacation, a cruise vacation with friends, make it happen, because a cruise is such an exciting vacation, it's best to share the experience with friends.

Tip Number Five: Purchase Travel Insurance
This is one option that many first-time cruisers forget. Get advice from your cruise-only travel agent, and ask about travel insurance. You can never forecast when an unfortunate event or accident will happen. If, for example, you're on a cruise in the middle of the ocean, and you have a heart attack or some other unforeseeable incident, the last thing you want is to be air-lifted from the deck of the ship by the coast guard and face a $50,000 expense. Anything could happen; the airline could lose your luggage, you could accidently fall and break a bone, a family member could die, forcing you to cancel your cruise....for peace of mind, buy travel insurance, and avoid unexpected expenses.

Tip Number Six: Avoid motion discomfort
One of the biggest concerns of first-time cruisers is that they worry about getting sea-sick. Motion discomfort is not something to worry about. Today's ships are so large and have the latest technology in stabilization, chances are you will not experience motion discomfort. Some people, however; do have some sort of motion discomfort, and there are some very simple ways to prevent or fight against this issue. Try not to buy Dramamine, the patch, or any sort of drugs, this will only cause you to not fully enjoy your cruise experience. Some natural and proven remedies include the following: If the discomfort is focused on your stomach, eat an

apple and saltine crackers, this will calm your stomach acids from causing discomfort. If the discomfort is focused on your head, equilibrium, purchase wrist-bands from any pharmacist prior to your cruise just in-case. SeaBands is a brand that offers these wrist bands that will trick your brain into NOT falling for the equilibrium-issues. Avoid consuming alcohol the first couple of nights to allow your body to develop "sea-legs". Alcohol will greatly exaggerate motion discomfort. If all of these natural remedies fail, make a visit to the doctor onboard and ask for "the shot" which will cure your motion discomfort for the duration of your vacation. The drugs like Dramamine and the patch have side effects that may disrupt the quality of your vacation.

Tip Number Seven: Purchase shore excursions on the ship

Many people fall for the trap that they can get a better deal on their shore excursions on their own. While seasoned travelers might be able to save money arranging their own shore excursions, the average person will most likely spend the same amount of money and end-up with a lesser quality excursion. As a first-time cruiser, choose the shore excursions offered by the ship, that way you'll know the excursion is sanctioned by the cruise line, you'll return to the ship in time, you'll avoid the pitfalls of less-than-honest tour guides and you can be confident the excursion will give you your money's worth. Many of these cruise ships visit the same port week after week, so they have developed relationships with proven and tested excursions that offer the best possible experience. Yes, you could probably save money buying an excursion at the pier in port, but you could also end up with a less-than-honest tour guide that might rip you off. The excursions offered on the ship may cost more money than if you booked it on your own, but again, when you try to beat the system, the chances of being ripped-off, or getting back to the ship late, could ruin your whole vacation.

Chapter 12 - *Nine Cruise Secrets Revealed*

For those cruise vacationers who have been on many cruises over the years, you might know some of these secrets of cruising, however; it's my challenge here to come up with cruise secrets that avid cruisers may not be aware of.

Secret Number One: Always seek out a Cruise Expert agency to book your cruise.

I have a few friends that regardless of my advice, continue to fall for the mistake of booking their cruise directly with the cruise line, or with a travel agency that doesn't specialize in booking cruises. Not that there's anything necessarily wrong with booking directly through the cruise line, it's simply in your best interest to find a Cruise Expert agency, because they are aware of and granted by the cruise lines based on their booking volume, special perks, upgrades, discounts and amenities only offered to high volume cruise agencies.   You may get a great deal on your cruise booked directly with the cruise line, and it may even be the same price quoted by a cruise-only agency, but what you may not know, is that that same cruise booked through the cruise-only agency can offer a special amenities package that the cruise line does not offer. You could save money. You could get an upgrade, and you can receive unbiased advice from a cruise-only travel agency. It does not cost anything extra to book through a cruise-only travel agency, and I think you will be pleased with the results the next time you plan to book a cruise. Tap-in to the upgrades, discounts, special amenities and other nice surprises the next time you book a cruise with a cruise-only travel agency.

Secret Number Two: Order more than one entrée.
When you are onboard a wonderful cruise ship and dining in the main dining room, why limit yourself to only one entrée? This is a little secret many don't know, which is you can order multiple entrees if you see several option on the menu that appeal to you. Go ahead, the next time you're in the dining room, order two entrees, or two soups, or two desserts, you're on vacation!

Secret Number Three: Book Shore Excursions online, before your cruise.
Many cruise lines now offer pre-booking shore excursions well before your cruise date. You may not save money doing this, but here's the key....if you wait to book your cruise once you board the ship, you may find that the best shore excursions are sold out. Don't find yourself in this situation, plan out

which excursions you may like weeks or months before your cruise, and secure your excursion tickets before they are sold out.

Secret Number Four: Use the showers and steam room in the spa.
The bathroom and shower in your stateroom may be very nice, but I have found that the showers in the spas sometimes have water-pressure. Also, many of the spas have a steam room that is free to use in the men's and women's changing areas. I love a nice steam to wake me up for the day.

Secret Number Five: Change-out bed linens and pillows.
Chances are you will find your bed and linens to be very comfortable, but if you discover you're not entirely comfortable with your mattress, the linens or pillows, talk to your room steward and explain your concern, because often times there are special mattress-toppers, linens and pillows your steward can find to make your bed fit your comfort needs.

Secret Number Six: Never purchase bottled water onboard the ship.
I'm amazed when I see passengers spend their hard-earned cash on something like bottled water. The modern cruise ships have incredibly high-tech water filtration systems onboard, so the water right out of the tap in your stateroom is going to be exceptionally purified and clean. When you pack for your next cruise, buy a nice water / juice bottle and pack it in your luggage. Fill your water / juice bottle using the sink in your stateroom. One extra little trick I do, is bring several boxes or packets of your favorite Crystal Light or the new MioEnergy "liquid water enhancer" and flavor your water, add some ice to make it cold and ta da.....you have a refreshing drink that doesn't cost you a penny onboard the ship!

Secret Number Seven: If you don't like your table-mates?
It happens; sometimes you may get placed at a table with people who might not fit with your idea of good dinner companions. At the entrance to the dining room, ask to speak with the Restaurant Manager or Maître-d, and simply request to be place at another table. You will be discreetly moved to another table.

Secret Number Eight: Who to talk to for extra-special perks.
If you are celebrating something special like a birthday, an anniversary, or anything you can think of that could be considered "special"; there are two people specifically, that you should request to meet face-to-face, the Hotel Manager and / or the Cruise Director. You see, both the Cruise Director and the Hotel Manager are given certain authority to authorize special perks like

flowers, champagne, upgrades, shipboard credits. The secret is to be very apologetic when meeting with let's say, the Hotel Manager. You might want to say something like; "My wife had a very difficult year at her job, and besides booking this cruise, I wanted to figure out something special to help her relax better and truly celebrate on this vacation....I feel like I dropped the ball already....do you have any ideas?" Watch as the Hotel Manager puts his imagination to work and releases the purse-strings of perks that he has access to. The secret is not to ask for special perks, but ask his or her advice.

Secret Number Nine: Gratuities
Most cruise lines now offer automated gratuities to make it simpler to thank and tip the service crew that clean your stateroom and bring your food in the dining room. For those, however; who want to have more control of who receives a gratuity from you, and how much you give, you can visit the purser's desk and ask for the automated gratuities to be removed from your end-of-cruise invoice. Once this has been done, you can determine how much you want to tip certain people that have made your cruise an excellent experience. This is a personal issue, and I often enjoy rewarding those who go the extra mile by personally handing them an envelope with my cash-gratuity inside. The automated gratuity system is convenient for those who don't know how much to tip, and who should receive a tip. I like to tip the old-fashioned way, and personally hand that waiter, maître d, or cabin steward my personal thanks with cash in an envelope.

Chapter 13 - *How to choose the right cruise line, itinerary and ship*

Choosing the right cruise line

For the sake of simplifying this process, I have selected 19 of the most popular cruise lines that cater mostly to the U.S. market. There are certainly more cruise lines out there that cater to the European markets, German market, and specialized niche cruise companies like river cruise lines. The following are the nineteen cruise lines I have selected for this chapter to feature:

- Cunard Line
- Crystal Cruises
- Seabourn Cruise Line
- Silversea Cruises
- SeaDream Yacht Club
- Azamara
- Disney Cruise Line
- Oceania
- Regent Seven Seas Cruises
- Windstar Cruises
- Viking Cruises
- Norwegian Cruise Line
- Holland America Line
- Celebrity Cruises
- Princess Cruises
- MSC Cruises
- Royal Caribbean International
- Carnival Cruise Line
- Costa Cruises

To clarify and simplify the process of choosing a cruise line, I have created a chart divided into four sections labeled, Ultra Luxury, Luxury, Premium & Resort, and finally Mass-Market. I like to put these categories into a triangle where the top section is Ultra Luxury because of the exclusivity of that demographic. The next one down is the Luxury Market, then the Premium Market and finally the Mass Market is at the bottom because this is the largest demographic. Several of the cruise lines like Norwegian Cruise Line, for example; is in two different categories because they have a ship within a ship concept that reaches two separate demographics, Mass Market and Premium Market. Also, Cunard Line reaches two of the demographic categories because the ships are designed for a larger luxury market and a very select ultra-luxury market.

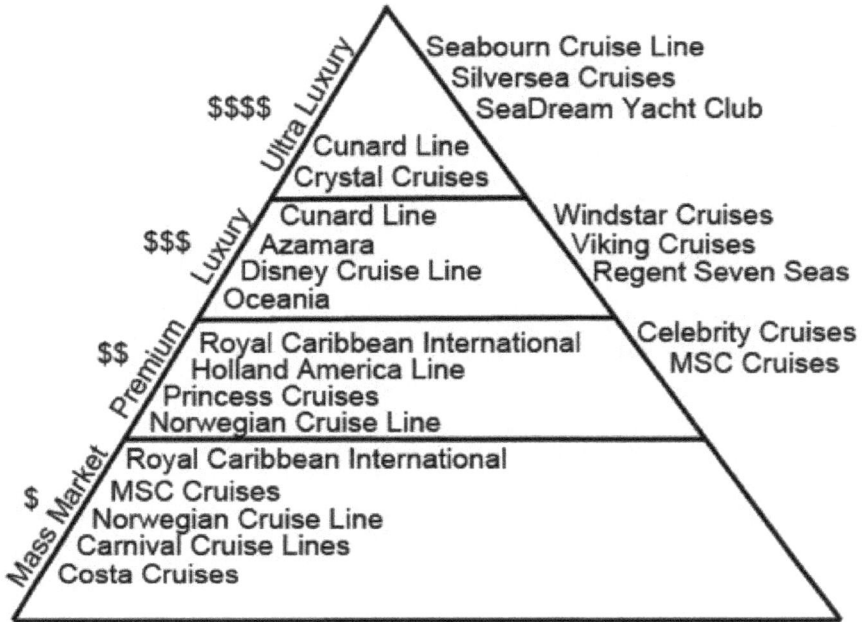

Choosing a cruise line depends on which demographic or section you can afford, or you believe you fit in that market. There's four categories to choose from, the top Ultra Luxury category being the most exclusive and most expensive, to the bottom category which is the largest market and is priced to be more affordable to the masses. So you must decide where you best fit-in between the four categories, and start to make your choice from there. See the graphic below to help you visualize the different categories.

Keep in-mind that the top Ultra Luxury cruise lines often have longer itineraries that visit more diverse and exotic parts of the world. The two bottom categories usually visit more common and more popular destinations, and often stick to three, four to seven night itineraries. The best value is relative to which category is affordable to you.

Choosing the right Itinerary
Today there are cruise ships all over the world in & out of most major ports. For a first-time cruise, you might want to try a cruise that's closer to home, and if you live in North America, in the United States, you have many options including: the Caribbean, Mexican Riviera, Alaska, Bermuda, and New England / Canada cruises. The most popular itinerary for first-time cruisers is the Caribbean. Now, in the Caribbean there are three basic

options, either the Western Caribbean, the Eastern Caribbean or the Southern Caribbean. See the chapter in this book describing the Eastern and Western Caribbean itineraries to help you decide which one is best for you. Some advice, however; for first-time cruisers is to choose a cruise that has more sea days as opposed to a port every day. The reason for this is that to fully enjoy and appreciate a cruise vacation, it's best so experience the ship at sea, which is what these floating resorts are designed to do. Sea days are often more relaxing, invigorating, and there's much more to do on the ship as far as activities. Southern Caribbean itineraries, on the other hand, are usually more port intensive, and these huge ships dock for the day and passengers scramble around the ports which can be very tiring, especially if you have a port every day, which, trust me, is exhausting. When you have a cruise or two under your belt, then you'll know better what I'm writing about, so my advice is to take it easy, choose a cruise with fewer ports, you'll thank me.

Choosing an itinerary is truly one of the highlights of developing your vacation because the entire world is at your feet and there are hundreds of options. This is a time for you to dream a bit. Where, in the entire world, would you like to visit? Perhaps you want to see the beautiful scenery of Alaska? You might have always wanted to visit: Italy, Greece, Bermuda, South America, Asia, the Bahamas, Aruba, Jamaica, Norway, Hawaii...the list can go on and on, it truly depends on 'what is your dream?'. Of course certain destinations may cost more to get to, and some happen to be longer cruises which can bring up the cost, but it's your vacation, it's your dream, and that should be the root to choosing an itinerary....where do you want to go for your vacation? You may have to be practical, and as I suggested earlier, choose a cruise closer to home.

Something else to consider is, what do you like to do on your vacation? Do you prefer shopping, beaches, adventure, scenery, or history? Certain itineraries are made for those who love to go to the beach, if that's you....you might like the Western Caribbean which has excellent beaches and water sports available. You may love to shop for bargains, if so, choose the Eastern Caribbean, where you will find great deals on jewelry, electronics, watches, silver, gold, or vanilla extract. If you enjoy history, choose an itinerary that visits San Juan or Mexico where you can see fascinating forts, rain forests, and ancient Mayan ruins. In this book I wrote out a story of how I saw a beautiful painting at the mall of a magical, quaint fishing village at the base of a giant and powerful mountain. I told myself, "I want to go there someday"....so years later I lived out that dream and visited

Reine, Lofoton in Norway, which was a dream come true. My wife's dream since she was a little girl was to go to Hawaii. I was thrilled to have the opportunity to take her on a cruise aboard the Pride of America to Hawaii! There are cruises that will take you nearly anywhere in the world you'd like to go like: the Great Wall of China outside of Beijing, the Fjords of Norway, Tahiti, Rio De Janeiro, even Antarctica.

If you are truly seeking a bargain for your next cruise, ask your Cruise Specialist about a repositioning cruise. When a ship is repositioned from the Caribbean, for example, to Alaska, there are often unique cruises you can tap into that will offer tremendous discounts and value. A repositioning cruise is for those who are flexible with where they go on vacation, and can offer a rewarding experience.

Choosing the right cruise ship
Each cruise ship, even within the same cruise line, have a unique environment onboard, and your Cruise Specialist will be able to assist you with choosing the right ship. When choosing a particular ship, remember that there are often a number of ships with different cruise lines that go to the same or similar itineraries, but the ship you choose may make or break your cruise experience. Cruise ships all have their own unique qualities, so it's up to you and your Cruise Specialist to select the ship that will best match your requirements for the perfect cruise vacation. Some ships have more children onboard, while others may be more focused on couples or mature adults. There are ships that are more carefree and others that are more sophisticated. Your Cruise Specialist knows the intricacies of each ship and cruise line, so lean on their knowledge of the ships. Even ships within the same cruise line might have a reputation for a specific culture onboard that could make the difference in which ship might be best for your requirements.

There are three things to consider when choosing a particular ship: price, itinerary and onboard amenities or culture. Newer ships often have more up-to-date amenities onboard and are priced on the higher scale, whereas older ships that have not been updated might have more bargains available. Cruise lines are scrambling to update their older vessels, but sometimes it's simply better to choose the latest, newest cruise ships with the latest designs and structural amenities. An example is the difference between the Freedom-class ships with Royal Caribbean and the Oasis-class ships. These ships are vastly different with the Oasis-class having a massive open atrium with actual plants, trees and grass grown onboard, and a spectacular aft boardwalk area with open-air shows.

What about the size of your cruise ship? This is another feature to consider. Today, the average new cruise ship is around 90,000 tons, but some ships are as large as 240,000 tons, which is unimaginably huge. If one of your concerns is motion discomfort during your cruise, you may want to select a larger ship. If you prefer more intimacy, then choose a smaller ship. The ships today, are so technologically superior to older vessels when it comes to stability, so a newer, larger vessel would be the best choice if motion is a concern. The larger vessels, on the other hand, often cannot make it into certain ports, so if the itinerary is a priority, then you might have to go with a smaller ship.

Notice the vast difference in size between Royal Caribbean's first ship at about 23,000 tons and the latest Oasis of the Seas at over 240,000 tons.

Chapter 14- What do the experts say about budgeting for a vacation

How to cruise FREE

Yes, you read that correctly, in this article you will learn the secret to cruising for FREE. It may not be as easy as you would hope, but I'm going to give the information here for you to decide how feasible it is.

First step is to contact a "cruise-only" agency that specializes in selling cruises. Determine a date you would like to cruise, and talk to the cruise agency about the specific requirements they have for creating a "group" booking. Generally speaking, a group of 30 paying passengers would allow for two TC's, or "Tour Conductors". The legwork lays with you to pull this together, and create or form a group of fellow travelers to join you on a cruise. To achieve the "Tour Conductor" status, you must put together a group of at least thirty people to receive a "TC" cabin, which is basically a FREE stateroom. You will still have to pay the port fees, and onboard expenses for drinks, gratuities, etc. and depending on your situation, or your charisma and leadership abilities, rounding-up thirty people may not be a challenge. Developing "TC" status and leading a group can be very rewarding, and if you plan out the details carefully with your cruise agency, you might be able to negotiate and plan a way to get your port fees and onboard expenses covered too. I'll leave that up to your imagination as to how that could be accomplished.

You would be surprised at where you might find enough people to form a group. Take a look at people you know from your church, school, Facebook friends, family reunions, bowling league, or social group, and you might find the thirty people or more. Of course if you are a super-social-butterfly, you might even be able to come up with a hundred people or more. The larger the group you are able to put together, the more amenities you will qualify for. Some have even gone as far as to produce a cruise-group as a fundraising opportunity for their favorite charity, where "X" amount per passenger would be allocated towards the charity. The more creative and influential you are the more people you'll be able to attract into your group.

A word of warning; steer clear of emails or offers in your mailbox promoting a free cruise. There are some common scams that suck people into timeshare "opportunities" that say they are offering a wonderful cruise for free as long as you agree to attend a meeting. These often sound so great, but in reality you are paying more than if you simply booked a cruise through your cruise agency. Additionally, these "free cruise scams" offer a substandard cruise experience on a not-so-well-known cruise ship to the Bahamas. If it sounds too good to be true, well.....you might want to steer clear of this.

Traveling in a group can be fun and very rewarding for those who choose the legit way to cruise for free. It's up to you to put the group together, so go ahead, put the plan in motion and make it happen!

In 2015 Author, Barry Vaudrin, hosted a group of about 80 passengers aboard the Celebrity Summit to the Eastern Caribbean

Chapter 15 - *Eastern vs. Western Caribbean – What's the Difference?*

For many years there were two main Caribbean itinerary options including either the Western Caribbean, or the Eastern Caribbean. It truly depends on which cruise line you choose, because Royal Caribbean, Carnival Cruise Line, Princess Cruises, and Norwegian Cruise Line all have their own private island to offer their passengers the private island experience, in both the Western and Eastern itineraries. Let's take these two itineraries and find out what each has to offer.

Eastern Caribbean
The Eastern Caribbean itinerary, generally speaking, offers the ports of St Thomas, San Juan, St Maarten, and in some cases, Grand Turk. These ports all have a diverse range of highlights and offer excellent excursions and fun sites to see. St Thomas in the Virgin Islands is a beautiful island with one of the ten most beautiful beaches in the world called Lover's Beach. The shopping experience in St Thomas is also excellent where bargains can be found in silver items and other jewelry. The people are also very friendly in St Thomas. I remember years ago, and I don't know if this is still practiced by the locals, but, if you needed to go somewhere and you hold up your index finger in the direction you'd like to go, on the side of the road, chances are a local will stop, greet you with a friendly smile and offer you a ride.

San Juan is also included on the eastern Caribbean itinerary, and often can be the port of embarkation for deeper southern itineraries, but that's another story. San Juan is the oldest city on U.S. territory and is the port city of Puerto Rico. The historic district is right in the same area the cruise ships dock, and within walking distance of El Morro Fortress, a military fort dating back to the 1500's. About an hour bus-ride from the port of San Juan, is the beautiful rain forest, which is a popular excursion for vacationers and cruise ship passengers.

Philipsburg, St Maarten is the capital of the Dutch-side of the island, and also where the cruise ships dock. The other side of Saint Maarten is the French side that offers great shopping bargains and fabulous beaches, but be aware of the French-side beaches where it's common to see topless sunbathers. In the not-to-distant past, cruise ships had to "tender" into the 40-square mile island of St Maarten, because there was no dock, however;

over the past few years, new docking facilities have been constructed to allow up to at least five or six large cruise ships to dock at once.

Western Caribbean
Perhaps the most popular itinerary for first-time cruisers is the Western Caribbean which offers ports like: Jamaica, Grand Cayman, and Cozumel. The Western Caribbean itinerary has the best possible snorkeling, beaches, and water-sports options.

Jacques Cousteau labeled the waters of Cozumel to be among the clearest waters in the world, which is fantastic for divers, swimmers, and those who like to snorkel. The waters are as clear as swimming-pool water, and you can often see nearly one hundred feet to the bottom. Cozumel also offers excellent shopping for Mexican craft items and jewelry.

Grand Cayman Island is another fascinating port with unique history and good shopping, but not necessarily thrifty shopping. The famous Seven-Mile-Beach in Grand Cayman is a dream for those who love to lay out on the beach and enjoy swimming and water-sports. Unique to Grand Cayman is the population of seas turtles and visitors can visit a unique town called "Hell", so you can actually send a postcard from "Hell".

Ya Mon, Ire Mon....Jamaica has several ports including Ocho Rios, Montego Bay, and now the Falmouth Cruise Port. Cruise passengers have some excellent and informative shore excursions to choose from like, Dunns River Falls where you can climb the falls, which is a lot of fun. You might choose to visit a plantation that produces sugar, rum, or coffee. One word of caution, however; be sure to only go into Jamaica on a shore excursion organized by the ship, to avoid confrontations with locals selling everything from braided hair, drugs, or prostitution, and there are some common scams and con-artists who prey on tourists.

In short, the Eastern Caribbean offers more of a cultural, historical, and shopping experience, whereas the Western Caribbean offers better water sports, beaches and fun in the sun. Both itineraries have their unique highlights and are excellent choices when cruising the Caribbean. The question to ask yourself when considering which itinerary to choose....are you a shopper or do you prefer the beach?

Chapter 16 - *Why Cruise During a Challenging Economy?*

A question I often hear is, "When is the best time to cruise?" Of course this is a loaded question because the "when" is relative to the needs of the vacationer, however; there are in fact times of the year that are better than others to embark on a cruise. There are certain itineraries, which rely on the seasons, like Alaska, for example. The optimal time of the year for an Alaska cruise is June, July, August, because of the weather. Cruise lines have ships in Alaska starting in May and usually ending in September. June through November in the Caribbean tend to have an increased potential for hurricanes, but the beauty of a cruise vacation is that the ships are mobile and can often avoid rough weather. In addition to weather-related seasons, there are also financial seasons to consider, hence the title of this chapter, "Why Cruise During a Challenging Economy". Basically when the economy is humming along in the positive, cruise lines adjust their revenue profiles and charge more for a stateroom. When the economy takes a dive in the negative, the consumer has less disposable cash and cruise lines adjust their budgets and offer staterooms at discount rates. Cruise line have an arsenal of options to lure the consumer into booking a cruise even during challenging economic times. In addition to lowering the cruise rates, cruise lines may offer interesting amenities to attract business, like onboard credits, complimentary gratuities, free drink packages, free shore excursions, or cabin upgrades. Because of the steep discounting and amenities offered, choosing to cruise during rough economic times allow for the best value to the consumer. Value, is also a relative term when thinking about the consumer, because some people are impacted differently during a tough economy or even a great economy.

What if the economy of a major market crashes dramatically? Let's take the United States, as an example...if there was a catastrophic event, which caused a major crash to the economy, the cruise lines have tricks up their sleeve to survive. Simply the nature of the cruise business, where the revenue-earners are the ships, if the American market dried-up for one reason or another, the ships are mobile and can be easily moved to a market that is strong. Cruise lines have the advantage of being mobile so they can seek out the strong economies and avoid the weak economies. The North American market has mostly been the leader when it comes to supplying cruise buyers, but that may not always be the case, so in the event of a turn-down to the American market, cruise lines are strategically placing their ships in different emerging markets around the world. One particular emerging untapped market is China. As I am writing this book at this very moment May 16th, 2015, Royal Caribbean International is placing the Quantum of the Seas in the Chinese market cruising out of Shanghai. Costa Cruises is sending the Costa Serena and the Costa Fortuna to cruise out of Shanghai as homeport. Princess Cruises is sending the Sapphire Princess to homeport out of Shanghai. There are more cruise lines and ships that will be calling on the Chinese market, because economically, China has seen an explosion in capitalistic ventures. The Chinese market is ripe for the picking and could prove to be an even larger market than the North American market, simply based on the sheer masses in China that currently have more money to spend. The American travel agent has shown skepticism in the decision for cruise lines to send major ship tonnage to China, but most of that skepticism is based on the unknown and intimidation. Yes, travel agents have expressed intimidation when trying to understand the Chinese marketplace because cruise lines can't seem to send ships to China fast enough to keep up with the demand. North American travel agents should welcome the massive growth of the China-based cruises because it opens up an entirely new market to American travelers. Similar to cruises to Europe, the Mediterranean, Greece, the Chinese market has tremendous potential if marketed correctly. There are incredible treasures in China for cruise vacationers to discover like: the Great Wall of China, the Forbidden City, Tiananmen Square, the Terra Cotta Army, the massive Three Gorges Dam and the elusive Yangtze River to name a few.

Another potentially exciting cruise destination is Cuba, and cruise lines are ringing their hands and getting ready for the possibility of Cuba opening up to American vacationers. Politics does have an impact on the cruise industry in ways sometimes subtle and sometime dramatic. In an effort to offer something new to the cruising consumer, American politics may be the catalyst to opening trade with Cuba. Only 90 miles south of Florida, Cuba has been closed to American tourists, but that may change as politicians work their magic to improve relations with Cuba. If millions of Americans are allowed to enter and explore Cuba as tourists, this will potentially make a huge positive impact on the economic landscape of Cuba.

A challenging economy may open up new doors to the consumer as unique incentives are offered yet if it's a tough economy, some people may simply not have the means to spend their valuable resources on a cruise. Disposable income is a relative term, some may have it, others may not, however; it's important to understand the overall value of a vacation. Is a vacation worth the sacrifice of spending "non-disposable" income? There are always options to consider. Perhaps a shorter vacation is more viable than a longer vacation. A little vacation is better than no vacation, and cruise lines offer shorter weekend cruises of three-four days and some offer five-night cruises. In a challenging economy there are many tips the consumer can take advantage of making a cruise vacation more affordable. This book has numerous tips and suggestions for getting the best possible deals when booking a cruise.

Chapter 17 - *How Men See Cruises / How Women See Cruises*

Considering the book written a few years ago, Men are From Mars Women are from Venus, by author John Gray, it's clear that men and women think completely different about nearly everything, including the choice of a vacation. In my own life, my wife Terri, has been on many cruises with me, however; she longs to go to an exotic resort with a beach and just do nothing for a week. That's tough for me as a cruise guy to swallow the fact that my wife would rather go to a ...cough cough...resort. Don't get me wrong, my wife Terri has completely enjoyed the many cruises we've been on, but I think she would just like to try out a resort one time just for the experience. If I could swing a resort gig, I'd jump at it in a heart-beat if it means giving my wife a vacation she desires. A few years ago, I did organize a special cruise to Hawaii for my wife, because it was her life-long dream to go to Hawaii. That Hawaii cruise aboard the Pride of America was a huge hit with my wife and she completely enjoyed the fulfillment of her dream to vacation in Hawaii. I think my wife enjoys the cruises, but when we cruise together, it's always rush here, rush there, do this do that and I think she feels like she is busy during her cruises with me, which is why she'd like to know what it would be like to sit at a resort on a beach for seven days with no agenda other than relax, enjoy the beach and fine dining.

When I use to sell cruises, I discovered an interesting trend. Those seeking to book a cruise were often men simply doing what their wives told them to do, which was to look into booking a cruise. These are first-time cruisers shopping for cruise rates, mostly men, trying to get the best deal. Having never cruised before and on assignment by their wives, these men were often not terribly excited about booking a cruise but it was the vacation of choice for the woman in their life, so they were going through the motions. I have found that typically, it's the women in a marriage or relationship that prefer a cruise, whereas the men would rather do a more traditional vacation of booking a hotel or resort in the Caribbean, Las Vegas or Mexico. The men are reluctant to choose a cruise as a vacation, however; after the cruise, it's the men who have an epiphany and the wives have to drag their husbands off the ship when the cruise is over. Let's examine why men get hooked on cruising after they have their first cruise experience. Men are attracted to machines, and a cruise ship is indeed a very sophisticated machine. A man also appreciates the task of hunting for the best deal and the best travel options to satisfy his woman. A man might also be attracted to the fine dining and all the steak and lobster he can eat during the cruise.

A man will enjoy the adventure of experiencing the different ports and the efficiency of killing two birds with one stone, meaning he can save money on his vacation budget and provide for the travel expectations of his wife.

Women have a different image of a cruise vacation than men. The one word that describes why a woman would choose a cruise is "Romance". Women are drawn-in to the perception of "romance" attached to a cruise vacation. A woman is drawn to a cruise because she sees all of the romantic things to see and do while onboard, like: the fine dining, the shows, the sea, the tropical islands and beaches, and the thought she can spend quality time with her man in a wonderful environment where nearly all her needs are met. Speaking of women and cruising, there is an interesting phenomenon that I have observed on the hundreds of cruises I've been on. This is a general observation and it doesn't always apply to all women. It may be related to the effect of "romance" associated with a cruise, and a few other elements, which I will describe, but many women tend to become more amorous while onboard a cruise ship. Having stood on the gangway to greet every single passenger on embarkation day, I would clearly see, on occasion, that some women experience a sudden wave of emotion and feelings of anticipation that turns on like a switch. I would like to see extensive testing conducted on this observation. Wouldn't this testing make an interesting television show? So men, take notice of this interesting phenomenon that just might affect the woman in your life the moment you step aboard a cruise ship.

I spoke about this phenomenon with a Cruise Director, and he had an interesting angle. Consider this; a cruise ship is like being in the womb. There is the sound of the heart-beat on a cruise ship, or more accurately the engines and the subtle movement of the ship at sea. Onboard a cruise ship numerous physical and emotional needs are met, for example; no need to worry about food, paying the bill after dinning, and a comfortable place to stay is taken care of. The desire for fun and entertainment is provided as well as the desire for adventure and seeing new and wonderful places in the ports. Cruise ships offer the element of romance because so many needs are met by both men and women. Think of the basic human needs, food, shelter, water, companionship, human touch, security & safety, comfort, limited stress....the cares and worries of life are minimized to such a degree on a cruise ship, what remains is an element of freedom, relaxation, free-time, and numerous opportunities for entertainment and one-on-one time with that special someone, very much like being on a date for an extended period of time. The mixture of this "being in the womb" effect, combined with fabulous gastronomical options, a whirlwind of entertainment, and new experiences helps to flip on the switch of romance between men and women. Because women are particularly prone to romance and matters related to "feelings" and "emotions", this is a phenomenon that men should take notice of, and be prepared for. Keep in-mind that all of this magical mixture prevalent on cruise ships, can also impact single women and men who embark on a cruise vacation. The television show "The Love Boat" was indeed the perfect title representing life aboard a cruise ship.

Introduction to Cruise Reviews Section

In this section I have included the cruise reviews of numerous cruise experiences as a Cruise Journalist. Live vicariously through the Cruise Journalist as he experiences the various cruises. From the author's first cruise as a cruise journalist to his experience aboard the Costa Mediterranea, there are some fascinating stories and observations. In the following pages you will experience through the eyes and ears of the Cruise Journalist, various cruises from the Caribbean to Alaska and beyond.

Author's Cruise Review of Norwegian Pearl

I wish I would have kept a writing blog during the cruise on the Norwegian Pearl, but I was too busy, and I didn't have a lap top yet. I did complete the editing of the Norwegian Pearl Experience for Cruising Authority so if you haven't listened to the show, I want to encourage you to do so, because we have some nice interviews with key people on the ship like the Captain and the Cruise Director. This cruise on the Norwegian Pearl was interesting for me, because I had not been on an NCL ship in a long time and this was my first experience with Freestyle Cruising. I must admit that I have not been a fan of NCL lately because I felt the corporation had struggled with it's identity for many years, and I had heard the quality of the onboard cruise experience for passengers was inconsistent. I also felt there were other cruise lines out there that offered a similar product with a far greater sense of direction, consistency and focus, so I would always direct cruise business to other lines within the mass-market and premium category. In the past I was a huge fan of NCL, they were among the first cruise lines out there that offered a great cruise product, and then of course they brought on the SS Norway and did a great job of managing that classic ocean liner for many years. Then NCL was sold to an Asian company, and I saw many odd changes to the line to the point where it looked as if NCL was searching for it's identity or trying to create a new identity, and I felt over the years NCL lost steam and momentum within the competitive cruise market.

After experiencing first-hand a cruise on the Norwegian Pearl, I am now convinced NCL is doing something right. They have developed an innovative concept that other cruise lines are starting to copy called Freestyle Dining and Freestyle Cruising. Up until a few years ago, the traditional dining experience on a cruise ship was centered around your scheduled dining time, either first or second seating. There were dress codes, every seven-day cruise had at least two nights where everyone would dress up to attend the Captain's Gala dinner or farewell dinner. Each

passenger was also assigned a table that they would eat at every night for dinner, at the same table and with the same waiter. With NCL's Freestyle Dinning, passengers basically decide WHEN they want to eat and WHERE they want to eat with multiple dining options and restaurants. There's also no dress code, if you want to go the entire cruise without a tie and jacket, that's perfectly fine on an NCL ship.

I wondered how this Freestyle Dinning would work...I thought there might be lines to get into a particular restaurant, or there might be some confusion related to where to eat etc. but I did not see any issues like this. In fact I kind of liked the idea of going to eat when I was ready and hungry rather than having the dining time forced upon me and wandering into the dining room like sheep for feeding time. Onboard the Norwegian Pearl, dinning was similar to how we would choose to dine at a restaurant at home...we simply decide when to eat and where. Freestyle 2.0 was a big hit in my book and obviously other cruise lines feel it's the way of the future as well, because they are offering similar flexible dining experiences. NCL's corporate offices may be struggling with identity issues, but onboard the ships the crew have a clear focus...to offer the best possible service and experience to passengers. The NCL logo where the fish are all swimming in the same direction except for one fish...that one fish representing NCL, is a great concept and a way for NCL to differentiate themselves from all the other cruise lines out there. Great job NCL!

That was all I wrote in my blog about this experience aboard the Norwegian Pearl.

Author's Cruise Review of Eurodam

It was a short cruise out of New York City aboard a brand new ship called the Eurodam, Holland America's first Signature-Class vessel. I brought my wife, who has never been to New York so I was thrilled to show her around the usual spots like Times Square, the Brooklyn Bridge, ground zero, the Empire State Building and the Statue of Liberty. It was a whirl wind trip, but well-coordinated like a fine time-piece. Cruising Authority the Talkshow has become the most listened-to cruise-related talkshow anywhere and I came across a number of people who enjoy the show, so I had a taste of celebrity status during this trip. That celebrity status was elevated a bit as my wife and I toured all over New York City in a private stretched limo. What a joy it was for me to treat my wife with the luxuries known mostly to the famous and wealthy. By the way, if you're ever in New York City, call New York Limo Guys for all your transportation needs, and you'll get around town in style.

The ship was wonderful! Check-in at the pier was short and effortless. Once we had our boarding pass, we crossed the gangway onto the ship and we immediately went to our stateroom 4180 on Deck Four aft, all the way to the back of the ship. The stateroom, at first glance, looked very cozy with a

smoked-mirror behind the bed, a dark tanish textured carpet, a little sitting area with a vanity, flat-screen TV and a luxurious verandah. The bathroom had a bathtub and the coolest shower mechanism I've seen. The bed, one of the Signature of Excellence features, was very comfortable and the sheets were soft. I thought the little fruit tray in the room with a menu to choose which fruits you preferred to be delivered each day was a nice touch. The fresh flowers in our stateroom offered an extra touch of luxury. You can have the most luxuriously appointed stateroom, but what really makes the whole experience complete is an attentive and gracious steward. Our Steward gave us a little tour of our stateroom and made it clear that he was there to help us with anything we might need in our room. Throughout the cruise our steward also called us by name, and was always very friendly and accommodating. He made the best towel creatures I've seen on a cruise ship. Each evening our bed was turned-down to perfection, it was like an artistic masterpiece the way he made our bed ready each evening, so much so we almost didn't want to mess it up. Our room was very modern and crisp, yet very comfortable, and the lighting throughout the room was just right. The private verandah was of course a luxury and my wife and I enjoyed spending time out there watching the wake of the ship. There are different categories of cruise lines, from mass-market, to resort-style, then perhaps premium and finally upscale and luxury....Holland America Line falls within the "premium" market, however, sometimes, in our stateroom, we felt the level of service and comfort was more upscale than premium, especially when our breakfast was served in our stateroom.

One particular observation that stood out with me as I walked around the ship was the stateroom corridors adorned with great photos of Holland America Line ships past and present. As an ocean liner buff, I was really distracted by all these photos, in a good way. My wife had to often come to an abrupt stop as I had to gaze at the many photos throughout the corridors. This was an extra nice touch I thought, considering my last cruise on the Oosterdam with Holland America, had rather plain corridors. I wish Holland America Line would offer a booklet with all the photos from the corridors in it.

The decor throughout the ship was very classy and elegant with a modern twist. Of course Holland America Line is known for having exquisite artwork and antique artifacts in the lounges around the ship. Eurodam was built on a popular "Vista-class" hull design, similar to the Oosterdam, Noordam, and Westerdam, except on the Eurodam there is an additional deck added with special spa suites, and a structure on Deck 11 where there is an Asian restaurant and lounge. Additionally, Eurodam's decks square off all the way aft rather than tapper-off like the other Vista-class ships in the fleet. It's my understanding, however that the three other Vista-class ships will undergo a transformation to square-off the decks just like Eurodam adding to the tonnage of those ships and additional staterooms too. There are subtle differences throughout the Eurodam that differentiate her from her sisters and I imagine that this vessel will be among the favorites in the fleet because of her charm and cozy décor.

I'm a huge fan of going to the spa, and the Eurodam's spa is awesome! I absolutely love the thermal suite and Hydro pool. In the thermal suite there are a number of thermal curvy tile benches facing the floor-to-ceiling windows offering a great view of the sea. These benches are heated, so when you lay on these things you can feel a soothing warmth on your back, and the benches are contoured to your back and really comfortable. This thermal suite also has two steam rooms, one that is not too hot and the other that is warmer. My favorite thing to do is get all steamed-up and then lay on one of those thermal benches…ooh that's my happy place, especially when the ship is at sea! Then, it's nice to wade into the hydro pool and let the bubbling jets relax the muscles and soothe the tension away. Eurodam has an extra deck of spa suites with a special spiral stairway entrance directly into the hydro pool area.

The ship is certainly beautiful; however, it's the crew and staff onboard that make the ship sparkle. The Indonesian and Pilipino service staff are very gracious and helpful with a smile. This is the one element that sets apart the Holland America Line fleet of ships from the rest of the cruise industry, the nationals onboard from Indonesia and the Philippines. There are second and even third-generation nationals working on the ships giving the cruise line a very traditional and warm feeling of continuity among all the Holland America Line vessels.

Dinning is very special on the Eurodam. It's like they bring out their finest china for every meal in the main dining room and particularly the Pinnacle and Tamarind restaurants. The waiters are very unobtrusive and efficient, so you rarely miss a step in your conversation with other table-mates.

Some other observations I made throughout the ship are as follows: The internet center was moved up to the Crows Nest area, a theater was placed where the internet center is on the other Vista-class ships. The Queens Lounge was a bit dark I thought. The production show was just ok, the singers and dancers did a great job, but I was disappointed with the fact that a sound track was used rather than a live band or orchestra. The production show was uninspiring, too much like all the cruise ships shows I've seen in the past, except for a few cool upgrades to the staging and projected images, and some other high-tech elements. The live music in the Ocean Bar was nice with Sean Bell on the vocals and piano. Sean seemed to develop quite a following of groupees who loved to dance. Most of the decking was the simulated teak deck, except for the promenade wrap-around deck which was real teak. Eurodam also incorporated a new trend in the cruise industry…private cabanas. Passengers can rent for the day or by the hour a private area of deck within their own cabana with lounge chairs, fruit, bottle water, and an iPod docking station for their own private music. There were a number of specialty restaurants aboard Eurodam, an Italian restaurant, an Asian restaurant, and of course the Pinnacle Restaurant. I also noticed you can get pizza by the slice at the aft pool area. Holland America effectively combined many great new amenities and features aboard their newest ship the Eurodam, which I think is going to be a big hit!

Author's Cruise Review of Seven Seas Mariner

Early morning June 17th we packed our bags, my wife Terri and I, and my son Jacob departed Minneapolis non-stop for Vancouver to embark on an Alaska cruise adventure aboard Regent's Seven Seas Mariner. I have been on about 300 cruises over the years, I love being at sea, I love cruising, and enjoy every chance I get to be on a cruise ship, so this opportunity to cruise on the upscale luxury Seven Seas Mariner in a

penthouse suite was without question a delight and a joy. I do have some experience with the upscale luxury cruise products, having crossed the Atlantic as a passenger aboard the QE2, and then living and working aboard QE2 as Stage Manager in 1992 was a dream come true for me. My luxury experience also includes the QM2 and I've visited ships with Crystal, Seabourn, Royal Viking, the old Sea Goddess ships, and a few others. I guess you could say I've been a student of luxury ocean travel, because I have studied the history of the trans-Atlantic era for many years. Oddly enough, considering all the cruises I've been on, this was my first Alaska cruise, so what better way to experience an Alaska itinerary than on a first class luxury ship. What was truly exciting for me was the opportunity to bring my wife and my eight-year-old son on this Alaska cruise. Of course every chance I get to treat my wife to a luxury cruise experience is a huge joy for me. The one concern we had, however, was bringing our son Jacob on this luxury cruise, because normally Alaska cruises attract an older more refined demographic, and additionally, the upscale lines, like Regent Seven Seas Cruises is perceived to be an environment that would be boring and unfit for kids. Our thoughts were that other cruise lines like Royal Caribbean or Carnival may be better suited for families with children because they have the facilities onboard for kids. We decided to take a leap of faith and rely on what we had been told about Regent's Seven Seas Mariner, and that during the Alaska season there are many families with children who cruise on this ship. We also heard that the Seven Seas Mariner has some wonderful youth programs during the Alaska season. In short, we were not disappointed, because our son Jacob had an enjoyable experience, and there were indeed about 50 children in Jacob's age-group onboard our cruise.

The Ship

The Seven Seas Mariner has a length of 709 feet, a beam of 93 feet, and a draft of 21 feet carrying 700 passengers and 445 crew in a 50,000 ton hull

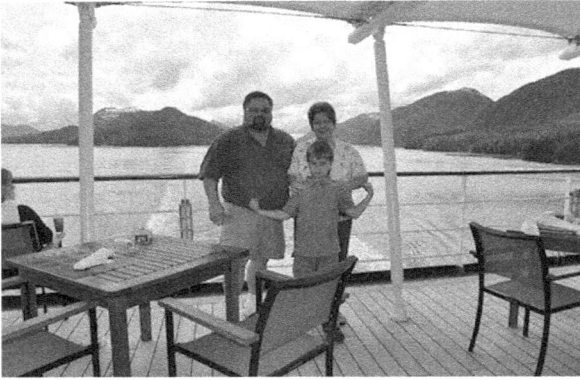

built at Chantiers de l'Atlantique, St. Nazaire, in France and first launched in 2001. The Mariner was the first cruise ship built as an "All-Suite" vessel with only balconied staterooms for it's guests. I have a particular appreciation for ship designs, and how they look aesthetically from the inside and outside, and I can say that I was pleased with the overall design of the ship, with it's sharp bow and sculpted stern. My wife made a comment that this was the first time she didn't get turned around or lost on a ship, because of the well laid out design of the public rooms. Indeed it is easy to navigate around the ship because of her more intimate size. The atrium seems to connect all the public areas quite nicely. Deck Five has the Purser's Desk and the Tour Desk, as well as a place to purchase future cruises. As you go aft there's a bar and a very comfortable lounge for pre-dinner cocktails before you arrive at the entrance to the main restaurant called the Compass Rose, and the more intimate Prime 7, which is a steakhouse. On Deck Six you'll find the upper-level to the main show lounge forward, a perfume shop in the atrium area, then as you walk aft thru what could be considered the main boulevard through the ship, there is a disco, a café, computer center, library, and a conference room. Further aft is the Signatures Restaurant and the Horizon Lounge, which has windows that look out over the stern of the ship. I really like the deck area just outside of the Horizon Lounge that has some wicker chairs and sofas, where you can watch the wake of the Seven Seas Mariner and really find a connection to the sea. On Deck Seven forward are the Spa and the fitness rooms, and then as you work your way aft thru the atrium you'll find the casino and some shops. Decks Eight, Nine and Ten are suites, then on Deck Eleven is the pool deck with a decent, heated pool with three hot tubs. Further aft is the La Veranda restaurant, and then past the restaurant is a nice deck area to enjoy a meal outside. Finally, Deck 12 has the Observation Lounge, which is the perfect venue for watching the scenery, listening to some live music with a coffee or tea.

The Seven Seas Mariner seemed to handle the seas very well...I could tell that she had the characteristics of a world-class vessel, comfortable in nearly any sea conditions which is important when the ship is making those deep sea trans-oceanic voyages. We had fairly calm seas during our cruise. There was one evening, however, where we could feel the motion a bit, and I was quite happy with the way the ship handled the seas.

The Itinerary

I've been to Alaska, but never on a cruise, so it was an adventure exploring the ports of Ketchikan, Juneau, Skagway, and Sitka. Seven Seas Mariner docked in all of the ports except in Sitka where there is no dock, and we had the opportunity to tender into town. I enjoy tendering sometimes, because it gives me a chance to see the ship away from the dock at anchor. We only participated in shore excursions in Ketchikan and in Juneau. Alaska is such a rustic, scenic place, and the ports, although quaint, parts of the towns seem to be built specifically for the tourists that arrive by cruise ships. There is a lot of history in these ports, so it's fascinating to explore their origins and heritage. Those we met who live in Alaska, love it there and say they will never leave. Why leave? Alaska can be remote and attracts those who enjoy adventure, the mountains, the sea and the great wilderness.

We enjoyed a wonderful shore excursion in Ketchikan. Our excursion departed around five in the evening and we took a motor coach to the

George Inlet Lodge where we enjoyed a spectacular fresh crab feast that would put Red Lobster to shame. These were huge, fresh, boiled crabs, and we could have as much as we wanted. After we feasted on the wonderful crab legs everyone in our group was served a delightful cheesecake for dessert. The motor coach ride to the lodge took about 40 minutes, but it was the transfer back to the ship that was particularly memorable because we boarded a floatplane that flew over some very picturesque terrain. Our pilot pointed out some interesting things as we flew back to the ship.

In Juneau I wanted to choose an excursion that would be fun for my eight-year-old son Jacob, so we took the helicopter and dogsled adventure. This was an amazing excursion, one of the most exciting I have ever taken. A representative of the excursion met us at the gangway in Juneau, where we boarded a motor coach for a short ride to the helicopter port. We were given some instructions about the helicopter ride and told to put on an inflatable life vest and special boots that fit over our shoes. Then we were assigned a pilot and taken to our helicopter. It was truly an adventure to fly in this helicopter up, up, higher and higher, over the tops of the mountains and glaciers. The scenery was spectacular, and I was snapping pictures and video, hoping my camera battery and memory card would hold out till we arrived at our destination way high up on top of a glacier. We slowly descended upon a snowy area where our dogsled camp awaited us. What a thrill it was to see my son Jacob and my wife absorbing this amazing experience. Being from Minnesota, we are no strangers to snow, but what was slightly unexpected was how deep the snow was up there on the glacier. Now it was clear to me why they had us put on these boots over our shoes. We had a short orientation about the dogs and then introduced to our trainer, Jennifer, who would take us on our dog sledding adventure. There were two sleds attached to each team of dogs. The trainer rode the first sled, and my son drove the rear sled. Basically he had to stand on the sled rails, and then stomp on the break when it was time to stop. My wife rode in the front sled with the trainer, and I rode in the rear sled while my son stood on the rails as the "musher". Apparently the dogs absolutely love to pull the sleds around, so we didn't feel so bad being passengers on their sleds. We would stop a few times to let the dogs rest. The whole experience was a huge thrill for my son, and he still talks about how he ran behind the sled and got to mush the dogs. I think we sledded a couple of miles and then returned to the camp. After our ride, the trainer, Jennifer, unhooked and introduced us to her dogs. Jacob had a great time petting the dogs. Soon it was time to board the helicopter and fly back to Juneau. Again, the flight back was spectacular as our pilot skimmed the tops of mountains and

glaciers. What a view! Even if you don't have children, be sure to take the helicopter and dogsled adventure.

We just walked around Skagway and panned for gold at a museum along the river. In Sitka, we didn't go on any excursions, we just walked around town, however; we did visit the Raptor Center and saw some American Bald

Eagles up-close. We also went up onto the top of the hill where the papers were signed to officially make Alaska one of the United States. Sitka does offer some exciting excursions to a volcano and some wonderful fishing and whale-watching tours by boat.

It wasn't a port, but we did visit the Hubbard Glacier, and the Captain spun the Seven Seas Mariner around a few times so we could get an eyeful of this picturesque and spectacular glacier. I think we were about a mile from the glacier, which was fairly close. The larger cruise ships aren't able to get quite as close as we did.

If your cruise ends in Seward like ours, be sure to take the train into Anchorage. All I can say is WOW! The scenery, the mountains, the glaciers, and the train ride itself was incredible.

The Dining
I had heard so much about the excellent dinning on Regent's ships, so I was looking forward to experiencing it first-hand. Without a doubt, I was not disappointed; the dining experience was excellent! There were of course numerous choices, however, I ate a lot of fish during this cruise. It's a personal thing, I'm just not a big beef or steak eater. I had lots of halibut and Alaskan Rock fish, and although I've never like salmon, I even tried the Salmon and loved it. I guess there's a difference if the salmon is fresh and doesn't have any fishy taste. Speaking of fresh, I was told by the Executive Chef that the fish is extremely fresh because he hand-picks the never frozen fish from selected vendors right in the ports. My wife, on the other hand, was in her element as she indulged each evening on the finest steaks she's ever had. The level of service was excellent, and I was very pleased with how the

waiters took care of our eight-year-old son. We ate in the main restaurant onboard called the Compass Rose several times and enjoyed the food and service, then two nights we made special reservations to eat in Prime Seven and Signatures which are more exclusive dining venues. There are no cover charges for Prime Seven or Signatures, however, because there is limited seating, it's important to get your reservations in when you first board the ship. I really enjoyed the selection of wines served each evening, and again there was no additional charge for this. I would say the overall best dining experience we had was in the Signatures restaurant. The mushroom soup was spectacular, and when our main entre arrived, the waiters presented our plate in grand style by unveiling our dinner covered with a silver dome. It was like, here's your dinner....Ta Daaaa! I personally like the more French-style of dinning with the exquisite sauces. We also had breakfast a number of times in La Veranda on Deck 11 aft. The selection of fruits, meats, vegetables, breads and cheeses was excellent. They have an egg omelet station where a chef will prepare your omelet just how you like it. I even indulged in some wonderful caviar. To me one of the signs of luxury is fresh squeezed orange juice...ahhh that's the best! It's very evident that the chefs aboard the Seven Seas Mariner go to great lengths to provide the best possible dining experience weather you eat in La Veranda on deck or in the exclusive Signatures or Prime Seven restaurants, or in the elegance of the main Compass Rose dining room. Another wonderful signature of luxury is dining in your suite. We ordered room service on several occasions for breakfast and once for dinner, and each dining experience was perfect. I decided to really test the room service one morning by ordering my eggs prepared a certain way that was not offered on the room service card. I happen to like eggs Benedict, so when it asked how I want my eggs on the little card placed out on our door the night before, I wrote down that I wanted eggs Benedict. Sure enough, the next morning right on time, the waiter set up a lovely breakfast table in our suite, and there it was, eggs Benedict. Having experienced some of the finest eggs Benedict around the world, I can now say that the eggs Benedict on the Seven Seas Mariner was exquisite!

Onboard Entertainment

Having been a Cruise Director and an entertainer on the ships in the past, I always pay close attention to the entertainment, and I was impressed with the singers and dancers and the orchestra onboard Seven Seas Mariner. The main show lounge was very comfortable, with excellent views from every vantage point in the room. The sound was excellent and the lighting was done very well. I liked the stage which stuck out into the audience a bit, allowing the singers and dancers to get closer to the audience. A huge plus, in my book, was the full orchestra providing the music for the shows as opposed to a sound track, which in my opinion cheapens the overall production quality. The only criticism I might have with the entertainment is the lack of variety of the entertainment in the show lounge. The shows were all with the singers and dancers, there was no comedian, or illusionist, the shows revolved around the talent within the singers and dancers. Not to diminish the quality of the talent, which was excellent, I just felt that there should be more variety in the type of entertainment. Of course throughout the ship on sea days, particularly, there were fun little games set up in the atrium area for passengers to participate in. Makeshift bowling, darts, and golf putting were set up in the atrium and the passengers seemed to enjoy the activities. On an Alaska cruise, however, the primary form of entertainment is the view from the decks while cruising through the Inside Passage, or Hubbard Glacier. Throughout the cruise there was a professor of Alaskan history that talked over the PA system from the bridge, explaining all the sights we were seeing. There was also a lecturer on ocean liner history in the Horizons Lounge….oh wait…that was me giving an informal lecture on the history of the trans-Atlantic liners.

Children and youth program
The children's program on the Seven Seas Mariner was particularly important for us because we have an eight-year-old and we wanted him to enjoy the cruise to Alaska too. We were concerned that he might be bored on a ship with no hardware facilities for kids, but the "software" or youth staff, made up for the lack of physical play areas designed for kids. The youth staff was awesome! They kept the kids busy with activities and projects. The kids also learned about Alaska during their cruise in a fun way. My son will be talking about riding the float plane, the helicopter and the dog sledding for years, so this cruise to Alaska with our son turned out to be a great experience for all of us. We were a bit concerned because of the upscale luxury element onboard the Seven Seas Mariner and the more refined passenger compliment, but that concern quickly faded when we saw there were about 50 kids in the same age group as my son. We did, however, have one incident when a woman scolded us as parents for not controlling our son better, but this woman, with her nose in the air, I think, was out of line. The ship was moving and my son was exaggerating the movement of the ship a bit and he purposely ran into a bulkhead…he was just being silly, and he was just being an eight-year-old boy, so this woman's comments were ridiculous, as if her excrement doesn't stink, to say it as civilized as possible.

Our Penthouse Suite

As much as I've cruised over the years, this was the first time I had the pleasure of staying in a Penthouse Suite on a ship. I was thrilled to treat my wife to the luxuries of a Penthouse Suite, and we certainly enjoyed every moment. We were in Suite number 836 on Deck Eight midship. This suite was 376 square feet, and the balcony was a huge 73 square feet, that's a total of 449 square feet of luxurious accommodations. The Seven Seas Mariner was the first ship to be constructed with all suites with balconies, so there are no interior staterooms or suites with just a window. Our suite had a walk-in closet and a fancy bathroom with a tub and marble counter. I was able to peek in the suite next to ours, which has a bathroom that was renovated during the recent 20 million refit in January of 2009. Apparently not all the bathrooms received the refit, which included a walk-in shower as opposed to a tub and shower like we had. We had nothing to complain about, however, with our spacious bathroom. I'm sure my wife felt like a queen for the week in our suite, because she had her own vanity for fixing her makeup. The king-size bed had wonderfully soft cotton sheets and we had a choice of feather or cotton-stuffed pillows. I think one of the best features of our suite was the floor-to-ceiling windows looking out to the sea, perfect for an Alaskan itinerary with so much to see. There was a decent television in the room connected to your online account so you always know what you're spending onboard, and they have free movies to watch. With a DVD player connected to your TV, you can also check out DVD's from the library, which is a great service. Our suite also had a nice desk for writing letters. I used the desk of course to put my laptop so I could go online and write on my blog and keep up with my emails. With YFi throughout the ship, it makes it easy to stay connected to your friends and family or business online. We also had personalized stationary that said, "From the Penthouse Suite of Mr. and Mrs. Vaudrin, aboard the Seven Seas Mariner". Our suite also had a complimentary box of fine chocolates, and a bottle of Champaign. Each day at around 4pm a waiter would deliver a tray of giant shrimp cocktail to the living room area of our suite. Our stewardess was wonderful because she was so friendly and made us feel at home in our Penthouse suite. There are much more expansive suites aboard the Seven Seas Mariner, however,

what we had was just right. Category B suites and above even have butler service, which I think would be very interesting, because they unpack your luggage and pack your things the night before. The butler acts as your own personal concierge and takes care of dinner reservations and shore excursions or perhaps you want a private car to take you to a fine restaurant in one of the ports.

Definition of Luxury
When I set out to go on this luxury cruise aboard the Seven Seas Mariner, I wrote out my definition of luxury to see if I could find a match while cruising on this ship. I was not disappointed. In fact, if I would have written out a wish list for the perfect Alaska cruise, I am pleased to say that every one of my expectations were not only met but exceeded. Below are my three definitions of luxury:

1. When Comfort Exceeds Expectations

2. When you are able to exclusively obtain an experience or something of high quality

3. When you discover and receive a genuine-level of exceptional care and service from someone.

It was a pleasure to cruise Alaska aboard the Seven Seas Mariner! I enjoyed my morning routine of visiting the steam room in the spa, and my wife got her nails done in the salon. I splurged and treated myself to something I had always wanted to try, a Four Hands Massage. I get a massage at least a couple times a month and one of my fantasies was to have two therapists work on me at the same time. I was able to fulfill that fantasy during this cruise, because they had that particular service on the menu, a Four Hands Massage.

You can have the fanciest ship or hardware, but what truly makes a luxury cruise a luxury experience is the people and the level of service they provide. All of the crew and staff we encountered were very friendly, and very service oriented. Whenever we would say thank you to our stewardess, she would often say, "It's my pleasure Mr. Vaudrin or Mrs. Vaudrin". The Executive Concierge, the General Manager, the Captain, the Executive Chef, our waiter genuinely treated us as special guests in their home. In essence the Seven Seas Mariner was their home. We obtained something of great value during this cruise, we also discovered a genuine-level of exceptional care and service, and the comfort of our Penthouse suite and throughout the ship exceeded our expectations. A cruise, anywhere around the World, and particularly Alaska, aboard the Seven Seas Mariner was indeed a luxury experience and I think this ship and her crew would exceed your expectations too.

Looking back on this cruise aboard the Seven Seas Mariner, it was a very memorable experience, particularly because I was able to share the experience with my wife and my son. I produced a video of this experience and included a unique challenge for my wife and I to see if we can enjoy this cruise without gaining weight. During the cruise I took specific supplements that were designed to block carbs along with multi-vitamins. Interestingly, the result of our test was that I did not gain weight even after enjoying the fabulous dining onboard, while my wife Terri, did not take the supplements and she gained five pounds. So it is possible to cruise and not gain weight.

Author's Cruise Review of Nieuw Amsterdam

There are many cruise products out there to choose from when it comes to planning a family vacation, and a few years ago a Holland America Line

cruise might not be on the radar for parents to consider, however; within the last ten years more family amenities, features and programming have been integrated into their ships and is evident on the Nieuw Amsterdam. For nearly one hundred and forty years Holland America Line has established itself as a solid, reliable, classy company, starting out as a Dutch national passenger shipping line, operating trans-Atlantic crossings and world-wide itineraries mostly for transportation like most other shipping companies in the early nineteen hundreds, through the fifties. Of course the passenger shipping industry faded as the jet aircraft took over the trans-Atlantic route, and a few of these "national" passenger shipping companies, like Britain's Cunard Line, the United States Line and Holland America Line, shifted their services from transport roles to cruising. I recently took my family on a cruise aboard the fourth ship in Holland America Line's history to bare the name Nieuw Amsterdam. Launched in July of 2010, the beautiful "vista-class" Nieuw Amsterdam is Holland America Line's newest ship incorporating all of the "Signature of Excellence" amenities and features that first-time and return passengers have come to enjoy over the past several years. My wife Terri, and my nine-year-old son Jacob, accompanied me on the eastern Caribbean itinerary aboard the Nieuw Amsterdam with the great anticipation of enjoying a wonderful vacation together as a family.

As a Cruise Industry Journalist, I was very busy onboard throughout the whole cruise aboard the Nieuw Amsterdam gathering video and audio content for my Cruising Authority website at www.cruisetalkshow.com and admittedly, I didn't relax as much as I should have. My wife helped me with getting the videos, so she worked extra hard on this "vacation" along with me. We did have our moments where we enjoyed time together as a family on shore excursions and some meal times. For us it was convenient to check our son into Club HAL while we worked on getting the video content together. Most passengers with children however; could use the "Club HAL time" away from their kids and enjoy the pool, the spa, or laying out on deck.

My son enjoyed Club HAL, which came as a surprise to me because they didn't have the water slides and water parks like some other cruise ships. Club HAL has rooms onboard the Nieuw Amsterdam dedicated to certain age groups; there was a child care area for little kids then a "tween" room for kids up to about 12 years old then a teen area. The "tween" room is where my son hung out for various planned activities. This "Tween" room had an authentic New York Taxi Cab for the kids to play in and around. This cab allows for the kids to use their imagination and pretend to drive everywhere. These days, I guess if the kid's facility has enough video games, that's sufficient to entertain these younger passengers. I know Club HAL also had numerous other activities to keep the kids busy like Spy Night and Paper Airplane Night, and a Club HAL version of the Olympics as well as a pajama party. Even though there are no water slides, my son swam for hours in the Lido Pool area on Deck Nine midship. As a parent it made me happy that my son was having a good time on this cruise, and I could count on Club HAL to provide the activities for him to enjoy himself. Jacob is nine years old and was given the opportunity with our permission of course to check himself in and out of Club HAL. I think my son enjoyed that freedom and responsibility to be able to leave if he was bored and go to our stateroom. Boredom, however; was not in my son's vocabulary during this cruise when he was engaged and plugged into Club HAL.

Dining onboard the Nieuw Amsterdam was a treat for all of us as a family. Since we were on vacation, if my son wanted pizza, we gave him the freedom to go for it, and on Deck Nine aft there is a little pizza place called "Slice" where pizza was available throughout the day. I enjoyed the mornings as a family because we usually ate together in the Lido, and of course there was a plethora of options including, eggs, omelets, sausage, bacon, breakfast rolls, cereal, and my breakfast of choice in recent months, oatmeal. There were fruits and juices and pancakes, nearly any breakfast you can imagine was available in the Lido each morning. We also ate from the Terrace Grill at the Lido Pool area for lunches. I was impressed to be able to have a turkey dog or a salmon burger rather than the usual beef hotdog or hamburger. Our first night onboard, as a family we had reservations in the Tamarind Restaurant, which was delightful! Even my son enjoyed some of the unique options and he was adventurous enough to try a little caviar. The service, presentation and quality of the food in Tamarind was excellent and worth making reservations in advance to eat in this place. There is a charge to eat here, and it's worth the extra few dollars to experience this Asian fusion dining. To truly go over-the-top and indulge in fine dining at it's best, without question the Chef's Table eight-course meal in the Pinnacle dining room was exceptional. We dined on the best Versace tableware, had the best wine sampling for each course, and I ate things I normally wouldn't care for, because it was prepared with exquisite culinary skill and craftsmanship. Particularly delicious was the Frappe of Lobster and Porcini Bisque, wow, that was such a delightful and smooth taste! This evening at the Chef's table was the first time I had ever indulged in the delicacy of Goose Liver and I was surprised there was not a "liver" taste to it. We also had Sea Bass with Caviar, Veal and completing the evening with the "Dialogue of Chocolate Seduction" which was seductive!

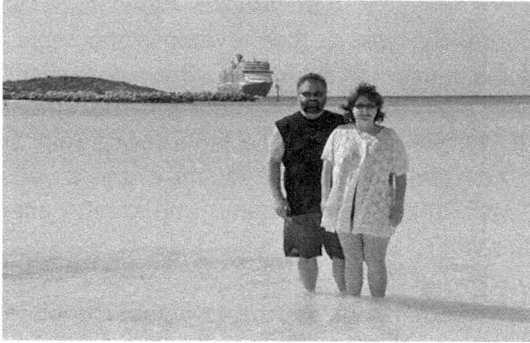

For the Manhattan Dining room I would recommend either first or second seating rather than the new "As You Wish" dining, because chances are you'll have a different wait staff each visit who will not have the opportunity to know you and your general preferences. We elected to dine in the Manhattan Dining room twice with As You Wish reservations and I wouldn't recommend it. The reasoning is because the wait staff has numerous tables at different levels and times of their course which may be somewhat challenging for the wait staff to accommodate the varying schedules efficiently. We felt that our waiter rushed us through our dinner and even brought out two courses at the same time, like for example our salad and entrée arrived at the same time. This may have been an isolated incident, however; we noticed that both of our experiences in the Manhattan Dining room were similar. Additionally, although the wait staff was very efficient, I felt that our waiters acted with more of a robotic precision rather than the more personable and friendly manner you would expect when enjoying a fine-dining experience. Again, I think if we had a regular wait staff each night, we would get to know them and they would get to know us, and there would be a more personable exchange, which we felt we missed in the "As You Wish" dinning experience. One more observation about the Manhattan Dining Room was the level of noise when the room was full. Wow, it got loud and difficult to carry on a conversation with someone across the table. I think part of the noise is from the design of the room, which acoustically allowed for sound to bounce all over the place because of the smooth surfaces. I think that perhaps if you are able to get a table away from the center two-level-high section of the room, in a corner, you may have a better experience with regard to the basic dining room volume and maybe enjoy your conversations with your tablemates easier.

This voyage aboard the Nieuw Amsterdam took us to the Eastern Caribbean ports of Half Moon Cay, Holland America Line's private island and beaches, St Maarten, San Juan and finally Grand Turk Island. I am convinced that Half Moon Cay is one of the top three private beaches owned by a cruise line with it's soft, white, powdery beaches and beautifully colored water. Holland America Line has done a great job of building play areas for kids and families with a fun water park and now a new two-level high pirate ship bar. From the pirate ship's top deck you can get a great view of the whole island. As a family we didn't get off the ship in St Maarten and elected to hang out and swim in the Lido pool while most of the passengers took off for excursions. We did, however; go on the Rain Forest Drive while in San Juan. I had been to San Juan about fifty times but never visited the rain forest, so this was my opportunity to do something I had never experienced. I was a little concerned that my son would get bored, and in fact he didn't want to go, but fortunately he found a friend his age on our bus and he had a great time exploring the observation tower and the lush trail through the forest. We stopped at a waterfall and climbed around together, which I think my son really enjoyed. The rain forest tour was a success! Finally, with our visit to Grand Turk, we decided to go on the horseback riding adventure and swim. This was my first time to Grand Turk and my son's first time riding a horse. My son was so funny, as I tried to take video of him while he was riding the horse, and he kept telling me he cannot look back because he was concentrating on driving the horse. The tour was very organized and I got a kick out of the operators of the tour as we were all being assigned a horse to ride. I felt like I was in high school waiting to be chosen to play on a particular team, as the operator would size up the various people in our group and then select a horse they thought would be best for that person. I would guess that the children in our group were assigned horses that were more obedient and docile. I was told that these horses came from Jamaica and were retired race horses. After a ride along the beach to the lighthouse, we returned to the little coral so the saddles could be changed for riding in the ocean. The operators would take small groups to the beach on horseback, and into the ocean up to our knees. The horses would plow through the water and even run through the ocean which was quite exhilarating. If there was one moment during our cruise that I was glad we had travel insurance with Access America, this was it. You never know what could happen, and even though we were all safe and there were no

accidents or injuries, I had peace of mind knowing that if there was a problem, we would have been taken care of.

While in Grand Turk, I happened to be in the right place at the right time and was able to meet Winston Scott, who was one of the astronauts from the space shuttle program. We happened to be in Grand Turk during the grand opening of an exhibition celebrating the splash down of the John Glenn space capsule in 1962 just off the coast of Grand Turk Island. There was a mock-up of the John Glenn space capsule and some very informative placards explaining the history of the space program and how Grand Turk Island has been a pivotal place for NASA and the U.S Military.

Holland America Line has certainly evolved over the past ten years or so in order to gain a wider and more diverse demographic which includes a less elderly yield. The entertainment for example, appeals to more discerning passengers with a taste for higher quality and more professional entertainers. I think what Holland America Line has done with the entertainment is excellent. They are working with a shore-based entertainment company that provides top quality and talented musicians that have the flexibility to stand on their own as entertainers. As an example, there was a quartet of violinists that alone performed an entire concert in the Explorers Lounge, and their talent was also utilized in the bigger, combined shows with singers and dancers. The same can be said about the four-man group called Cantare, who were also utilized in a number of other shows during the cruise. I enjoyed the grand finale show where Sandy Patti's "Love in Any Language" is sung as crew and staff from all over the ship come together to bid farewell.

Was I unhappy with any aspect of the cruise? Holland America Line creates such a comforting environment, it would truly be a challenge to find unhappy passengers, however; on our cruise there was a very small number of passengers who were experiencing gastro-intestinal issues or norovirus, so the crew had to work extra hard and longer hours to make sure the ship was sterilized and absolutely spotless. Hand sanitizer was used at the entrance to all the restaurant areas so it was mandatory for all passengers to sanitize their hands when entering the dining venues or entering the ship from shore. The buffet in the Lido was on lock-down so no passengers could help themselves to food, rather the food was served by the crew. No salt and pepper shakers were available on the tables, but individual packets were available upon request. The biggest disappointment for my wife and I was the fact that the spa with the thalassotherapy pool and the thermal beds and hot tubs were unavailable and closed throughout the duration of the cruise. This was a precautionary measure to minimize the risk of spreading this GI disease. I wouldn't of course blame Holland America Line for this, because they were in fact taking extra stringent precautions to prevent further spreading of this highly contagious virus. After speaking with the Hotel Director, he informed me that their extra stringent measures were effective in preventing further issues, which overall, allows for more passengers to fully enjoy their cruise.

I think the new "Signature-Class" vessels, the Eurodam and Nieuw Amsterdam, both of which I have cruised on, are the maximum size of ship that Holland America Line should build. The cruise industry has plenty of larger ships, and Holland America Line maintains that "premium" standard, even with ships as large as the Nieuw Amsterdam. Both the Eurodam and Nieuw Amsterdam are wonderful ships, well built, with classy interiors and with truly exceptional crew members. With ships of this size, however; there is a magnified "feeling" that this is a very large company and I think the more intimate, personalized, experience onboard is watered down a bit. Don't get me wrong, the crew onboard do an excellent job and the ships never feel crowded, in fact I think Holland America Line has mastered the art of providing an excellent, comfortable, classy and "premium" vacation experience. It's like the "feeling" you get when you live in a small town, compared to living in a larger metropolitan city. It's that "small-town" feeling that causes passengers to become so loyal to Holland America Line. For the discerning vacationers, Holland America Line delivers. For families with children vacationing aboard any of the Holland America Line vessels, you can be assured that your kids will also enjoy a fun and memorable vacation.

Interviewing Cruise Journalist Peter Knego

Author's Cruise Review of Silver Spirit

Enter the world of Silversea and you are embraced by a refined, unobtrusive blend of modern design and a sophistication reserved for the affluent

individuals who are accustomed to concierge and butler services, fine dining, exquisite wines and exotic destinations. Today the world often seems like it's shaking with political and economic fallout all around us, yet when you board the Silver Spirit those

cares of the world fall away, and it's like entering an oasis of peace. I recently boarded the Silver Spirit for a seven night cruise through the Italian Riviera, however; I missed the first couple of days because of transportation and logistics. We boarded the Silver Spirit in Taormina, Italy on a beautiful day in May. The ship was anchored in the harbor perfectly contrasted with the ancient Italian culture, and beckoning us to open our imagination to the upscale experience awaiting us. As a Journalist, I usually travel with my wife, but this time my Father-in-law, Richard, assisted me with my video work. It's interesting, Richard is a retired minister and now works in an executive position with Kids Against Hunger, so this level of luxury was very foreign to him. Can you imagine how thrilled I was to watch Richard experience the fine dining and exotic excursions?

The Silver Spirit is Silversea's newest and largest vessel with luxury accommodations for 540 passengers. At 642 feet long and 36,000 tons, Silver Spirit is not a small vessel, however; compared to most of the newbuilds today, she is on the smaller more intimate size. With 376 European crew members serving the 540 passengers, the crew to guest ratio is higher than on most other cruise ships. It is this exclusivity that is so appealing to Silversea passengers, in a ship that offers amenities and services for a few hundred as opposed to a few thousand passengers. I didn't see crowds of passengers nor did I wait in any lines for dinner. The feeling onboard the Silver Spirit was close to being at a private club or yacht, but the most distinguishing element was a relaxed, carefree, precise environment to indulge in the good life...whatever that may mean to you.

I enjoyed the dining experience, knowing that each meal was made-to-order, and a testament to the expertise of highly trained chefs, with the best possible ingredients. Every evening, complimentary fine wine is served and the wine glass is kept full throughout the meal. The attentive waiters made me feel like they enjoyed their job and were sincere when they often asked if I needed anything. The reason I mention this is because on the many cruises I've been on over the years it's not uncommon to notice that many wait staff personnel are on automatic pilot, and work as if they are on an assembly line just doing their job. This was certainly not what I experienced onboard the Silver Spirit, the waiters and waitresses were genuinely focused on providing exceptional service. I counted at least six different restaurants onboard the Silver Spirit from the main Restaurant on Deck Four to the Italian La Terrazza on Deck Seven and the Pool Grill serves a wonderful "Hot Rock" dining experience on Deck Ten overlooking the pool. The Hot Rock dining gives the guest an opportunity to cook their own meat on a hot slab of rock served at your table, so you can have fun preparing your fresh fish or steak cooked exactly how you prefer. Rudi Scholdis, Silversea's Culinary Director, was onboard our voyage preparing mussels using beer, at an exquisite poolside buffet. Setting the standards for Silversea's cuisine fleet-wide, Chef Rudi has demonstrated his culinary expertise for Royalty including Queen Elizabeth, Prince Charles, and Heads of State like Bill Clinton, King Kayd of Saudi Arabia, Israeli Prime Minister Netenayu, and numerous Hollywood stars. Since Chef Rudi has prepared fine dining for all these famous world-

personalities, why not for me? On a Silversea voyage you can ask the same indulgent question, "why not you"?

Luxury does have a certain "feel", a certain "taste", and even a familiar "sound", relative to the distinguishing senses of those who can afford it. During my experience aboard the Silver Spirit, I savored the aroma of luxury, even as a mere Journalist. For me, there were numerous and specific moments that caused me to be more than content, for example; I enjoyed the spa onboard, particularly the steam room and sauna that each had a large window looking out to the sea. I'm no elite, and I may have been pretending to be someone I was not, but it did feel good to have the ability and freedom to ask for a glass of champagne while in the relaxing thermal bath on deck by the pool. During our visit to Rome, my Father-in-law and I embarked on a special shore excursion lead by Rosalba Iocca, who was no ordinary tour guide. Yet another example of Silversea's commitment to provide the very best for guests, Rosalba was an expert in Roman history, she studied archeology, but her greatest asset as an expert Roman guide was through her intimate contacts at Vatican City and the Coliseum. Rosalba lead our bus group ahead of the masses waiting for hours in lines to enter the museums and the coliseum, circumventing the system and quickly ushering our group immediately into the many museums, the coliseum and so much more as if we were VIP's or someone special. It's no coincidence, our tour guide to Rome was the best there is, and I'm certain the Shore Excursions people at Silversea go to great lengths to plan, coordinate, and capture the best guides, tour routes, buses, and VIP access for Silversea guests.

Whatever your definition of luxury is, the perks of being a Silversea passenger are obvious, but sometimes the perks are subtle. The beautifully appointed suites, the butler service, wide corridors, fine dining, classy interior décor and the refined-level of service among the crew stand out as an obvious statement of luxury, however; I noticed a few small details and perks that might get overlooked. Mini news-of-the-day printouts from the country of your residence are placed in the slot just outside your suite each day. If you are from the U.S.A. you'll receive news applicable to what's happening in America, if you come from Britain, you will receive a news-flyer focused on news in Britain. I noticed the shape of the silverware in the restaurants, particularly the handles, had a unique feel that better conformed to your hands. For those passengers who were residents on the world cruise, there was a special engraved plaque just outside your suite with your name and the country you are from. Many cruise ships have the internet available, but through MTN Satellite Communications, there were more Wifi hotspots throughout the whole ship, so you could access the internet on your laptop or internet device from the pool if you choose. Security is tight on all the cruise ships throughout the industry, however; I did appreciate the precise, yet unobtrusive manner in which security was conducted at the gangway. I was delighted to see a set of quality binoculars in our suite so we could explore the horizon or get a close-up view of the port we were visiting right from our private veranda. The fresh flowers, over-sized fluffy towels and the personalized stationary in our suite was a nice perk. The scented oil sticks in our bathroom were not only nice to look at, but created a rich, subtle fragrance. Obviously the Silver Spirit scored high points from my perspective, and when you look at the popularity of Silversea among the affluent, it's clear to see the expectations of luxury, are continuously met by a wide range of people from around the world.

I enjoyed the hardware of the Silver Spirit and appreciated the consistency of quality in the ship's design, the artwork onboard, and the fittings that provide the atmosphere and ambience of luxury. I've said this many times and it is also true aboard the Silver Spirit, you can have a fabulously luxurious ship, yet it's the crew and staff that make up the personality of a ship. A highly trained and fine-tuned crew, complete the element of luxury on any ship. The crowning jewel aboard the Silver Spirit is the crew and staff that contribute to the overall sweetness of luxury on this ship. I want to encourage you to indulge and savor the sweetness of luxury aboard the Silver Spirit or any of the ships in the Silversea fleet. Pick out an itinerary anywhere in the world and you should be able to find a Silversea ship that goes there.

Colosseum in Rome...Wow!

Richard, retired pastor, visits the Vatican

Author's Cruise Review of Gota Kanal

For over 137 years the Gota Kanal Steamship Company has been in operation, cruising the canals, locks and lakes that cut across Sweden, and today provide a classic and cultural experience for passengers who embark on the journey between Gothenborg and Stockholm. The company's prized vessel is the M/S Juno, first launched in 1874 and continues today as the world's oldest passenger vessel with sleeping accommodations still in operation. M/S Wilhelm Tham is the next oldest vessel in the company's fleet of three boats, launched in 1912. Finally, the youngest boat in the fleet is the M/S Diana, built in the Finnboda shipyard not far from Stockholm in 1931. Borton Overseas, in Minneapolis, Minnesota recently offered me an opportunity to experience this iconic journey with Gota Kanal, aboard the Diana's first cruise of the season from Gothenborg to Stockholm. As an ocean liner and classic passenger ship enthusiast, cruising the canals of Sweden on an eighty-year-old vessel like the Diana had a certain romance to it.

Boarding the Diana in Gothenborg and being greeted by the staff pier-side on a red carpet, was a great introduction. Upon presenting a boarding pass, your name is checked to see if it is on the passenger manifest, then Kjerstin Lundwall, the Guide and Tour Manager, welcomes travelers and vacationers aboard, while a crew member carries your luggage and escorts you across the gangway. The moment I stepped aboard the Diana, I felt as if I were stepping back in time to a simpler era. With 28 cabins on three decks and a passenger capacity of about fifty, it was clear this journey would be an intimate, and exclusive experience. There were

many notable passengers, according to Captain Ake Foghammar, who have experienced this Gota Kanal journey, including Hans Christian Andersen, the famous author and poet, the King of Sweden and Teresa Heinz the wife of U.S. Senator John Kerry, to name a few. On this particular voyage there were two governors from a couple of Swedish providences, a couple from Australia, and a good mix of people from Germany, Switzerland, Sweden, the U.S. and England. One couple purchased a new Volvo from the factory in Sweden, and chose to also see the country aboard the Diana with Gota Kanal. The CEO of the Gota Kanal Steamship Company, Hakan Gullberg, was also onboard, celebrating the first cruise of the season. Mr. Gullberg said his company is part of the Stromma Group, one of the largest tourism companies in Sweden.

The history of this steamship company is fascinating, and equally amazing are the locks and the canal that stretch across Sweden. The first lock was

built in 1800 with very primitive technology, yet very ingenious techniques, and hard labor. The lock and canal system transformed Sweden's commerce, allowing for more cost-effective transport of goods and materials from east to west and back again. Wooden log fenders line the sides of Diana, protecting the hull, as she occasionally glances against the lock. Passengers on the Gota Kanal vessels will experience these locks and canals, and gain an up-close appreciation for the rich history that envelops each little town along the journey.

From the comfort of a wicker chair, the teak deck of the Diana, the gentle hum of the motor and sounds of the water trickling by; all these elements will calm the senses and offer a relaxing, enchanting experience. The Diana still maintains her wooden railings with brass fittings and continues on like she has done for eighty years. Unique to a Gota Kanal journey is the intimacy and community that develops onboard among fellow passengers. With the absence of television, internet and modern-day electronics, the main focus is relaxing onboard, fine dining and a sense of community. At 268 tons and with only 28 cabins, Diana is not a large vessel, so gathering on deck, the main lounge, or at meal times are the perfect opportunity to engage in conversation with fellow passengers. The community onboard, the dining, and the culture of the locks and canals are the featured entertainment.

A fascinating element to the Diana is the extraordinarily small passenger cabins. Some of the old cruise director jokes on cruise ships about how small the passenger's cabins are, comes to mind as I sit in my tiny little room A14, on the Diana. The sleeper cabin on a train is larger than the sleep compartments aboard the Diana. Don't get me wrong, the beds in these compact cabins on the Diana, are very comfortable and the linens are wonderful, however; most passengers will only use these rooms to sleep and maybe freshen-up using the small wash basin. Reminiscent of the Victorian era, occupants will enjoy the classy wall-trimmings, hard wood

framing, a cold and hot water washbasin with a wooden cover, and brass hooks for hanging a coat or bathrobe. There's also a very shallow closet for hanging a suite or dress. With so little space to even stand in these cabins, a suggestion is to pack a smaller carry-on suite case and slip it under the bed for storage, because the larger bags will not fit. For the passenger accommodations on the Bridge and Sheltered Decks, cabin doors can be propped open with a hook allowing for fresh air to circulate, or the door can be opened completely offering a view of the passing scenery. For privacy the cabin doors can be closed or a curtain can be slid in-place while the door is open. Cabins have no toilet or shower, so passengers must use a community bathroom and shower located on each deck. These tiny bathroom facilities are also very compact, yet well maintained and cleaned throughout each day. A good perspective on these tiny cabins is that passengers will not spend much time other than freshening up or sleeping, rather; more time will be spent on deck socializing with fellow passengers and enjoying the sites of this historic lock and canal system.

Cruising the locks and canals aboard any of the Gota Kanal Steamship Company vessels is saturated in the Swedish culture, which includes traditional Swedish cuisine. The highlight of each day aboard the Diana, for example; was breakfast, lunch and dinner. A common element to Scandinavian dining is fish prepared in many ways including pickled, fried, baked, poached, and certain menus include specially prepared raw fish. Onboard the Diana we enjoyed a fixed menu, however; for those with special dietary requirements and made arrangements in advance, vegetarian entrées were available. Seating was assigned during lunch and dinner, yet for breakfast, which is buffet-style, passengers could sit wherever they wish. A classic tradition is the ringing of the dinner bell. The waiter or maitre d' will walk the decks ringing a bell or gong to announce that it's time for dinner. Some of the characteristic sounds onboard during lunch and dinner is the click-clacking of the dumb-waiter delivering the prepared

meals from the galley below. Dining aboard the Diana was a first-class experience with crisp white table linens, fine tableware, and the wait-staff are dressed in white jackets with black and gold epaulets and gold buttons. Fine spirits, cognac and wine, were also

available for an additional cost to enhance the dining experience. There was the occasional beef or poultry entrée, however; the majority of cuisine was fresh local fish. The Chef in the galley, one deck below, prepared each entree with artistic flare and included fresh cooked vegetables, potatoes and the perfect accompaniments for each main dish. The dinning room itself aboard these Gota Kanal vessels, has an intimate, friendly and classy ambiance, yet without exception, passengers will enjoy a delightful social experience, a highlight of this special Swedish journey.

The crew aboard the Diana were genuinely proud to serve each passenger. In Stockholm, at the conclusion of our cruise or journey across Sweden on this historic and charming vessel, with the red carpet rolled out just past the gangway, the entire crew of the Diana stood in line to shake our hands and hug us as if we were family. At the very beginning of the journey when we embarked on the Diana in Gothenborg, as I stepped aboard for the first time, I felt like we were about to experience something special, and upon disembarkation in Stockholm my premonition was clear and accurate. I think my fellow travelers also experienced a camaraderie unique to this journey, where the rich heritage and culture of Sweden came alive aboard the Diana. The Gota Kanal Steamship Company, and the crew of the Diana indeed offered somewhat of a time-travel experience reminiscent of a simpler era. It was clear that the folks who live in the small towns along the canal passage saw the Diana as a gleaming and proud representation of their rich culture and heritage, and consequently, our fellow passengers clearly experienced that sense of exclusivity and pride of participating in the journey.

Author's Cruise Review of Pride of America

Since my wife, Terri, was a little girl, one of her wildest dreams was to one-day experience a magical vacation to Hawaii. When I married Terri, the girl of my dreams, I told her that I would show her the world. Following through with my promise, I've taken her to China, Norway, the Caribbean, and Alaska, but the dream destination from her childhood still called out to her. Millions of people dream of going to Hawaii, a destination of romance often seen in movies and television. The time was now for my wife Terri, a small-town mid-western girl, to live out her dream of vacationing in Hawaii, however; because she's married to a Cruise Journalist, we embarked on the perfect Hawaiian cruise aboard Norwegian Cruise Line's Pride of America. Cruising the Hawaiian islands aboard the Pride of America is a gleaming, dreamy, unique experience within the cruise industry because of the ship, the itinerary and the American crew who work onboard.

Hawaii is such a friendly place where the locals make you feel like family. The customary orchid lei and a warm "Aloha" greeting, set the tone for a relaxed feeling as you board the Pride of America. You'll soon get use to saying "aloha", which means both hello and good-bye, and you'll also find yourself saying "mahalo", the Hawaiian word for thank you. A cruise departure from Honolulu has risen to the top of my list as one of the most beautiful ports to cruise out of. Pride of America departs at 7:00pm just as the sun is setting, and the lights of Waikiki glisten with the Diamond Head landmark as a backdrop.

Pride of America has a comfortable, welcoming interior design with rich colors and American-themed décor. The two main dining rooms are called the Liberty and Skyline Restaurants, both have a very elegant setting; Liberty with a very patriotic red, white and blue décor and Skyline with an art deco design. Norwegian Cruise Line invented Freestyle Dinning, so with twelve dining venues the chances of going hungry are slim. Our favorite restaurants were Jefferson Bistro, offering French cuisine, and Teppanyaki that has an entertaining and talented Japanese chef cooking on a grill surrounded by about eight hungry passengers. Seven of the twelve dining venues had an extra charge, ranging from $10 - $25 dollars per person. If you have a particular craving for pizza anytime and anywhere on the ship, just call it in and make your order, for five-bucks a piping hot pizza will arrive just like back home. I like to think of myself as a pizza connoisseur, and I must say that the pizza we ordered was perfect!

Accommodations onboard are comfortable with a refrigerator and the usual amenities available in most fine hotels, and many categories have private verandahs. My wife has instructed me to find out how we can buy one of the Pride of America beds, because they were so comfortable. From sea to shining sea, America the beautiful is seen in the interior design and décor with samples from the South, the East, the Midwest and the West Coast. I was impressed with the Guest Services area on Deck Five with it's grand stairs, red carpet, white banisters, columns, and an atrium dome with frescos lining the ceiling area that reminded me of the artwork I've seen in Rome. A fantastic image of the Great Seal from the United States of America, covers the floor of the Guest Services area, and makes a patriotic first impression when boarding the ship.

The Pride of America certainly makes a bold and proud impression as a physical resort at sea, and yet it's the fantastic Hawaiian itinerary that is perhaps the biggest attraction. Pride of America is the only cruise ship in the industry allowed to embark passengers in Honolulu, cruise the Hawaiian islands and disembark passengers again in Honolulu on a seven-day itinerary. Unique within the cruise industry, the Pride of America is a U.S.

registered vessel that fully complies with the Jones Act of 1920, a United States Federal statute regulating maritime commerce between U.S. ports. The usual choices for internationally operated cruise ships to cruise the Hawaiian Islands requires embarkation for example, from the mainland, which is a four-night voyage at sea just to get to Hawaii, then these ships can cruise the islands, but must make the journey back to the mainland again, resulting in a cruise length of at least fourteen days. Pride of America, on the other hand, is exclusively allowed to offer a seven-night cruise beginning and ending in Hawaii, so her itinerary is unique. Embarkation is in Honolulu and the first port is Maui, where the ship is docked for two full days. Next, Pride of America cruises to the Big Island of Hawaii to Hilo, then to Kona. Finally, passengers have another full day and a half in the beautiful port Kuaui, before returning to Honolulu. Our favorite ports were Maui and Kuaui, mostly because these islands seemed more lush and tropical. After departing Kauai around 1:30pm, make sure you're on-deck at 5:00pm because Pride of America cruises along the Na Pali Coast, offering an incredibly beautiful and scenic view of the rugged mountains.

The highlights of this Hawaiian itinerary, and what most passengers want to see when they go to Hawaii are the volcanoes, the whales, the beaches and to experience a Hawaiian Luau. Whale-spotting is seasonal, only in the winter months from November through May, because this is when the Humback Whales migrate from Alaska to Hawaiian waters for mating. Perhaps the most popular excursions offered are to see the active volcanoes on the Big Island from Hilo. My wife and I rented a car in Maui and we explored the island a bit. The ship tenders into Kona, and the visit to this quaint town is worthwhile because most of the highlights are within walking distance. A visit to Hawaii wouldn't be complete without experiencing an authentic luau. Norwegian Cruise Line has found an excellent luau production in Kuaui where the roasted pig and the show bring to life a traditional Hawaiian story with music and dancing by local performers. The food was delicious, and there was an open-bar included in the excursion.

One particular feature that makes the Pride of America one of the most unique ships in the cruise industry is her mostly American crew. With a crew ratio of 75% Americans and 25% international, I was looking forward to experiencing such a high concentration of Americans working on a cruise ship. With this unique U.S. registration, the ship must be operated under American labor laws, so the crew are paid overtime and wages just like any other company in America. The operating costs of the Pride of America alone, are equal to that of four internationally registered Norwegian Cruise Line vessels, which is why great care and attention is given to make sure passengers have the Hawaiian vacation of a lifetime. I boarded the Pride of America, not knowing what to expect, and after our cruise, I was impressed with the attentiveness and quality of service offered by the crew.

The most important objective for me on this cruise aboard the Pride of America was to make sure my wife Terri, was able to fully enjoy her Hawaiian dream vacation. I watched as my wife experienced the fulfillment of her lifelong dream of going to Hawaii, and this cruise on the Pride of America exceeded her expectations as well as mine. Hawaii is a beautiful place, and the Pride of America, in my opinion, is among the best ways to sample the islands and enjoy the perfect Hawaiian cruise vacation.

MSC Poesia Cruise Review

In a North American cruise market there are numerous choices and flavors of cruise lines intricately managed and fine-tuned to appeal to American vacationers, however; MSC Cruises offers something different. All the cruise lines have a bit of culture to offer, but most of these cruise companies based in the U.S. are distinctly "Americanized" and cater primarily to Americans and the North American market. MSC Cruises appears seasonally in U.S. waters and during the winter months of 2011 and 2012, the MSC Poesia gallops across the Caribbean like a strong and graceful Italian stallion at sea.

MSC Cruises is a family-owned company with it's roots in container shipping and a fleet of nearly five hundred container vessels making the Mediterranean Shipping Company (MSC) the second largest carrier in the world. In 2003 MSC Cruises invested 5.5 Billion Euros into a massive ship-building project to create an ultra-modern fleet, and today the line has twelve stylish cruise ships, including the MSC Poesia which debuted in 2008. The owner and his wife are intimately involved in the interior design of their ships, and aboard the MSC Poesia, it is very clear to see that a great deal of care went into the fabrics, the colors, materials, artwork, and layout of the ship's interior spaces. The "feeling" onboard the MSC Poesia is exciting with sharp, contrasting design materials like brass, glass, marble, indirectly lighting and colorful carpet details.

I took my ten-year-old son on a December cruise aboard the MSC Poesia to the Western Caribbean, so both my son and I were particularly interested in the quality of the kids programs. I'm happy to report that my son had an excellent time during this cruise. The ship had a large complement of families with kids, and I noticed the pools and pool deck areas were very popular on our days at sea. Of course we had excellent weather during our cruise. The MSC Poesia was full, however; because of the excellent configuration of the lounges, restaurants and deck areas, the ship didn't feel too crowded.

I'll have to admit that prior to my cruise onboard the MSC Poesia, I was expecting more Italian crew and staff, but it soon became clear that gone are the days when ships employed single-nationalities. I was not disappointed, and enjoyed the international mix of crew and staff from many nationalities, including Canadians, Europeans, and Indonesians. The passenger complement also included many Italians, Germans, French and Americans. This mix of passenger nationalities is a specific element that creates the international "feeling" onboard the MSC Poesia. During the

cruise throughout the ship and during the shows, announcements were made in several languages, so it's important to be tolerant and flexible, a trait which Americans tend to lack sometimes.

The dining was exquisite. I was impressed with the menu choices each night and the quality and taste of the cuisine. In our consumerism culture we have today, it can be easy to not fully appreciate the exceptional thought and planning that goes into preparing thousands of fine-dining experiences every day and night, however; the amazing Chefs onboard the MSC Poesia are able to make it happen with apparent ease. A big winner during our cruise was the lobster and Filet Mignon. When I cruise, my usual menu choice is the fish, and I was very pleased with the taste and quality. The salmon was from Norwegian waters and prepared just right. A common American impression of European cuisine is that the food is bland, but I did not experience this on the MSC Poesia. This is a cruise line with a strong Italian heritage so you can expect some great pasta, and those who love Italian food will feel at home onboard the MSC Poesia. The two main restaurants are on Decks Five and Six aft, and if I were to cruise again on the MSC Poesia, I would choose the restaurant on Deck Five because of the curvy passage from one end to the other. The restaurant on Deck Six had a straight passage from one end to the other that seemed to share traffic with the waiters more than the curvy passage. The cafeteria restaurant on Deck 13 aft was laid out well, however; if you arrive at certain peak times, you might experience lines. On one of the final evenings there was a delightful late-night buffet, and the lines were very slow as passengers took pictures. A tip for those wanting the chocolate and to see the ice and butter carvings, skip the long lines and make your way further aft where the sugary goodies are.

Because of the many languages represented among the crew and passengers, the design of the entertainment is filled with visual and musical acts. The shows were packed each night because passengers thoroughly and consistently enjoyed the entertainment. When the topic at the diner table is how great the show was the previous night, it's clear MSC Cruises is doing something right with planning great entertainment and hiring talented performers. The acts included juggling, acrobatics, dancers and opera singers, and I particularly liked the show lounge with it's purple decor and high-tech stage.

When you cruise on the MSC Poesia, be sure to reserve a balcony stateroom, so you can enjoy the ocean breezes. Our stateroom 10124, was comfortable and efficient. The cabin stewardess was friendly, and always said hello when she saw us passing through the corridor. Our room was spotless, the bathroom was always clean with fresh towels. My son actually discovered how the stewardess knows if we are in the room or not, there's a tiny light outside the door near the ceiling panel that indicates the room is occupied. Your room key card is used to turn on the lights in the room, so when you leave the room and take your card, the lights turn off saving power.

How does the MSC Poesia compare to other cruise lines in the Caribbean? Keep in-mind that the MSC Poesia is a high-volume passenger vessel, yet MSC Cruises does a classy job of making sure everyone onboard is treated with white-glove service. There is an aura of Italian culture onboard the MSC Poesia that even the well-traveled individuals will appreciate. Considering the fine dining, classy décor, excellent entertainment and attention to details, a vacation on the Italian Stallion at Sea, the elegant MSC Poesia, will offer an experience that will delight the senses. Contact iCruise at www.icruise.com to book your next cruise vacation and check out the great deals MSC Cruises has to offer on any of their beautiful ships.

Hurtigruten Coastal Cruise Review

At an art gallery in Eden Prairie, Minnesota about 1995, there was a painting that caught my eye, that would lead me to a magical place in Norway many years later. Passionate about the cruise industry, I have been on over 300

cruises around the world and have even worked on the ships as a Cruise Director and Entertainer. Today, as a Cruise Industry Journalist, I set out to find creative and fascinating cruises and itineraries that will be of interest to the listeners of my talk show and viewers

of my videos. Back to the painting I saw back in 1995, at first glance this beautiful scene was of a mountain that rose out of the sea with a quaint fishing village at the base of this magnificent, magical, and mountainous rock. I thought it was a fictitious location, because the image was so powerful, so I inquired further only to see the gallery manager bring out the actual photo from which this painting was based on. I've travelled all around the world and had yet to ever see a sight as magnificent as this place and told myself one day I want to go there to see it first-hand. On a business card from the gallery, I wrote the name of this beautiful village with the intention to research more about this remote location in Norway called Reine Lofoten. And so finally in October of 2010 I saw an opportunity to possibly journey to Reine. I considered which cruise lines might visit Lofoten, and finally determined the best option was with Hurtigruten, which has operated passenger ships along the Norwegian coast for over one hundred years. I called this the Hurtigruten and SAS Experience because what better way to get to Norway than on a Scandinavian airline. Join me on this journey where we experience the "Most Beautiful Voyage" aboard the Hurtigruten ships and get to Norway in luxury with SAS.

From the U.S. it's a full day and a half of travel to get to Kirkenes, our initial port of departure with Hurtigruten aboard the Nordlys. It certainly was a pleasant experience in Business Class aboard the SAS trans-Atlantic flight from Chicago to Copenhagen. The seats in this section have video and movies on demand, there's a plug to charge your lap top if you so choose, and what I found to be truly fascinating was the electronically operated seat which reclines to a near horizontal position for sleeping at the touch of a button. Dinner was exquisite. This was the first time in my hundreds of flights all over the world where I could select my entrée from a menu of choices. I decided to have the Halibut and a fine wine. There's also a special snack bar open to Business-class passengers where they have fruit, candy, chocolate, drinks and sandwiches available throughout the eight and a half hour flight. We enjoyed a nice dinner then decided to sleep through the flight since we were traveling eastbound. Flying on an SAS trans-Atlantic flight was the perfect way to prepare for a trip to Scandinavia.

After four different flights, we finally arrived at Kirkenes Norway in the Arctic Circle. After a long day of traveling it was a pleasure to stay one night at the Rica Arctic Hotel in Kirkenes. This hotel reminded me of an Ikea, in fact most of the items in the room seemed to be from Ikea. I liked the wood floors and the comfortable beds. Norwegians seem to like wood floors. Most of the airports we went through in Norway had wood floors. Speaking of floors, my wife enjoyed the "heated" floors in some of the bathrooms we encountered. The Rica Arctic Hotel had a very typical Norwegian buffet breakfast that included an assortment of fish, cheeses, breads, meats and some eggs. We could board the Nordlys at around noon, so we caught the bus at the front of the hotel around 11:00am. My wife has been on a number of cruises with me, but this "voyage" with Hurtigruten was an entirely different experience for her. I somewhat knew what to expect, because I read a lot about Hurtigruten prior to this trip, and I understand the concept of a multi-functional passenger vessel. I was looking forward to the experience of being on a "working" passenger ship because there is more of a "purpose" rather than simply a round-trip "bus tour" through the Caribbean like most cruise ships….not that there's anything wrong with what cruise ships do.

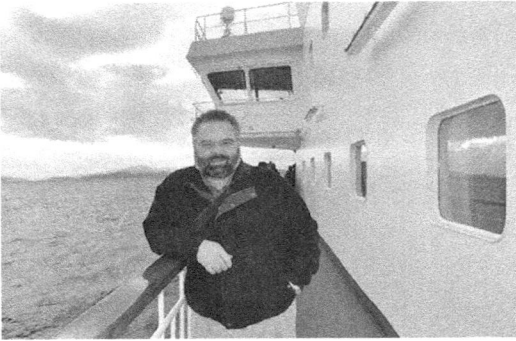

Boarding the Nordlys with Hurtigruten was a far different experience than boarding a cruise ship. There were no lines, no other passengers in sight, only the Nordlys' fascinating fold-out gangway awaiting our arrival. Most of the Hurtigruten ships have a self-contained robotic gangway and a huge cargo hatch that open up onto the pier. We stopped for a photo then climbed up the gangway into the lobby of the ship. The Hotel Manager and another staff person greeted us. It was an absolute requirement, apparently, for us to have our hands squirted with anti-bacterial hand sanitizer as we boarded. We checked in, were given our room keys, and headed off to our little sanctuary "cabin" for this first leg of our five-night Hurtigruten journey. Our itinerary included two nights on the Nordlys, then three nights in Lofoten, and finally another three nights aboard the Trollfjord where we would disembark in Bergen.

Cruise Ship, Ferry, Cargo or Passengers ship?

I set out on this Hurtigruten Experience to determine where these ships fit within the cruise industry. The Hurtigruten ships can be broken down into several classifications, and there certainly is an element that resembles a cruise ship, however, when you look at the full picture, these ships are very different than your typical cruise ship. The Hurtigruten ships also carry automobiles, but I wouldn't say they are one hundred percent car ferries either. The same applies to cargo, mail and these ships act as a passenger transport as well, bringing local passengers on short hops between point A and point B along the coast of Norway. I have heard a number of explanations for these multifunctional ships and their true nature, which range from "Ro Ro Ships" to "Hybrids" and "Working Vessels", however, I place these ships in the "Coastal Passenger Liner" category....oh wait that's not an official category. In the days of the trans-Atlantic liners, the ships were "working" vessels that carried passengers, cargo and mail from point A to B, which is quite different from what the cruise ships do today, but very similar to what the Hurtigruten vessels do. The Hurtigruten ships often visit up to four or five ports a day. These are short visits that last between ten to fifteen minutes to an hour or so, but mostly these visits are comparatively shorter than what you would expect on a cruise ship. So a note to typical cruise ship passengers, the Hurtigruten ships are not in the ports for extended periods of time, and barely long enough to go ashore to see the sights. There are some exceptions to this where the ship will stay long enough for an excursion, but overall, a voyage should focus on the beautiful scenery as the ship cruises along the coast from port-to-port.

The ports and scenery

A Norwegian coastal voyage aboard a Hurtigruten ship is a very visual experience. I often saw passengers quietly cuddled up in a chair, reading a book, in the observation lounge, watching the scenery pass by. Photographers could often be seen on deck near the bow or on the aft decks adjusting their apertures and depth of field on the incredible panorama of peeks, mountains and seascapes. Sitting in a cozy chair on the main promenade, my wife would laugh at me, as I would suddenly jump out of my chair to head outside to snap a photo or two. The scenery is so amazing it's like sensory overload at times, and I would often scramble to the open deck to capture the moment either on video, a still shot, or both. Because the ships are not in port long, it's best to sign up for the excursions, but often there were not enough participants for the tours so they were canceled, leaving me to fend for myself using a taxi to visit the sights. A few of the ports we visited stood out as being particularly memorable. We stayed one night in Kirkenes and had an opportunity to see the town a bit. Apparently the main industry in Kirkenes was iron mining, however, that industry has slowly shut down over the last few years leaving many without jobs. I was told a new tourism industry was rising up for that area, with tourists from Norway, Germany, England and France. In the winter season you could go dog sledding, or visit a hotel made of ice.

Hammerfest was a fascinating port that I enjoyed very much. As we approached the city aboard the Nordlys, we passed by a huge natural gas facility, which provided power and energy to the entire region. Hammerfest is also known to be the World's most northernmost town at 70 degrees 39' 48"N in the arctic region. There are ten thousand people who call Hammerfest home. This is the place where my wife and I experienced an amazingly rapid change in weather. It went from cold and clear to colder with near snowy and blizzard conditions in a matter on a couple of minutes or so. We watched as a wall of snow and wind hit us. In Hammerfest, I became a member of The Royal And Ancient Polar Bear Society. With only about 200,000 members this is a very exclusive club with members all around the world. The only way to become a member of this elite and exclusive club or society is to visit Hammerfest, and apply for your membership in-person. Elvis Presley wanted to become a member and sent one of his buddies to Hammerfest to acquire a membership for him, but he was declined because applicants must physically be there to apply for membership. This exclusive society seeks to preserve the polar bears and the unique and delicate ecology of this arctic region. It was fun to tell my wife that I was able to literally take her to the top of the World.

Before the Nordlys arrived at Svolvaer, Lofoten, we went on a special Sea Eagles Safari, an excursion that brought us up close to this mighty bird. We boarded a smaller boat that took us into the kjellfjord where these sea eagles nested and hunted for food. Our guide inflated the fish bait with air, then threw them out into the water near the boat so the Sea Eagles would swoop down, grab the fish out of the sea and fly off to enjoy their meal. We were able to take pictures of this amazing bird as it buzzed right past our boat and nearly grabbed the fish out of the hand of our guide. The Seagulls were everywhere and they too were fun to watch.

The Nordlys stopped at the little town of Stokmarknes where my wife and I experienced a very interesting museum. The 1956 built Finnmarken was a Hurtigruten vessel that had been retired and turned into a museum. What was unique about this museum was the Finnmarken vessel was hoisted up onto land in a cradle so that you can actually walk under the hull of this ship. To me that was really cool to see a big ship like this on land and to walk under the hull, to be able to touch and see the propeller and rudder was a thrill. You can go aboard the Finnmarken and see her old staterooms and lounges. As a ship buff this was a highlight for me. I really enjoyed this museum!

Unimaginably beautiful Reine, Lofoten

A highlight of our Hurtigruten and SAS Experience was our three-night visit to Lofoten. After two nights cruising the coast of Norway aboard the Nordlys we disembarked in Stamsund, Lofoten at 10:30pm, rented a car and drove for about an hour south, in the dark and in the rain, to a quaint and amazingly picturesque town called Reine. Of course it was dark when we drove down to Reine, so we really couldn't see much until the next day when we woke up in our little rorbuer and looked out the window. We checked into a rorbuer or boat house at about midnight in a wonderful place called Reine Rorbuer which is like a resort or bed and breakfast cottage in the middle of a fishing village that has been in operation since about 1785. The little rorbuer we stayed in could very well have been nearly two hundred years old, however it was rebuilt, refurbished and fitted with modern facilities, so it was very cozy. I have been all around the World and I am not exaggerating when I say Reine, Lofoten is perhaps the most beautiful and scenic place I have ever seen with my own eyes, and it was the fulfillment of a dream to visit this place. As I mentioned at the beginning of this article, it was a beautiful painting that inspired me to one day journey to this place of Reine, Lofoten, and finally that dream became a reality and I was not disappointed. It truly was a magical place and I felt like I was in a dream as I marveled at the scenery. I could almost sense that there was a spiritual echo among the amazingly picturesque mountains, where God was saying, "Look what I have made for you"! The Managers of Reine Rorbuer, Hans van Kampen and Daniella de Vreeze were gracious hosts, and one day Daniella, a chef, prepared a special Norwegian dinner for us in their little rustic restaurant called Gammelbua. We also toured the fascinating fishery

next to Reine Rorbuer that has a long heritage of sending dried fish all around the world. We saw first-hand how the fish was prepared and processed. The Director of this fishery told us about the theory that God specially created the Reine Lofoten area as a perfectly balanced environment for the fish to flourish abundantly because of the warmer Caribbean waters coming from the south, that seem to blend with the arctic waters from the North. A delicate and perfectly balanced ecosystem that seems to indicate there was a great deal of intelligence and design to the environment, allowing fishermen for centuries to enjoy an abundance of quality fish to catch. I didn't want to leave Reine after three days, but we had to catch the Hurtigruten ship, Trollfjord in Stamsund, to continue our journey along the coast of Norway.

Another highlight of our voyage with Hurtigruten was our visit to Trondheim, which is the third largest city in Norway. As I mentioned earlier, the Hurtigruten ships do not stay in the ports very long and this fact was evident when we embarked on our excursion or bus tour of Trondheim, which lasted about two hours. Our bus tour quickly took us through town and up onto a hill where we could look out over the city. Next we visited a cathedral that has been there for over one thousand years. Trondheim is a historical and friendly community with a large university and a number of cultural centers and museums. After about an hour of touring the cathedral we returned to

Torghatten is a mountain with a hole in it

our ship the Trollfjord and shortly thereafter we enjoyed a chilly departure.

As we came closer to our final destination of Bergen the Trollfjord went through some beautiful passages and fjords. Our ship crossed the Arctic Circle 66 degrees 33' North, on October 19th in the morning, and we were issued an official certificate indicating this accomplishment. Among the many rock formations and mountains, we came upon an interesting mountain that literally had a hole through it. I thought as we went further south the weather would improve and we would experience a little warmer climate, but this did not turned out to be true on our cruise because it was colder, with sleet and snow, which can be expected for this time of year. We were blessed to experience the first snow of the winter season when we arrived in Bergen. The hillsides near Bergen were covered in a fresh coat of beautiful white snow allowing for some nice photos. Bergen is the second largest city in Norway, tucked in the hills along the coast. We met up with a third cousin of mine who lives in Voss, near Bergen, and had a delightful Chinese dinner and visit with her. We walked around town through some of the shops and a mall.

Our journey with Hurtigruten had ended and the next morning we were off to the airport to fly home via SAS. Flying on SAS was an enjoyable experience because of the care and service of the friendly flight crew. During our eight and half hour flight from Copenhagen to Chicago we watched a few movies and entertained ourselves to stay awake so we could have a good sleep when we finally arrived at home again in Minneapolis. What type of person embarks on a Hurtigruten voyage? I'm going to come out and say that your typical cruise passenger might be disappointed because of the more specialized elements to a Hurtigruten voyage. There are no casinos, there is no formal entertainment or show lounges, the port visits are short, and the onboard amenities are comfortable but minimal. The dining is Eurpoean-style which some Americans may not understand. Europeans dine at a more leisurely pace, and the menu each evening is fixed to a set course as opposed to multiple options. Breakfast and lunch are buffet-style. Expect a lot of fish and cheese. A Hurtigruten voyage will appeal to those who enjoy the quiet, scenic, go-at-your-own-pace routine. Photographers and those who enjoy a rich Norwegian cultural experience will feel very comfortable on a Hurtigruten journey. For those who have a desire to visit an ecological and environmental wonderland, a Hurtigruten voyage will fulfill the quest for natural beauty, spectacular panoramas and abundant wildlife. As I compare our Hurtigruten voyage with our Alaska cruise we did in 2009, I can now say with complete confidence that while Alaska is very beautiful, a Norwegian coastal voyage with Hurtigruten is magnificent and the scenery pushes and exceeds my expectations to a higher level than I had anticipated. We have heard many people say, after we tell them of our trip to Norway, that a Norwegian coastal cruise is on their bucket list, and it should be, because I cannot imagine anyone visiting Norway like we did and not return feeling completely overwhelmed with the incredible scenery. Other cruise ships may visit Norway, but you can truly become entrenched with the culture when you embark on a Hurtigruten voyage. The Hurtigruten vessels have an all-Norwegian crew onboard and in fact, Hurtigruten is a Norwegian company with a genuine and rich Norwegian heritage and history. The artwork onboard all the ships reflect Norwegian artistry at it's best. Cruising on any other cruise line along the coast of Norway would be like going to the grocery store and buying frozen fish for dinner, as opposed to going out with the fishermen on their boat to catch the fish, and preparing the fish dinner right there on the boat.

For those who have a Norwegian coastal cruise on your bucket list, do not delay, make your plans sooner than later to experience for yourself this incredible voyage, this beautiful journey with Hurtigruten. Your expectations will be fulfilled and you will come away with memories of Norway that will inspire you and fuel your imagination. Embark on a southbound or northbound itinerary or do what we did and custom-design your own itinerary so you can have an extended visit to a particular village or town of your choosing. Expect to be enriched by the culture and beautiful scenery.

Viking River Cruises – Yangtze China River Cruise

On August 19th, 2009 my wife and I flew from Minneapolis to Chicago, then to Beijing, China, to participate in a cruise / tour adventure with Viking River Cruises, and their Imperial Jewels of China 12-day excursion. This excursion included six nights in luxury hotels and five nights on their river vessel called the Viking Century Sun. We flew into Beijing and spent three nights in the Raffles Hotel, then we flew to Xian (pronounced 'She Hon') and stayed in the Shangri-La Hotel for one night. Next we flew to Chongqing (pronounced 'Chong King') and we boarded the Viking Century Sun. Once aboard the Viking Century Sun we visited Shibaozhai, then to Qutang to see the Lesser Three Gorges, next we cruised to Sandouping where we visited the fantastic Three Gorges Dam. Our next city was Jingzhou, a city that Viking River Cruises sponsors a school, where we had the opportunity to visit the children and see their classroom. Finally the Viking Century Sun arrived at Wuhan, and this is where we disembarked the vessel. From Wuhan we flew to Shanghai and spent two nights in the Westin Bund Hotel.

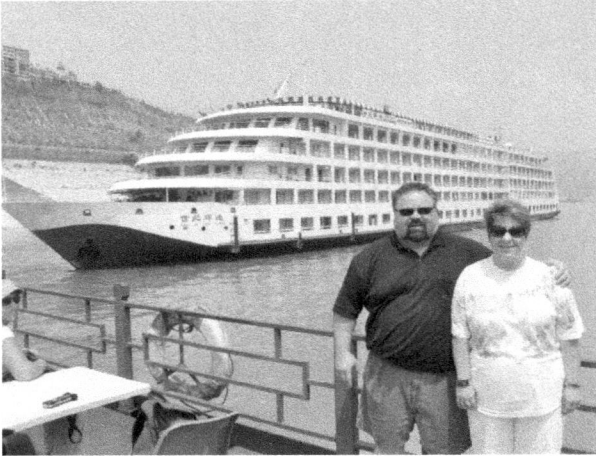

Food / Dinning

Viking River Cruises goes to great lengths to bring it's passengers and tour-groups to the best restaurants in the area. In Beijing we dined at the same restaurant that Nixon ate, as well as President Bush when they were in Beijing. For those with a western palate, you might have to be somewhat adventurous because there are many unique flavors to experience. The dining, however; was excellent. Especially breakfast in the hotels we have stayed at...the variety is amazing; of course the restaurant must accommodate many different tastes from all around the world. Americans will be happy with the eggs and bacon, or cereal of your choice, or you may want to eat what the Chinese eat for breakfast, like noodles and mushroom or some sort of fish. There have been some occasions when I personally didn't care for the food served at lunch, however, dinner seems to be the meal of choice for the Chinese, with a great variety of meats prepared in unique ways. I like to have a soda for dinner and in China on this tour, it seems the choice is limited to either water, Sprite, Coke, or local beer. Only a few restaurants offer diet, or Coke Lite, and on this tour the first drink is included but the second drink is usually not and you must pay extra for another glass or can of whatever. Many evenings dinner was served on a "lazy susan" a circular plate on the table that spins allowing people to eat family-style. We did eat a lot of Chinese food, and it only made sense since we were in China. It's a good thing we like Chinese food, however, we noticed that the Chinese food in China is often a little different than what we eat at our local Chinese restaurant in America. We found the Peking Duck in Beijing to be very tasty, but we noticed it wasn't like eating chicken, because the tradition is to put the duck meat on a tortia with some onion and a dark sauce.

Hotel stays during the tour portion of the trip:

Our first hotel experience on this tour arranged by Viking River Cruises is similar to the dinning experience where they put passengers in the best

hotels in the area. Our first hotel was in Beijing. After a long 13 hour flight from Chicago to Beijing, we were very eager to get into our room to relax a bit. My wife and I thought we were put in the wrong room at first, because it was very spacious, the décor was exquisite and the amenities were first class. It was as if we were in the Presidential suite of a five star hotel, and in fact this was a five star hotel. The bed was a large king-size canopy bed, which was very nice with fine linens and comfy pillows. I think there is a difference in the packages offered…we happened to be in the premium land-package, so be sure to choose the premium option to really experience luxury accommodations, it really is worth it.

Our first Hotel was the Raffles Hotel in Beijing. This is the same hotel that accommodated many of the dignitaries during the Olympics, and many U.S. Presidents have stayed in the Raffles Hotel. Back to our room, we had a large wooden desk for writing letters or using the computer (I brought my own lap top) , a large flat-screen television, another small writing desk, and a cabinet for displaying interesting articles. The bathroom was very nice with a tub with water jets, two sinks, a large shower and of course a toilet with a bidet. Actually this suite had two bathrooms, one was in the entry corridor. Use of the internet was free, however, it seems as if the Chinese Government may be blocking certain social media sites like, Facebook, Blogs, Youtube and a few others. This was a problem for me since I had planned to blog about our trip so my listeners to my show could follow us in a virtual way. All of the staff in the hotel were very professional, very detail oriented and their hospitality skills were finely tuned. Score another high mark to Viking River Cruises for scoping out the best hotel in the area. The very first evening when we arrived we used the hot tub in the spa area to relax a bit after a long flight, which was very soothing. Then we went to our palatial room, changed for dinner. This first night we were on our own for dinner, so my wife and I walked around the corner from the hotel and were amazed at the thousands and thousands of people in the streets. We ended up trying out a Big Mac and a chocolate shake at McDonalds....and our basic impression was that it all tasted the same as back home. It was an interesting cultural experience to be among the Chinese people that first night.

Our accommodations in Xian were very nice, not as opulent as the Raffles in Beijing, but very comfortable. Finally, Westin Hotels operated the hotel in Shanghai and we found the bed to be the most comfortable bed we had experienced in China. The bathroom was very large with a huge tub right next to the window, which offered a nice view from 15 stories up. Internet was not free in this hotel but the price was reasonable. Again it was frustrating that the government of China had blocked certain social media websites and of course I could not contribute to my blog.

Our River Vessel, the Viking Century Sun

We arrived at our cruise-portion of the cruise / tour and boarded the Viking Century Sun in the evening. It was a long walk down to the pier and we had to walk across about four other barges to get to our vessel, that's the way it is on the river. For me, being a cruise guy, it was a thrill to finally get aboard the Viking Century Sun. Actually, let me mention that I found it difficult to determine whether to call the Viking Century Sun a 'ship' or a 'boat'. It's on the Yangtze River and was not designed for the open sea, and most vessels on the river are considered boats or barges. The Viking Century Sun was certainly not a barge, and yet I struggled with calling it a 'ship'. I asked the Hotel Director onboard, what he thought the designation should be and he suggested it should be considered not a boat, or a ship, rather a 'vessel'. Anyways, back to our arrival to the Viking Century Sun. There were numerous crew members with smiles, who greeted us as we were navigating the various barges to finally get aboard the Viking Century Sun.

What a thrill it was to finally get aboard the vessel knowing that we were going to be there for five nights as opposed to moving from hotel to hotel.

The Viking Century Sun has six passenger decks and carries about 300 passengers in 150 staterooms, all of which have a private balcony. Built in 2006, the vessel was still very new, and we noticed that the crew onboard were constantly cleaning every nook and cranny. Our stateroom was very nice, and in fact we were upgraded to one of the four suites onboard. Our room had ample desk and drawer space, and a special glass-top desk, which was perfect for setting up my mobile office, including my laptop and camera gear. The linens on the bed were very nice and soft, however, the beds themselves were very firm. I personally like a bed that is not too firm, however I can't complain because we enjoyed the sanctuary of our stateroom. The bathroom was one of the largest we've had on a cruise. The toilet and the shower had a sliding panel to act as a door, and there were two sinks, a his and hers. Every couple of nights we would find a little treat or gift on our pillow, like a hat that says Viking River Cruises on it, or a cute little Chinese silk bag.

I'd like to offer some observations of the stateroom and perhaps a recommendation for the cruise line. There was no refrigerator in the stateroom, which is a common amenity on most cruise ships and hotels these days. I travel with medications that need to be refrigerated, which is why I thought this should be highlighted. Particularly on the Yangtze where it can be very hot and humid, I would suggest maybe a dehumidifier in the room, and a fan. The air conditioning on the Viking Century Sun was probably operating at its best, but on the really hot and humid days, that is when a dehumidifier and a fan would come in handy. Overall, I would definitely say the vessel was comfortable.

The dining onboard the Viking Century Sun was very good, and at par with many of the hotels we stayed at prior to embarking on the vessel. The waitresses and waiters in the dinning room were all very bubbly and went to great lengths to remember your name and what many of your preferences were. Service was very quick and efficient, and the staff truly cared about tending to your requests. There was only one evening when I ordered the fish, and I didn't care for the taste, the sauce had a fishy taste to it and the fish tasted fishy which wasn't normal for this type of mild white fish. Breakfast each morning was very good with a chef available to make you an omelet or scrambled eggs to order, or even pancakes. There was also cereal and breads and many of the usual western-style breakfast items. Two nights were dedicated to Chinese food, and the other evenings the choices were western-style or international entrées like beef and pasta and chicken. The chef was German, so there was somewhat of a German-style to the dining. The presentation was excellent and most people would definitely enjoy the dining aboard the Viking Century Sun.

A cruise on the Viking Century Sun is unlike your usual cruise experience with big production shows, rather the entertainment onboard was structured more to learn about China and the Yangtze River. There was one night, however, where the crew put on a decent show that was fun to watch and very colorful. The lectures onboard were very informative, and helpful because most people who travel to China want to know and experience the culture. Viking River Cruises offers a wonderful cultural experience that turns out to be the highlight of the cruise for most passengers, and that is the visit to the elementary school in Jingzhou. In fact, Viking River Cruises sponsors the school, which is one opportunity for the company to give back to the community in a very positive way. I highly applaud Viking River Cruises for their sponsorship program with the local school. Everyone in our group completely enjoyed this day where we visited the school. The children put on a little show of music and dancing for us and then we broke-up into smaller groups and visited different classrooms. It was obvious that these children really look forward to meeting the "Westerners", and the passengers enjoy the interaction with the kids. I performed a magic trick and the kids seemed to like that. There's an opportunity to give donations to the school, and most passengers drop in a few bucks. My wife and I brought a big bag of story cubes to give to the children at the school, and they really liked this little gift. So do not expect the big production shows and entertainment like on most cruise ships, the location on the Yangtze river in itself is entertaining and enriching, and I don't think the big production shows would be missed.

I noticed from a logistics point of view that operating a western-style cruisetour on the Viking Century Sun would be a huge project because of cultural differences, however, Viking River Cruises was able to pull it off with flying colors. I tried to understand how the operation of this vessel worked on the Yangtze in China, and discovered that the vessel, the Viking Century Sun, was actually leased by Viking River Cruises with a local Chinese businessman who owns the vessel under a company name, New Century Cruises. I think it's a clever operation and a brilliant way to offer a cruise product in China. I don't think the Chinese government would allow an American company or foreign company to set up shop on the Yangtze River, so what Viking River Cruises has done is quite the achievement. I took some time to explore another river boat on the Yangtze that has about eight boats and often promotes it's product to westerners. The boat seemed nice from the inside, but on the outside they look a bit raw. I also happen to know that they utilize westerners as cruise directors so they can better serve their passengers. This company I am referring to looks like they do a fine job, and I discovered they are building a vessel that will become the largest cruise vessel on the Yangtze, out-sizing the Viking Century Sun which is currently the largest passenger vessel. I can't say anything for their cruisetour packages other than they probably offer a similar package to what Viking River Cruises offers, however, having been a cruise industry professional for many years, I did have an experience which has brought me to the conclusion that Viking River Cruises without question has the best cruisetour product available in China and on the Yangtze. Unlike the other cruise company I'm referencing; Viking River Cruises offers a consumer-friendly and travel agent-friendly system for booking your cruisetour to

China. Let me give you an example. A few years ago, someone came into my office and said they wanted to book a cruise to China on the Yangtze. I was very excited to offer my expertise as a cruise industry professional, however, I ran into some challenges trying to get information and book my clients on a Yangtze cruise. I never was able to book these people because it was too obscure and complicated. This was before I knew about Viking River Cruises of course. The bottom line is that it was very complicated trying to decipher which tour operator to try and book with. What makes Viking River Cruises rise above as my choice for the best company to work with is that they offer an amazing product that is contained within one simple westernized company as opposed to numerous tour operators and sub-companies.   I can book the entire cruisetour experience to China with one company, and have the confidence that everything is handled by one company with no surprises.

The Tours

Unique to Viking River Cruises are the tours they offer and the local guides who hold your hand throughout the whole trip from the first moment you arrive at the airport.   The tours are carefully chosen to offer the best experiences, allowing passengers to see the most popular sites as comfortably as possible. The buses are all air conditioned and comfortable, the transfers are all taken care of by your guide, in fact the guide even checks you into your hotels, you simply receive your room key and you're off to your room.   The same is true for your intra-China flights, your guide checks you in and gets your boarding pass, so you can just board the plane without any hassles. It's a smooth seamless process that the Viking River Cruises guides have perfected. Another unique element to the tours is the electronic "Vox" device that is given to each passenger.   The "Vox" is basically a receiver that you put around your neck that has a comfortable earpiece, allowing each individual to hear what the guide is saying, so the guide does not have to speak loudly over the crowds. In fact you have the freedom to wander around while listening to your guide explain the history and details about the place or site you're visiting. As long as you keep your guide in-sight as he holds up his Viking River Cruises flag, you're never lost.

The Great Wall of China

Wow, the Great Wall is a spectacular sight to see first-hand. You can read about it and see pictures, but to actually walk on the Great Wall is truly a remarkable experience considering how old and how long this structure is. From the entrance to the best-preserved sections of the amazing Great Wall in the Badaling Hills, you have a choice to either walk up to the eastern direction (the right) or to the western direction (on the left) the latter direction being the most difficult. My wife and I chose to take the more challenging route on the left because we were told the views were better, and I could get better pictures. Both my wife and I carry a little more weight than we should so we were both concerned that this tough walk and climb was going to be too much for us. I think the adrenaline-rush we experienced as we were finally standing on such a monumental staple of China, and one of the wonders of the world, kept us going and we were victorious in reaching the top. It was no easy climb, that's for sure, and both my wife and I were beat. It's a good thing we brought oxygenated water and our favorite energy drink to give us the endurance and boost of energy we needed to make our way to the top. The views were indeed spectacular! The steps on the Great Wall are somewhat irregular, so it was a good thing they had solid handrails built in. If I were to offer any criticism of this particular tour that Viking River Cruises coordinated, I would suggest they allow more time to wander and enjoy the Great Wall. After our visit to the Great Wall we also stopped at the Sacred Way of the Ming Tombs and the place where the 2008 Olympics were held, so needless to say, it was a long day of walking and climbing and sightseeing.

The Terra Cotta Army Museum

I was particularly fascinated by the Terra Cotta Army Museum in Xian, pronounced (She-Hon). Again, the tour seemed to move a lot faster than I

would have liked. I was always way behind the group because I was taking pictures and video. It was a sobering experience entering the first giant building constructed over the archeological dig pits and seeing hundreds and hundreds of these Terra Cotta Warriors standing at attention for over 2,000 years! We learned how these clay warriors were created for Emperor Qin Shi Huang while he was still a boy. It's overwhelming to think that this clay army and thousands of other items were buried in chambers to honor one man, this Emperor, and to imagine the many years men and women must have labored to create such a vast array of items. We also learned from new aerial photos that over 600 additional burial plots are now known to exist around this area with countless items yet to be dug up and discovered. I was surprised to learn that the actual Emperor's tomb has not been dug-up, so there must be a vast collection of amazing riches still buried. The Chinese government has decided not to excavate the Emperor's tomb, however; if tomb-robbers were to ever figure out a way in to the tomb, only then would the government step-in to protect the area. The Emperor's tomb lays within a large man-made mountain, overlooking the area where the Terra Cotta Army was buried. Sounds like a job for Indiana Jones if you ask me.

The Three Gorges Dam

It truly is a monumental achievement for the Chinese government to construct the world's largest dam, and we had the opportunity to not only see this massive dam but to actually pass through the locks aboard the Viking Century Sun. I was amazed to watch as we went into the locks and saw our vessel lowered down to the next lock chamber. Both my wife and I had to go to bed however, because we traversed the locks at around 10:30pm and we were very tired. We did stay up to watch us go through the first lock which was fascinating. The next day we got on the Dam bus to go on the Dam tour, but first we had to go through the Dam security which was very thorough. Our Dam guide explained how the Dam was constructed and the purpose of the Dam, which was actually to help prevent flooding on the Yangtze, to generate hydro-power and to simply offer a better life for the Chinese people.   It would be pretty difficult for anyone to not be impressed by this gigantic human achievement.   Furthermore, it was impressive to learn that the Chinese government relocated millions of Chinese people along the Yangtze River in order to allow for the Yangtze River-level to rise up to about 175 meters above sea-level. So there are whole cities now underwater, and the local people were given new condominiums to live in on higher ground. It was very evident to see the massive construction of new condominiums all along the river.

Massive bridges were also being constructed all along the Yangtze River. The planning, the infrastructure that went into all the construction related to the Three Gorges Dam and the efforts to relocate millions along the river is staggering to say the least. There is one thing I can say for certain, and that is the Chinese people are very industrious, in fact we discovered that the state bird is the crane, because there were massive cranes on building-sites everywhere. We also learned there are over 400 MILLION people who live along the Yangtze River alone in China! That population is more than the entire number of people in the United States. China has a population of over one Billion people, and this fact became clear to us when we saw the masses everywhere.

Operas and Museums

We were treated like important dignitaries everywhere we went, and our guides always secured the best seats in the house, whenever we attended an opera, concert, or special production. In Beijing we saw the famous Peking Opera. In Xian we enjoyed the Tang Dynasty Dinner & Show, which was very colorful and well produced. Finally in Shanghai we saw an incredible Acrobat show, and I

am still amazed at the flexibility and balance these performers had. We also visited a number of temples, gardens and museums, one of which peaked my interest. In Wuhan we visited a museum that contained amazing artifacts from a wealthy man who lived over 2,400 years ago. This man had buried with him, a large, ancient, musical instrument that could still carry a tune. This device was built with many bells large and small, and it was incredible to learn that this ancient musical instrument survived being buried for thousands of years, and over a thousand years under water. I still struggle with the idea that this artifact did not corrode away, and yet it seemed to be in pristine condition. I thought it was amazing when I heard the whistle from the Titanic, having been at the bottom of the Atlantic for over 80 years, blown one time in St Paul, Minnesota. But to hear the sound from these ancient bells buried for over two thousand four hundred years...that was truly awe-inspiring.

Our Guide

If you embark on a trip to China be sure you go with a company that has a guide or tour escort that is there to watch over and take care of your every move. Our guide's name was Daniel, and he was very nurturing for us foreigners, and as mentioned before, he checked us into our hotel rooms, he acquired our intra-China airline tickets, and took care of all our transfers flawlessly. We were in a completely foreign country, none of us spoke the language, so it would have been a huge challenge to navigate around China like we did without someone there to escort us everywhere we went. Our guide even knew which restrooms (happy rooms) was the best choice throughout our journeys. The Chinese refer to bathrooms or toilets as "Happy Rooms", because after you use the bathroom you feel happy. This was a funny ongoing term to hear throughout the trip. The same guide who met us at the airport in Beijing when we first arrived, was also there for us when we finally departed back to the States out of Shanghai. Our guide also did his best to explain the culture of China, he was entertaining and informative, and being a local himself, he was able to express the intricacies of his culture in a way we could understand. I know some of the guides had to deal with passengers / individuals who were rather high-maintenance to put it as politically correct as I can. Thankfully, our group of 20 or so was not high-maintenance, and was a decent group of people. So my hat goes off to Viking River Cruises for selecting the best, most knowledgeable guides they could find.

Conclusion
For my wife and I, this amazing journey to China was a once-in-a-lifetime experience we will treasure, and thankfully, the entire trip went without any major issues or problems. On the flight from Chicago to Beijing, I did go through a little pain as I passed a kidney stone during the last three hours before arriving into Beijing, and my wife had a little stomach issue early in the trip, but for the most part, we stayed healthy, and thoroughly enjoyed the adventure. Of course we took extra precautions with supplementation, which I think was the reason we stayed healthy. We took the best possible vitamin supplementation, and Glucosamine for our joint health, as well as Echinacea and a special powdered supplement called IntestiFlora to boost our digestive immune system. We also took a potent and pure supplement called Omega 3, which gave us better blood circulation. While a few others experienced colds at the end of the trip, my wife and I stayed healthy.

Would I recommend a trip to China with Viking River Cruises? Absolutely! Let me give you some tips if you are considering a cruisetour of China. First, be sure to book your trip with Viking River Cruises or tell your travel agent to book you with Viking River Cruises. Secondly, be prepared to do some walking, you might even want to get on the treadmill or do some pre-trip exercises to get in shape. Bring a decent camera, and perhaps even take a photography class so that you can capture the best possible photos from your trip. Consider high-quality supplementation during your trip to avoid or prevent potential sickness. The last thing you want is to be sick while climbing the Great Wall of China or exploring the Forbidden City. Leave some room in your suitcase or bring an additional suitcase for souvenirs, because you'll want to bring home some interesting treasures. Our trip was in August and the temperatures in China were hot and humid, however, if you want to avoid the heat and humidity, try booking your China trip for October or November. Be prepared to be wowed and amazed by the masses in China, and with the masses come an incredible level of traffic. Before we experienced China and Yangtze River, our initial expectations were that we would see a lot of rural areas with rice fields and farmers, but the complete opposite is what we saw. China has a massive build-up of infrastructure, with massive bridges and vast colonies of tall condominiums and high-rises everywhere. I guess the high-rises should be expected with over One Billion people living in China. One thing is for certain if you plan your trip to China with Viking River Cruises, you will come to appreciate the ancient and fascinating culture of China, and return home with a unique perspective of this great country.

A look through a 600+ year old Pagota with a view of our river boat the Viking Century Sun docked

Queen Mary Long Beach Review

I've written so much about the Queen Mary which is now a hotel, museum and convention facility in Long Beach, California, but this time I'd like to offer a review of the ship as a hotel and attraction in southern California. This really does tie-in to the cruise industry too, because just aft of the Queen Mary is a cruise terminal where thousands of cruise passengers can depart from each week. While I was onboard the Queen Mary I often came across people wandering the ship that either just came off of a cruise or were just about to depart on their cruise from the Long Beach cruise terminal. Carnival Cruise Line's Paradise and the Carnival Splendor were docked at the cruise terminal throughout the weekend that I was visiting the Queen Mary. I need to remind my readers that I am passionate about the Queen Mary, her history and her future as an attraction in Long Beach. I know it sounds odd, but I had chosen a college in southern California because it was not far from Long Beach where the Queen Mary was. Since I was about 13 years old, I developed a unique interest in the Queen Mary, my friends in junior high school would tease me that I knew how many rivets and portholes were in the Queen Mary. I was fascinated by her size and engineering and history, then I discovered there were many other grand ocean liners during the trans-Atlantic era, when crossing the Atlantic by ship was the "only way to cross".

I spent the weekend aboard the Queen Mary Hotel with my wife and my son. For me this was a huge weekend because I was returning to the place I asked my wife to marry me, and I was going to have an opportunity to show my 9 year-old son the ship that has inspired me for so many years. Additionally, I produced an event aboard the Queen Mary during this weekend where I invited the listeners of my talkshow in the southern California area to come watch me interview a few people in front of an audience. The event was a huge success and everyone seemed to have a wonderful time. We were booked into the Eisenhower Suite; which is the same room that President Eisenhower stayed in when he crossed the Atlantic aboard the Queen Mary. This is a key selling point for anyone looking for a hotel to stay at while visiting southern California..the fact that you can book yourself into an original first-class stateroom from the days when the Queen Mary was in her glory crossing the Atlantic on a regular basis. The who's who list of celebrities and movie stars, statesman and royalty that stayed in the suites aboard the Queen Mary when she was in active service is spectacular. To think that you could stay overnight or several nights in the same room that Bob Hope, Winston Churchill, Liz Taylor, Frank Sinatra, Billy Graham, or President Eisenhower stayed in while crossing the Atlantic is more than intriguing. The Queen Mary Hotel has a rather new management company so the rooms have new beds and linens, which are very comfortable. New iPod docking stations have been placed in the rooms with flat-screen TV's and when you add the element of historical significance to your stay, it all adds-up to a memorable, comfortable visit.

The Queen Mary is a Historical Treasure and worth a visit. She's not just an old ship, the Queen Mary has an illustrious history that spans over 70 years. Most of her career has now been spent as a landmark in Long Beach, so she is a "place" where millions of people have visited, explored, and marveled at her size, her engines, her romance, and her history before she arrived in Long Beach. Ocean liners were mini cities or communities that had their own personality, and they were a microcosm of societal engineering. Today, Queen Mary is considered a building rather than a ship since she no longer separates herself from land, and she no longer becomes an island unto herself. The ship is still floating, however; which is nice, but gone are the days when passengers can feel the movement and energy of the ship as she pounds her way across the vast ocean. Queen Mary has been absorbed by the city of Long Beach as opposed to having the ability to escape to the sea, and yet if you squint, you can imagine what it was like when she was still an active ship.

What's there to do onboard the Queen Mary? Don't miss the opportunity to stay in the Queen Mary Hotel. You can also explore the museum and see the ship's last remaining propeller. There are plenty of great rooms and space for that special meeting, dance or banquet. You can take a self-guided tour or sign-up for an escorted behind-the-scenes tour. For those who want to experience a chill down their leg, you can try out the ghost tour experience. If you want a unique place to eat, the Queen Mary has many excellent dining venues, including the famous Sunday Brunch in the First-

Class Dining Room or Sir Winston's with a great view of the Long Beach skyline. Or you might want to do what I did and find a deck chair to relax and just soak-in the southern California sunshine from the deck of the Queen Mary.

There is an ongoing effort to preserve and protect the Queen Mary's original areas, decks, rooms and lounges, and I know it is a daunting task for any management company to take on, because she's not a building but a ship, and ships have unique maintenance requirements. The maintenance onboard the Queen Mary is staggering, and for the most part, I think the current management company has done a fine job, however, her exterior desperately needs to be painted and cared for.

I'd like to thank the PR department aboard the Queen Mary for their generosity to host our Cruising Authority event in the Verandah Grill. I'd also like to thank a few of my sponsors for this trip to southern California, which include: Advantage Rent A Car, AirTran, American Limousine and Disneyland. This trip to southern California would not have been possible without these great sponsors.

Is the Queen Mary Haunted?

This is somewhat of a subtitle and addition to my review of the Queen Mary which I think must be discussed to answer a question that has been stirring since the day Queen Mary opened up as an attraction in the 70's, is the Queen Mary haunted? I've heard the stories over the years about a ghost or two in the Pool area or some that may lurk in the old engine room areas and even some staterooms. Stories of an engineer that was killed by a watertight door in the engine room area and still walks the catwalks and deck-plates of the below deck areas is a common story. My favorite is one where a security guard heard noises in the pool area, so he went to investigate. The noises stopped, but he did see what appeared to be wet footprints from someone who had just came out of the pool, and yet there was no water in the pool. Some have seen a ghostly-figured woman in an old-style bathing suit, or have heard the voice of a little girl that wasn't there. Another interesting story is of a light bulb, in the area where the carpenter shop use to be located, which apparently turns on and off, even though there is no electricity or even a working bulb in the socket. The carpenter shop near the bow is of course where an occasional wooden casket was constructed. I've also heard the stories of strange yelling and the sounds of crashing steel and water flooding at the bow stem area deep in the ship.

These sounds were suspected to be ghostly remnants from when the Queen Mary during World War II crashed into, split in half and sunk the cruiser, HMS Curacoa. In October of 1942 the HMS Curacoa was escorting the troop ship Queen Mary with 10,000 troops onboard, and after a collision with the Queen Mary, 338 crewmembers from the Curacoa were lost at sea with only 102 survivors. Of course the Queen Mary could not jeopardize being torpedoed with 10,000 troops onboard, so she continued full-steam-ahead to her destination. There are many more stories of ghosts, sounds, creaks, growns, and even apparitions recorded by famous paranormal investigators.

I spoke with William Kane, who works on the Queen Mary as the designated Captain and historian, and I asked him about the ghost stories. I suggested to Mr. Kane that I thought it might be a PR stunt to draw visitors to the Queen Mary and I liked his answer which was, "We get reports all the time from people experiencing something paranormally....I will say we don't have ghosts onboard, rather we seem to have a lot of angels." So are the ghost stories and paranormal activity real? My opinion is complicated, but my basic answer is no. Allow me to explain my reasoning. I moved to southern California in 1985 to attend college, and I spent many hours, days, weeks, months exploring every little corner, bulkhead, storeroom, lounge and even the deep bowels of the ship where the old engine room and boilers use to be. Throughout the many years of exploring the ship, never did I see, hear, or sense anything that would be considered paranormal or ghostly, and I must preface this by saying that I happen to be a very spiritual person, and I am very sensitive to "spiritual" experiences both positive and negative. I have a few ideas for why so many people seem to think they are experiencing paranormal activity. First of all, the Queen Mary is a ship that is still floating, so there are going to be strange sounds related to a moving ship even subtle movements due to winds and tidal movement. Secondly, the Queen Mary's hull was constructed in 1934 – 1936, so she is over 80 years old and it would not be unusual to hear sounds related to plumbing, both new and old that exist deep within the bowels of the ship. Much of her interior spaces deep inside the hull have been dramatically altered or even cut away, so there are unique sounds of stress on the ship's structure as she continues to float in her private basin. I've heard the unique sounds of the ship's interiors mostly due to plumbing and subtle movement of the ship. I have been onboard the Queen Mary in several of her most "haunted" areas at all hours of the day and night, and I have never experienced anything that could be interpreted as paranormal. I watched a program on television where some highly respected "ghost hunters" set up a camera in a stateroom that was apparently known to have a poltergeist, and when the tape was played back it became apparent that someone accessed the room in a way other than the main cabin door, and they moved the blanket, but shut off the camera, then turned it on again. This was obviously someone who wanted to escalate or help to prove there are ghosts on Queen Mary, by someone who knows the ship and how to navigate some of the spaces between the walls. I am convinced that someone employed by the Queen Mary Hotel or the City of Long Beach has effectively tried to mess with paranormal researchers by producing sounds and voices that are seemingly from a child ghost in the swimming pool area. This deception could be done by bouncing sounds off the mother of pearl ceiling, with conveniently located speakers, to create the illusion of a resident ghost-child. I have definitely been the source of some ghost stories told by some of the cleaning staff. There were a few nights that I impersonated a ghostly sound behind a wall to the employee break area. This wall was not easily accessible, and in an area of the ship that no one goes to. It was fun scaring these staff members and hearing their response. Of course it was a mean thing to do, but I was in college with my college buddies and it was fun. I even heard the residual stories from that incident a few weeks later through a security guard. Knowing the ship's layout as well as I did, I was able to get into areas of the ship that even many security officers may not be familiar with, so I often had fun being chased by security officers with my buddies. It was an adventure and an adrenaline-rush for my friends and I. That being said, some unexplained incidents might be a result of my adventures.

Top: When I travel, I often ride in limos and visiting the Queen Mary in Long Beach by stretched limo was a thrill. Right: Jacob on his tour of the Queen Mary's engine room in 2010

Norwegian EPIC - *First impressions:*

Seeing the Norwegian Epic tower over the pier in New York was impressive,

in fact the Epic completely blocked the site of the Carnival Miracle docked in the next pier over. I knew the ship was going to be very big, and what seems to always be among the first comments when you talk to someone is "wow this ship is really big". Having also been aboard the Oasis of the Seas with Royal Caribbean, in January, which is a much larger ship at 240,000 tons, it was interesting to compare the two. Oasis is the biggest, but you'd hardly know the difference when ships get this big. I think as ships get larger, the ocean seems smaller, because the focus onboard these giants revolves around numerous options, more amenities, more dining venues, more entertainment, more staterooms and suites, and of course more people. The key is to build a big ship with excellent attention to passenger flow, and I think for the most part, NCL has succeeded in developing spaces and lounges that flow together well.

Wavy staterooms

One of the big discussion points as the Norwegian Epic is revealed in all her glory, is her "wavy", staterooms with curved walls and separate compartments for the toilet and the shower. My first impression when I arrived at my room 9248, a deluxe Balcony stateroom, was that it felt small and narrow. I liked the wood-like paneling, and the lighting. There's a large domed-ceiling above the bed that offered a soothing glow, which reminded me of something from the future. I discovered plenty of storage space, and clever baskets in a couple of the compartments, which are perfect for storing the dirty clothes after a long day at the beach or exploring the Mayan Ruins. The bed linens were nice, but the beds, themselves, were a bit too firm for my taste. The balcony was a decent size, and from what I understand, the air conditioning for the room, is connected to the sliding balcony door, and the air shuts off when the door is opened so passengers aren't wasting or blasting cool air into the hot and often humid Caribbean.

There has been much to say about the bathroom arrangement in the wavy staterooms, most of the comments being on the "uneasy" side. After speaking with seasoned cruise industry journalists who suggested that North Americans will have a problem with the bathroom arrangement, I came to the conclusion that maybe experienced cruisers might struggle with it a bit, but first-time cruisers won't notice anything terribly unusual. I have noticed when first-time cruisers board a ship for their vacation, everything is "different" and takes a little "getting used to", for example; the movement of the ship, the lips at the base of many doors, compact staterooms, even navigating around the ship. Because "things are different" on a cruise ship, many passengers won't notice or care that the bathrooms are unusual onboard the Epic.

I think the staterooms are smallish, even the suites. This is most certainly a high-density ship, and I think it will be interesting to experience the ship when at full capacity. Additionally, I think even a Deluxe Balcony Stateroom would be a squeeze for three or four people. I enjoyed the stateroom décor, and after spending some time in the room, I was pleased with the overall "feel" of the room. At a press conference someone asked about the little sink outside of the shower and toilet area with the tallish spout. The answer was that it was decided and chosen, several years ago, by Colin Veitch, the previous CEO of NCL, to install these unique sinks, so that he could easily fill his tea kettle. It was suggested, in somewhat of a joking way, that perhaps this is why Colin is the "previous" CEO and not the current CEO.

Entertainment

The live bands around the ship are also a huge plus in my book. Many of the cruise lines still use piped-in music or tracks, but NCL is using live music. There are numerous live music venues around the ship including a

"Blues" club. It will take a week just to experience all the unique entertainment onboard the Norwegian Epic. Another interesting thing I discovered onboard the Norwegian Epic is that the ship doesn't just have a Cruise Director, but also an Entertainment Director, because of the magnitude

of entertainment offered. Without question, Norwegian Cruise Lines has upped the ante industry-wide with their "branded" entertainment including Blue Man Group, Second City, Legends in Concert, Cirque Dreams, and Nickelodeon at sea. Entertainment on ships has certainly evolved over the last couple of years with full-scale broadway-style musicals, high-diving shows and now branded entertainment. I enjoyed Blue Man Group, it was so refreshing and cool to see on a ship this eclectic and wild show performed by these "Blue Guys". I have a theory about who the Blue Men are trying to be…..they are aliens from another world experiencing simple human interaction, and it's hilarious, particularly the scene with the twinkie and the volunteer (victim) from the audience. I found myself caught-up in the show, and that says a lot because I have seen the best of the best when it comes to big shows on cruise ships, having been a Cruise Director.

The Norwegian Epic will have wonderful entertainment options for families with children because of the Nickelodeon at sea experience and the spectacular water slides on the pool deck. The youth and the teens have their own spaces and rooms for hanging out and playing videos games and watching movies. There is a vast sports deck with bungee jumping, basketball, and NCL is even offering ice skating, which is a direct competitive move to compete with Royal Caribbean. Now NCL can say, "Hey we also have ice skating at sea". The Epic is packed from stem to stern with entertainment options from the shows, the live music and the very active bars with darts, bowling, and you can even play a game of pool on two pool tables. Freeze your butt off in the Ice Bar, enjoy dancing on deck with a giant TV screen, or find a quiet spot somewhere on deck for a romantic rendezvous, there's so many options. The key is that not only is there a multitude of options, but the quality of those options is excellent.

Dining

When I first experienced "Freestyle dining" on the Norwegian Pearl a couple years ago, I was skeptical, however, I was soon sold on the concept when I realized that I didn't have to go eat at a certain time if I didn't want to…I could eat later and have numerous choices of where to eat. The Norwegian Epic has truly taken Freestyle Dining to the level with a plethora of quality dining options throughout the ship. You can get pizza, fish & chips, a sizzling steak, sushi, Teppanyaki, Italian food, French food, you name it and they probably have it aboard the Epic. I think I heard there were 26 different restaurants onboard. During my short visit I didn't really have an opportunity to enjoy the fine dining in the restaurants because I was scrambling to get all my scheduled interviews, take pictures and video and explore the ship, so I just stopped briefly to grab a quick something and then I was off to my

The "actual" Travelocity Gnome

next meeting. I did, however; have a wonderful mushroom soup in the Bistro that is burned into my memory and taste buds. I don't think I heard any negative comments about the food onboard. I really enjoyed the Garden Café for breakfast on Deck Fifteen because of the vast options including: fruits, meats, eggs, cream of wheat, pancakes and waffles, cereals, breads, pastries, all divided into stations throughout the Garden Café, and you can't beat the views high above the sea.

Décor around the ship

I found the décor to be very whimsical and modern, with some classically elegant rooms for dining and socializing. The ship is very colorful but tasteful from the carpets to the artwork on the bulkheads. I didn't think the décor was over the top like you might see on a Carnival ship, rather I felt the tone around the ship to be fun, classy, and modern. I enjoyed the way the interior areas were broken-up into nooks and very usable spaces. There wasn't much wasted space on this ship at all, in fact the Norwegian Epic was designed to truly maximize passenger-flow from one area to another. There's even an escalator to assist with this passenger flow midship. I could see an evolution in cruise ship interior design onboard the Epic that I haven't noticed on other ships. I could see that a tremendous-level of thought went into the passenger areas. Gone are the days of boxy lounges and specific rooms; on the Epic, one room flowed and transitioned into another. I almost felt like I was in a casino in Las Vegas the way the various areas seamlessly came together. There was also an excitement in the air, not because this was a brand new ship, but I think the décor and laughter, the music and general pulse of the activity onboard promoted a sense of relaxation, and fun.

Conclusion

When I first saw the artist rendering of the Norwegian Epic, I thought there must have been a mistake, the ship looked comically top heavy and odd with decks 15 and 16 above the bridge area. After visiting the ship, I had a sense that the ship was very solid, and someone cleverly pointed out to me that this ship was built from the inside out. It really is what's on the inside that counts, and the Norwegian Epic is truly a ship that will make a big splash in a very positive way with singles, couples, and families. And speaking about single cruisers, The Epic has these very cool pod-like, staterooms for single passengers, and there's no single occupancy supplement which is excellent news for single travelers. I met with Mr. Paul Priestman who designed these single occupancy staterooms, and he was very proud of his work on these compact rooms. These rooms are almost patterned after the pod-like spaces in Japan where someone can sleep and clean-up and not much else. Mr. Priestman made these single rooms very comfortable, with fun lighting and clever cubbies for storage and hanging clothes. There's also a private shower and toilet, so there's everything you need to basically spend the week on this ship in your own small stateroom pod. It will be very interesting to see how passengers receive the Norwegian Epic this year while she is cruising the Caribbean. The hardware is very interesting, there's a lot to do, but more importantly, the crew and staff are all very excited about their new ship. I also heard that a majority of the crew onboard has their own room, which is a huge plus for those who work on the ship for months at a time. What makes an excellent cruise vacation experience is not just the fancy hardware, but the care and excellent service of the staff onboard, which I am confident the Norwegian Epic will deliver with style!

Brilliance of the Seas out of Dubai

Cruising around the world is a fascinating way to travel, especially if you have been on one particular cruise line a number of times in other parts of the world. As an example, I have cruised the Caribbean with Royal Caribbean many times, so when I stepped aboard the Brilliance of the Seas in the exotic and far-away port of Dubai, it was like coming home to a familiar place, even though I'm in a strange culture. The highlight of this particular cruise aboard the Brilliance of the Seas was the fascinating itinerary cruising from Dubai to Fujairah, (UAE) Muscat, Oman, and finally Abu Dhabi, (UAE). We cruised through the Straight or Hormuz twice, which has been in the news because of the instability of Iran and their military and nuclear programs. This cruise was an adventure. The ship offered all the usual Royal Caribbean amenities; food and entertainment, which was very familiar, while the places we visited were mysterious and intriguing.

I'm going to be very straight and honest about our experience with Royal Caribbean. I'm a fan of Royal Caribbean, I use to work at Royal Caribbean and when I was selling cruises I sent a lot of people on Royal Caribbean. I was impressed with the professionalism among the Guest Services staff and all the crew and staff I came across. The ship was very clean and well maintained. Two things stuck out with me, however; and that was the dining experience was not memorable, except for the one night we ate in Portofino, and the fact that so many amenities and services were monetized or commercialized. Back to the dining, our waiter for example, was excellent, and from the explanations of the food and the presentation by the waiter, you would expect the taste to be extraordinary....but in my opinion the taste and sometimes even the look of the food fell flat. I think the waiters are trained to hype-up the dining and get you ready for an incredible tasty experience, then when the food is there in front of me and I took a few bites, I felt it was good but not extraordinary. I liked the new plates and bowls, the service was excellent, it was the actual taste and sometimes presentation of the food that fell flat with me. I also must take into consideration that most of the passengers onboard the Brilliance of the Seas were from the UK, so there may have been some cultural adjustments to the preparation, presentation and taste, based on the palate of people from the UK, and the European market too. One more example: I usually take photos of the food, but on this cruise, in the main dining room, I did not. I'm not saying the food was poor, or not tasty, it just didn't stand out as being extraordinary, as it was built-up to be by the waiters and my personal expectations.

I am embarrassed to say that only one time did I set foot in a stage show during this cruise, and only for a few minutes. What I did see was excellent. Royal Caribbean does such a great job with their shows, the talent brought

onboard is top of the line. I have just seen so many shows in the many cruises I've been on, and the shows were later in the evening when I was tired and ready for bed. I think you can expect great entertainment onboard any of the Royal Caribbean ships, that is yet another part of the cruise that is very consistent. There were plenty of activities throughout the ship, and many familiar games and activities I use to host when I worked on the ships. The Brilliance of the Seas had one particular "Cool factor" activity, and that was the pool tables. Yes, you can play billiards on a ship, since these pool tables were rigged with gyros so they remained level no matter how rough the seas were outside. It was very fun to watch someone play pool as the ship is pitching and listing through the sea, and the pool table remained level.

Another area where Royal Caribbean stepped-up to the plate and hit a home-run was the Arabian White Night on deck. This was the third night of the cruise, we had been docked in Muscat, Oman all day. Many passengers, including me, went out and purchased the Arabian head gear which was in nearly every shop in Muscat. The band was playing on deck, there were ice sculptures, a fantastic dessert buffet, you could rent a special bong device where you could smoke some harmless, tobacco / drug-free mint. I forgot what the flavor was, but everyone seemed to enjoy pretending to get high on the bong. There were tents set up with pillows on the deck so you could live the dream of being an Arabian Sultan. It was a very fun event and my hat goes off to Royal Caribbean for producing such a creative activity.

The real treasure from this cruise, aside from the Brilliance of the Seas, was the unique ports, and the incredible sights to see in Muscat and Abu Dhabi. Muscat, Oman, did not seem like a place that was accustomed to tourists and cruise passengers scrambling around. We were docked in Muscat for

two full days, giving passengers plenty of opportunity to explore the city. The one thing I was surprised to see were the Indian shop keepers and product from India. There were few if any women that actually worked in the stores or shops, in fact, I think it was against the law in this town for women to work in a public place. At every turn throughout the city of Muscat it was clear that this was a very strict, religious community. Mosques and religious structures were everywhere, and there were large speakers throughout the city that broadcast prayers every morning. I was anticipating somewhat of an oppressive feeling in an environment like this, but that was not my experience. A pleasant surprise was the fabulous market-place or mall. There were no windows in this mall, it was a little on the dark side, but absolutely fascinating to walk through. We spent hours wandering through this mall. Again it surprised me that nearly every shopkeeper was from India. There were numerous shops that had identical nick-knacks, statues, clocks, nautical brass items, jewelry, linens, cashmere, silk, herbs, exotic spices....it was mesmerizing how much "stuff" these stores had in stock. Much of the product in these stores were useless junk, but one man's junk is another man's treasure. It truly was fascinating to walk through this mall, and I only wish I had brought money to spend, cause there were certainly some items I'd like to have, but then I tried to realize that most of this stuff was made in England or India, and the real challenge was to find items actually made in Muscat, Oman. I did find and purchased some silver earrings for my wife, that were made in Muscat.

We also visited Abu Dhabi. I truly enjoyed Abu Dhabi and was impressed by how clean and modern the city was. We went on one shore excursion during the entire cruise, to a fabulous mosque, which was very impressive. Entirely made out of white marble, and larger than the Taj Mahal in India, this Mosque was recently completed in 2007 I think. All of the women in our group had to wear black robes to enter the mosque. I think this mosque had

several Guiness world records, including the world's largest chandelier, which was spectacular. In fact, there were four of these giant chandeliers. Another world record was the massive custom rug manufactured specifically for this mosque. It was a massive structure and worth visiting. I was also impressed with the mall in Abu Dhabi. This mall in Abu Dhabi is far different than the seemingly ancient mall in Muscat. I enjoy walking through malls, and this one in Abu Dhabi was ultra-modern and had all the brands you would expect in a first-class mall anywhere in the world. I'm a movie fan, and asked if I could peek into the theater. The movie playing was Mission Impossible and it was subtitled in Arabic, in the latest stadium seating theater with the latest sound system.

Finally, we spent a whole day in Dubai before disembarking the Brilliance of the Seas the next morning. I had made special transportation arrangements with Dubai Exotic Limo, and visited several landmarks in Dubai, including Burj Al Arab, the giant hotel that looks like a huge sale, and the mall at the base of the tallest building in the world, the Burj Khalifa. First of all, if you ever plan a trip to Dubai, contact Dubai Exotic Limo who offers a truly luxurious experience of transport in an actual stretched limo. There are few stretched limos in Dubai. If you ask for a limo service, most companies send you just a "car" or van, but not Dubai Exotic Limo, where you are shuttled around in an actual stretched limo....the best way to get around in Dubai in my humble opinion. We also visited the world's most luxurious hotel, Burj Al Arab. At this moment, all I can say is Wow! Burj Al Arab is over-the-top spectacular, and one of the only seven star hotels in the world. It's a very exclusive building that is only accessible by crossing the gated bridge. Only hotel guests and special visitors who are invited by a guests can enter this exclusive and luxurious hotel.

I think the builders of Dubai have decided long ago to construct a city with the best of the best, the largest, tallest and most extravagant structures in the world. I thought our Mall of America in my hometown was impressive, but then visited the Dubai Mall and I was completely taken back by the size and range of stores and activities available. There's a complete ice-skating rink and the world's largest fish tank, all in the shadow of the Burj Khalifa, the tallest building in the world. The dancing waters in the lake at the base of the Burj Khalifa, rivals that of the dancing waters in Las Vegas. As you walk around the mall area in Dubai, you can't help but think this place is over-the-top and the best of the best. It reminded me of a massively expanded Fashion Island in Newport Beach.

I'm so thrilled that I can now check off my bucket list of places to visit, this amazing city of Dubai and the cruise aboard Royal Caribbean's Brilliance of the Seas was an adventurous and comfortable experience. Without question I would recommend a cruise with Royal Caribbean out of Dubai. For American's reading this, you might want to take note that on this itinerary out of Dubai, you will be a minority. Of the two thousand or so passengers onboard the Brilliance of the Seas, there were only one hundred fifty American passengers onboard. Most of the passengers were from the UK or Europe, so you can expect a culturally diverse experience on this itinerary among the passengers.

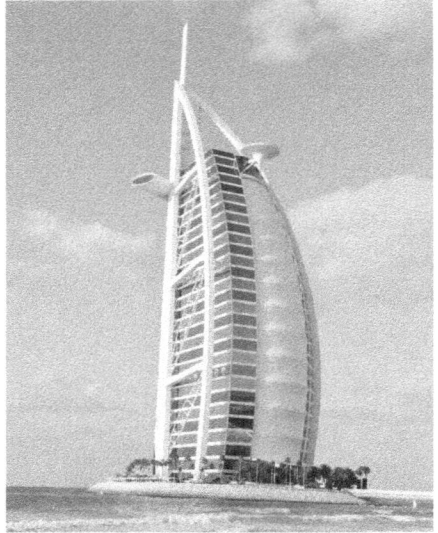

Top Left: Brilliance of the Seas has a fascinating pool table set on hydraulics so the surface is always level…compensating for the movement of the ship while at sea.

Left Middle: Barry cruising the Strait of Hormuz aboard the Brilliance of the Seas.

Left Bottom: The massive and beautiful Sheikh Zayed Mosque, built with exotic marble from around the world. Unfortunately, Sheikh Zayed passed away before he could see the completed mosque.

Above: The super-luxury hotel, Burj Al Arab in Dubai. Nearly as tall as the Empire State Building in New York, Burj Al Arab is the largest man-made structure constructed on a man-made island. For an average suite, expect to pay nearly $6,000 per night.

Burj Al Arab – Dubai

It is an interesting exercise to consider what the term "luxury" means to you. Everyone has their own perspective of what is luxurious, for example,

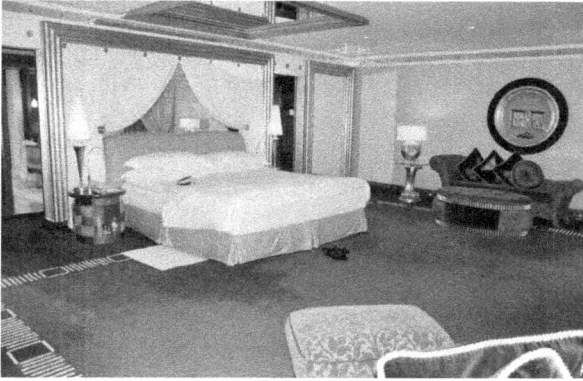

twenty-five cents given to a beggar on the street in India might be considered a moment of luxury to the beggar. As a Cruise Journalist, I developed three elements that define luxury: first, when comfort exceeds expectations, second, exclusivity or when you obtain something of high quality, and finally, when you receive a genuine level of care and service. Wrap all of these elements into one experience and I think you'll have a moment of lavish luxury. I experienced lavish luxury at the magnificent Burj Al Arab hotel in Dubai, which was one of those items on my bucket list to one day experience first-hand.

I cruised on Royal Caribbean's Brilliance of the Seas on a fascinating itinerary out of Dubai, and to top-off that great cruise, I stayed one night at Burj Al Arab. Dubai has become a bustling, high-energy, cosmopolitan city within only a few years. I'm convinced the builders of this modern city made every effort to out-do the great structures in America, by building the tallest building in the world, one of the largest malls in the world, the most advanced dancing fountain show rivaling anything seen in Las Vegas, and constructing the world's most luxurious hotel, Burj Al Arab. It's no wonder the Port of Dubai has attracted a few of the top cruise lines to position ships out of Dubai as their home port. It is this boom in cruising out of Dubai that sparked my interest to visit Dubai and see what all the fuss was about. I can now say that a cruise departure from Dubai is a must, because of the exciting things to see in Dubai, and for those who can afford to stay at the exquisite Burj Al Arab, I'd highly recommend the indulgence of a pre-cruise or post cruise stay at the world's most luxurious hotel.

What makes Burj Al Arab so luxurious? No expense was spared in the design and construction of the building, which is not much shorter than the Empire State Building in New York. It's the tallest structure in the world built upon it's own man-made island. Seventeen thousand square feet of 24 carat gold leaf was used throughout the hotel, imported marble, exquisite tiles and fabrics lavish guests in the public areas. The 202 suites ranging in size from 1,800 to over 8,300 square feet are lavishly appointed with the finest linens, the most comfortable beds, exquisite amenities, butler service

and spectacular views of the Arabian Gulf. I was impressed with the great steam and sauna in the men's spa area that had a specialized attendant who brought you a cool scented towel while you steamed or a cold bottle of water while you sat in the sauna. You know those little bottles of shampoo and soaps the hotels usually offer? Burj Al Arab offers guests, full-size Hermes products from Paris, like shampoo, body soap, cologne, after shave and deodorant. I also brought home the complimentary flip-flops and the very comfortable slippers with the Burj Al Arab logo that will continually remind me of the amazing comfort of this amazing hotel.

Access to Burj Al Arab is exclusively available to hotel guests, and the only way to get to the hotel is by passing through the secured gates and across the bridge to the island where the hotel stands, or if you so choose, you could arrive by helicopter, one thousand feet above the Arabian Gulf, onto the special rooftop heliport. I met a wonderful couple on the Brilliance of the Seas cruise and invited them to meet me at Burj Al Arab, where we enjoyed great conversation, and some tea in my suite served by my butler. My friends had to show a picture ID and I had to prearrange for my friends to enter the hotel where they were escorted to my suite. My suite was massive, with two levels, a sweeping staircase and chandelier, a fully-equipped office, two bedrooms, two very large bathrooms with a huge hot tub, a living room and dining room and kitchen. The suite was equipped with state-of-the-art electronics where at the touch of a special key-pad, I could control the lights, close or open the curtains, turn on the TV or call for my butler. A fleet of custom Rolls Royce Phantoms are available to transport me anywhere I want to go in Dubai, or I could rent an exotic sports car and explore the city on my own. During my entire stay in Dubai, I had the great luxury of having all my transportation needs covered by Dubai

Exotic Limo service. Anytime I needed a ride, a black stretched limo was waiting to pick me up at the airport, or take me to the ship, the hotel or into the city. When you visit Dubai make sure to have your transportation needs taken care of by Dubai Exotic Limo, it is such a classy and convenient way to get around Dubai.

Experiencing the luxuries of a seven-star hotel, Burj Al Arab, is not for everyone. Some may not appreciate the pretentious lifestyle and over-the-top amenities, which is intoxicating to say the least. For me, I was happy to gut it out, but now I can't wait to go there again and drink of the elixir of Burj Al Arab.

Dubai Exotic Limo Fleet posing in front of QE2

Queen Mary 2 Trans-Atlantic Crossing
The Real Ship of Dreams

Few ships over the past eight to nine years have received the world-wide attention and publicity that Queen Mary 2 has. In 2003, When Queen Mary 2 (QM2) first set out on her sea trials, she was the culmination of directives initiated by billionaire Mickey Arison, and designed by Stephen Payne, the perfect man for the job considering Payne was not only a ship designer, but a fan of the old ocean liners of the past. Recognizing that the aging QE2 was nearing the end of her sea going career, Cunard Line was about to be re-energized as a company with the first true ocean liner to be constructed in thirty years. When the original Queen Mary set out on her maiden voyage in 1936, the hope and dreams of an entire country followed her successful introduction into the trans-Atlantic market. The original Queen Mary became an instant celebrity because she represented a transformation out of an economic depression, and all eyes from England and America were on this incredible ship that seemed to have a soul capable of lifting the spirits of her passengers. That was another era when ships like the Queen Mary were ambassadors of an entire nation. Today, the Queen Mary 2 aspires to lift the spirits of her passengers, but in this age and time, she carries mostly the legacy of a glorious past, while forging out her own role in history as a ship of dreams.

With many books and articles already written about the Queen Mary 2, as a Cruise Journalist, I had my work cut out for me as I embarked on the journey of a lifetime on a trans-Atlantic crossing aboard this incredible ocean liner. Our crossing was scheduled for June 17th, 2012 from New York (or Brooklyn) across the Atlantic to Southampton, England. A special voyage like this means something different to everyone, but for me, this was the fulfillment of a dream. I had made numerous Atlantic crossings onboard the QE2 as a member of the crew, however; now as a married man I have wanted to share this unique experience of a trans-Atlantic crossing with my wife. Since 1977, I have had a passion for the original Queen Mary and studied all I could about her history. In 1997, I proposed to a woman on the deck of the Queen Mary in Long Beach, California, and she has now been my wife for fifteen years. As a Cruise Journalist, I have had the privilege and honor of bringing my wife all around the world on incredible cruise adventures, but this one experience of a trans-Atlantic crossing on the Queen Mary 2 was for me, the pinnacle of all my past cruise experiences. This was no 'cruise' aboard the QM2, it was a crossing that transcends the usual cruise vacation because of the nostalgia, the legacy and rich history of the trans-Atlantic crossing by ocean liner.

Considering the interest and passion I have carried for most of my adult life regarding the Queen Mary, the QM2 and the trans-Atlantic era, I will share with you my thoughts about this QM2 trans-Atlantic crossing in this very special review.

The ship - There is a difference between a cruise ship and an ocean liner. An ocean liner is built for a very unique purpose, to conduct line voyages across the ocean in all weather and sea conditions. Queen Mary 2 was designed and built to push her way through any sea conditions and she has the reserve power to make-up time lost to maintain a schedule. It was fascinating to notice the complexities of this massive structure, and like a finely-crafted watch all the parts work together for one purpose, comfortable transportation across the ocean for all it's crew and passengers.

The dinning - We dinned in the Princess Grill. One afternoon we ate in the Britannia Restaurant to capture the experience in this incredible room that is reminiscent of the trans-Atlantic liners of old. In the Princess Grill, service was exceptional. Our waiter staff paid very close attention to the details of properly serving our dining needs and requests. My wife enjoys sweet tea, so we asked the waiter staff to prepare her tea just the way she likes it, specially brewed just for her for lunch and dinner. The only observation I have that might be considered constructive advice would be the employment of mostly Indian service staff in our part of the restaurant. Don't get me wrong, I've been to India, I enjoy Indian food and I don't have any issues with people from India. At times it felt more like we were dining in an Indian restaurant as opposed to a British dining experience. There was even an Indian dish, Chicken Tikka Masala, available on the menu. Although the dining room staff and the menus in Princess Grill were excellent, my expectations were for a quintessential British experience. If that is your expectation too, I would suggest you prepare for a more international experience. This is not a criticism, simply an observation.

The Spa - The Canyon Ranch Spa onboard the Queen Mary 2 was a very exclusive experience that few onboard seemed to take advantage of. The thermal pool, steam room and sauna facilities were exceptional, and my wife and I thoroughly enjoyed the facilities. The thermal pool area was never crowded and offered a very relaxing environment where my wife and I indulged in relaxation and water therapy. I didn't like the eucalyptus smell in the steam room too much, but that's just me, I prefer pure steam in a steam room.

The suite accommodations - We were in Suite 10032 which is in the Princess Grill accommodations. Queen Mary 2 is broken-up into three basic categories of accommodations, Britannia Restaurant, Princess Grill and Queens Grill. The Grill accommodations of course are much more exclusive and offer a more upscale experience. Some of the most lavish suites available at sea are in the Queens Grill accommodations. My wife and I were quite pleased with our Princess Grill accommodations. There was plenty of space, a walk-in closet and a bathroom with a tub. Our suite also had a veranda, a mini-bar area and vanity desk area. In the Grill accommodations our stewards also were available to pack our luggage at the end of our crossing, which my wife was very pleased with, since she dislikes packing.

The experience - I must be honest and mention that although this crossing on the Queen Mary 2 had tremendous meaning and was very relaxing, there was one element I felt was lacking that truly gave a crossing that unique

energy, and that was speed. Queen Mary 2 only reached a maximum speed of about 22 knots, which is not much different than what most cruise ships cruise at. As an example, when I worked aboard the QE2, she pounded across the Atlantic at about 28 knots, which generated a unique feeling of purpose and power. Queen Mary 2 has the capability to achieve up to about 30 knots, and she would need to power-up her gas turbine engines built by GE to reach these speeds, but today the ship is more of a destination rather than transportation, so the journey has been stretched out to seven days as oppose to four days at sea. The weather was agreeable for the entire crossing, so we hardly experienced the Queen Mary 2 in challenging north Atlantic seas. There were times when QM2 navigated through patches of fog, but that was about it. I was also very introspective when we crossed over the exact spot where Titanic sank one hundred years earlier. I noticed we spent a lot of time in the Grill restaurant socializing with our adjacent table-mates typical of lazy days at sea. Despite the fact that my wife drank a considerable amount of ice tea, she was still able to take leisurely naps nearly every day. For those who have traveled the world and perhaps may not have even considered a cruise, a Queen Mary 2 voyage across the Atlantic is truly a unique experience that is filled with romance, history, a long legacy and cultural tradition that is a must for anyone's bucket list.

Contrasted with the original Queen Mary - I chose to attend a college in southern California so that I could visit the original Queen Mary in Long Beach as often as possible. I worked on the QE2 so I have a unique level of experience with Cunard Line's history, her ships and the fascinating culture aboard an ocean liner, which is very different than the culture aboard a cruise ship. The Queen Mary 2, without question, has inherited this culture unique to ocean liner voyages. Like the original Queen Mary, the QM2 has tall ceilings, large rooms and lounges that have the art deco look. Wood veneers and paneling adorn the QM2 throughout her public spaces, and although the veneers and paneling have the faux replicated appearance of real wood, the feeling of palatial interiors fit for royalty is evident. Queen Mary 2 is a solid vessel, a workhorse with a solid steel construction unique to ocean liners of the past. As times have changed, gone is the "class" system from the days of the original Queen Mary, however; the QM2 still maintains three basic social and economic levels of passengers with the dominant Britannia Restaurant-level of accommodations, then there is the Princess Grill and Queens Grill which all have separate dinning areas.

This voyage from New York to Southampton, again had a very special meaning for me personally, and the experience came around full-circle, when Captain Chris Wells conducted a surprise wedding vow renewal ceremony for my wife and I as we celebrated fifteen years of marriage. At this time, Cunard can now offer weddings at sea onboard the Queen Mary 2 to fulfill the ultimate romantic setting for any couple with the desire to "tie the knot" in a unique and memorable way. I long for the environment onboard the Queen Mary 2, an environment that coddles me like being in the womb. I miss life aboard this ocean liner and you will too, once you experience this unique culture exclusive to a powerful and luxurious ship like the Queen Mary 2.

This is John, a passenger traveling with his mother in the Queens Grill-class. John was on the Queen Mary 2 trans-Atlantic crossing because he watched some of my videos filmed aboard the Queen Mary in Long Beach. My videos sparked his interest in the Queen Mary and eventually the Queen Mary 2. My wife and I were walking out of the library onboard QM2 in mid-Atlantic, and I heard John ask, " *Are you Barry, the guy who makes YouTube Videos*?" I said "*Yes*" and he said he was on this crossing because he watched my videos. It happens often, and my wife rolls her eyes, as people come up to me during a cruise and recognize me from the many cruise videos I have produced over the years.

Ruby Princess Has Heart – The Love Boat is Alive and Well

February 10th – 15th 2014 the Ruby Princess with Princess Cruises embarked on a unique mission to the Western Caribbean to support the American Heart Association. Onboard were leaders with the American Heart Association as well as a few celebrity speakers all gathering to bring attention to heart disease and an updated method of CPR that focuses more on getting the heart to start again after a heart attack. Senior Vice President & Chief Medical Officer with Princess Cruises, Dr. Grant Tarling was onboard to produce an event to educate passengers and crew about "hands only" CPR using the beat from the song Staying Alive sung by the Bee Gees. Among the celebrities onboard this special cruise was Chef Marc Anthony Bynum, Ary Nunez who is a celebrity trainer and fitness expert. Four-time Super Bowl champion Jesse Sapolu of the NFL San Francisco 49ers told us his story of heart surgery and football. The beloved actor from The Love Boat television series, Bernie Kopell, who played The Doc on the show, entertained passenger with a Q&A session. The entire cruise event was created to support the American Heart Association and educate passengers and crew about heart disease.

I've been on hundreds of cruises, produced many videos and audio podcasts, and I have taken thousands of photos on numerous cruises over the past fifteen years, however; this was my first cruise with Princess Cruises, so I want to present to you my perspective on this Cruise With Heart aboard the Ruby Princess. I must admit I had preconceived thoughts about Princess Cruises and their ships, based on many reviews and articles written over the years. I'm very pleased to say that my expectations were exceeded and I was very impressed with the Ruby Princess. The Princess Cruise's Love Boat brand certainly remains alive and well onboard, evident by the great level of service among the crew. The dining experience was excellent, and I enjoyed the cuisine and décor of the restaurants. It's interesting as a 'student of the cruise industry' to witness the early beginnings of cruise lines and how they've grown-up over the past twenty years. In my humble opinion, Princess Cruises has aged well.

The theme for this cruise was all about creating healthy habits to take care of your heart and to learn the 'Hands-Only' method of CPR which has saved countless lives over the years. Passengers enjoyed the seminars from celebrity experts and catching photo ops with television star Bernie Kopell and NFL 49'er Jesse Sabolu. For those who have been on many cruises, these themed cruise events can truly be a delight to vacation and learn valuable tips on daily living and health.

A very meaningful and special surprise from Captain Fabrizio Maresca and Dr. Grant Tarling, was when they honored Bernie Kopell for his role on The Love Boat, by giving him a promotion from a three stripe officer to a four

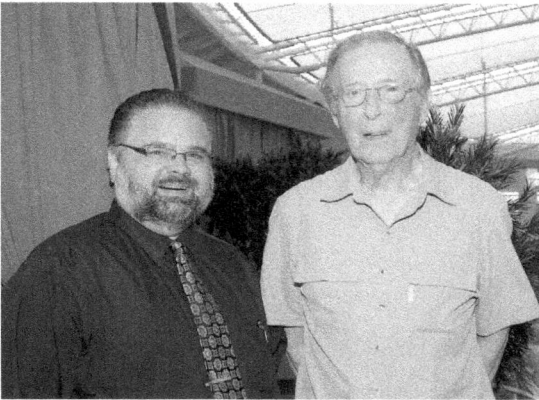

Bernie Kopell, actor from The Love Boat TV series

stripe commander for his years of service aboard The Love Boat and Princess Cruises from 1976 to present. In a short but sweet presentation in the Piazza atrium, Bernie Kopell was given a new officer blazer with four-stripes and a nametag acknowledging his nearly forty years of service. I'm going to continue writing about the massive impact The Love Boat television show had on the cruise industry, because I'm not sure it's too well known how significant this little TV show had on this multi-Billion dollar industry. I also planned ahead and through Cruising Authority, presented a Lifetime Achievement Award to Bernie Kopell. I'd like to give each of the main actors from The Love Boat, the same Lifetime Achievement Award, and hopefully soon, I will have that opportunity. For those of us that enjoy the cruise industry, we owe a great debt of gratitude for that TV show.

This particular voyage on the Ruby Princess was unique because it was a five-night cruise, allowing more people to experience a taste of Princess Cruises within five glorious days to the Western Caribbean ports of Grand Cayman and Cozumel. Typically, Princess Cruises operates longer voyages starting at seven nights and even ten to fourteen-day trips world-wide. I was thrilled to bring my wife on this cruise because it gave me an opportunity to take her to Grand Cayman, a port she had never been to. I chose the Stingray City and City Tour Excursion, which made stops at Hell, the Turtle Farm and then a boat ride out to the sandbar where Stingray City is. The weather was perfect; perfect water temperature, and perfect air temperature. The boat stops at the sandbar, and passengers jump into the beautiful water that is only waist deep, with perfect white sand, and stingrays swimming around our feet searching for a treat. Our guide took pictures of us holding the stingrays, feeding them, kissing them and we even got a back-rub from these strange sea creatures.

The next day, Ruby Princess took us to Cozumel where my wife and I embarked on a very unique and exhilarating excursion. Two world-class, America's Cup racing yachts, the American Stars & Stripes and the Canadian yacht True North. Each boat carried ten passengers that were all given jobs to drive the yachts, some tightened the main sail and some the forward sail, while others managed the ropes and even steered the boat. Both vessels

Incredible racing yacht excursion in Cozumel

competed in an actual race, so the passenger's felt the adrenaline as the wind swept these large sailing yachts across the sea at speeds of roughly ten to twelve knots. With the sea spray from the water splashing over the bow, the wind, and sound of the sails, this authentic race was very exciting and a lot of fun! I've been on a sail boat a number of times and I do know how to sail, but this was something special to operate and ride on this fine-tuned racing yacht!

Also unique to this cruise aboard Ruby Princess was that this particular cruise was during Valentines Day, perfect for couples to renew their vows and enjoy an incredibly romantic environment aboard The Love Boat. In the shops onboard I bought something special for my wife for Valentines day. I found a charm bracelet and picked out some meaningful charms that I knew my wife Terri would like. Of course the gift was a big hit; she loved it! So this cruise had many firsts...#1 first cruise with Princess Cruises, #2 first time cruising with my wife on Valentines Day, #3 first time my wife visited

Grand Cayman, and #4 first time on a racing yacht. My advice, make every effort to cruise with Princess Cruises, especially on Valentines Day!

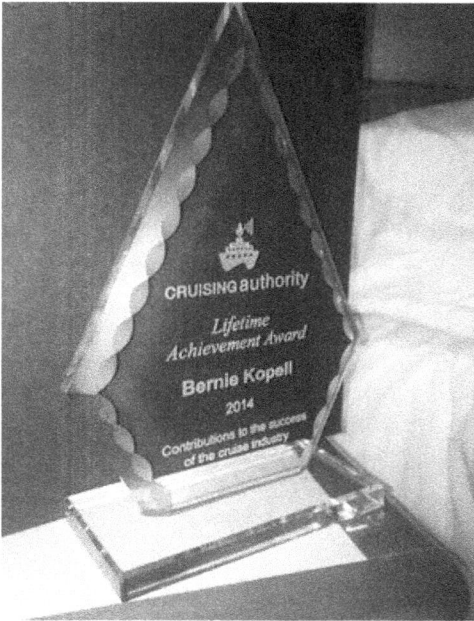

This is a Lifetime Achievement Award that Cruising Authority offered to Bernie Kopell for his contributions to the massive growth of the cruise industry from his role as The Doc, on The Love Boat TV series. It was a thrill to be able to present to Bernie this award. Most people have no idea the massive impact The Love Boat television show had on the growth of the cruise industry. I want to give this award to all of the original cast of The Love Boat, and I will, given the opportunity.

Quantum of the Seas Review

The World's third largest cruise ship, Royal Caribbean's Quantum of the Seas, arrives at the Bayonne Cape Liberty Cruise Terminal November 2014. Without question the incredible Quantum of the Seas is packed-full of technological wonders and innovations never before seen on a cruise ship. On a side note, you can build a cruise ship with high-tech gadgets, fantastic amenities, grand spaces, but without a highly skilled, friendly, service-oriented crew, that ship would just be a sterile thing to look at. The life-blood of the Quantum of the Seas is her incredible crew, in Royal Caribbean fashion, that exceeds the expectations of passengers every day.

Scheduled to be deployed to the Asian market in May of 2015, Quantum of the Seas will have a few months to WOW American passengers until sister ship Anthem of the Seas is launched into the market. The following are TWENTY incredible innovations introduced on the Quantum of the Seas:

ONE - NorthStar reaches 300 feet above the ocean for spectacular views.

TWO - Ripcord iFly allows passengers to simulate a sky diving experience

THREE – SeaPlex is an indoor room that has numerous uses including a basketball court, bumper cars, a disco and many other activities.

FOUR - 03B Network offers the fasted speed high-bandwidth internet WiFi connectivity ever seen on a cruise ship at sea. A low-orbiting satellite beams high-speed internet to the ship, so passengers can Skype, watch Netflix, stay in-touch on Facebook and keep up with email while at sea on vacation.

FIVE - Smart Art – throughout the Quantum of the Seas some of the artwork utilizes video, interactive and kinetic elements.

SIX - Smart Check-in is a feature that greatly improves check-in at the cruise terminal, allowing passengers to go from pier to ship in just a few minutes. Passengers arrive at the pier and are greeted by agents with iPads, ready to check in guests. After passengers check-in, then they go through security and then are issued electronic boarding passes. It's the smoothest, most efficient embarkation experience in the cruise industry.

SEVEN - Two70 is a new type of multi-purpose lounge with a unique, immersive experience, with a grand view of the ship's wake that stretches at 270 degrees across the back of the ship. Perhaps the most expensive and technologically advanced room ever constructed on a cruise ship, Two70 offers one-of-a-kind production shows with projected images and video on the giant glass wall, six Robotic one hundred inch screens enhance the visuals of the production shows. Performers are seen appearing through ceiling and floor openings in the staging. There's a gourmet restaurant, bar, library, all combined in this unique multi-purpose lounge that is busy day and night.

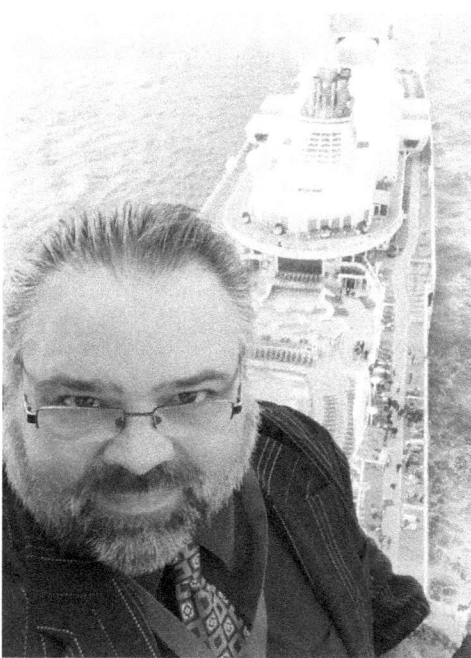

In The North Star 300 feet high

EIGHT - Robots at sea. Here's a first, now passengers can experience a robotic bartender at the Bionic Bar. The same type of robots seen on the production-line of a car factory, the Quantum of the Seas has the Bionic Bar and also utilizes robots to synchronized one-hundred-inch HD screens in the Two70 lounge for the production shows and other multi-media presentations.

NINE –The Royal iQ App for passengers allows passengers to customize their cruise vacation aboard the Quantum of the Seas...plan in advance activities and excursions before you board the ship and managed on your own phone with Royal Caribbean's iQ App.

TEN - RFID technology is wearable technology allowing passengers to enter their stateroom, purchase items onboard and book excursions with a unique rubber wrist-band electronic device worn like a watch.

ELEVEN - Dynamic Dining at sea. There are 18 different places to dine aboard the Quantum of the Seas offering more flexibility in dining than ever before. Times are changing, and no longer do you find one giant dining room on the Quantum of the Seas, rather, there are multiple dining rooms with different menus and décor, so passengers can choose where and when they dine. Most of the restaurants are included in the cruise fare, however; there are a few exclusive and unique dining options that have an extra charge....but the extra charge is worth every penny because of the celebrity chefs and the exclusive dynamic environment in the specialty restaurants.

TWELVE - The Loft Accommodations or suites are the largest at sea. First introduced on the Oasis of the Seas, the Loft Suites on the Quantum of the Seas are vast, with comfortable amenities and even concierge service.

THIRTEEN - Music Hall. There is usually lots of great music on a cruise ship, yet on the Quantum of the Seas, Royal Caribbean introduces a dedicated Music Hall just for live music and dancing.

FOURTEEN - Dreamworks Experience. Now families and kids can create special memories with their favorite Dreamworks characters like Shrek, Kung Fu Panda, the Penguins from Madagascar and more.

FIFTEEN - First wave-making pool at sea. Kids love to play in the water, and now on the Quantum of the Seas, they can experience fun in the sun in a wave-making pool.

SIXTEEN - Royal Theater Shows. Royal Caribbean introduces the full Broadway production of Mamma Mia. Sonic Odyssey and the Earth Harp is an immersive type of entertainment never seen on a cruise ship.

Passengers can feel the music of this amazing one-of-a-kind string instrument that stretches out above the audience.

SEVENTEEN - Lighting – Quantum of the Seas uses only LED or Fluorescent lights throughout the ship, saving energy.

EIGHTEEN - Quantum of the Seas is the first Royal Caribbean vessel to deploy a new and advanced full air lubrication system built into the ship's hull. This new system uses micro-bubbles to reduce the resistance between the ship's hull and the ocean, allowing the ship to be more fuel-efficient and even gain half a knot of speed.

NINETEEN - Silicone-based anti-fouling paint makes the ship's hull slippery as it passes through the ocean, allowing for more fuel-efficient operation.

TWENTY - Two giant stainless steel propellers and a podded system offers better fuel efficiency and optimized propulsion.

Quantum of the Seas is a One Billion Dollar vessel that is certain to WOW passengers for many years. There are of course more than twenty innovations on this incredible ship, but the ones listed in this article are some of the most notable.

Costa Mediterranea's Caribbean Review

Costa Cruises has recently positioned the Costa Mediterranea to cruise the Caribbean out of Miami on a seasonal basis, and vacationers are going to

truly enjoy, not only the Italian environment and culture onboard the ship, but also the unique itinerary. December 11th 2014, I had the great opportunity to sample the Costa Mediterranea shipboard lifestyle, and a fabulous itinerary, which includes: Nassau Bahamas, Samana Dominican Republic, Antigua Leewards Islands, Tortola British Virgin Islands, St Maarten Leewards Islands, Guadelupe Leewards Islands, and finally Freeport Bahamas. Having cruised all over the Caribbean, mostly Eastern & Western Caribbean, I had never been to most of the ports we visited. I've been to Nassau and St Maarten, but the other ports of call on this voyage were a treat to visit.

Some highlights and observations from these first-time visits are worth going into more detail. Samana, Domincan Republic was a delight to visit. With no pier for the giant Costa Mediterranea to dock, we tendered into this quaint village. There was a boardwalk that lined the crescent-shaped bay area with leisure and fishing boats anchored off-shore. Some locals were on the boardwalk area with shops filled with local crafts, nick-knacks and clothes items. Off in the distance and on a hill was a five-star resort called Gran Bahia Principe, and connecting several small islands were bridges for pedestrians. The locals have an interesting version of a rickshaw powered by motorcycle. I've seen rickshaws in India powered by a man pulling the cart, or perhaps a bicycle, but never a motorcycle. Facing the bay was a very colorful village of buildings, which looked more like a Hollywood set or façade, rather than practical buildings for businesses. I decided to walk to the resort on the hill and maybe walk out on the bridges that connect the islands. The resort access was strictly for guests only, however; I enjoyed the beautiful beach area before heading out onto the bridges. There were plenty of picturesque scenes to capture with my camera. I even came across some local boys jumping into the ocean from the middle of the bridge. The drop to the ocean was about forty feet so these boys were challenging their wits by leaping off the bridge into the ocean below, only to climb up and do it again. With Samana being our fourth day on the ship, I looked forward to the fifth day as we were in yet another port that was new to me, Tortola.

Again we tendered into the port of Tortola, where there was some construction work being done to lengthen and widen the cruise ship pier area. I spoke with April who works for the British Virgin Islands Port

My brother Paul's first cruise

Authority, and she told me they expect to have much of the pier expansion project complete by April 20th, 2015, and the land portion will be complete by the end of 2015. The land portion will include cultural shops, local bands, local shops and kiosks with local foods to try. It will be a complete

entertainment center for cruise passengers. Currently Tortola can accommodate two large ships at anchor, and one smaller ship at a pier, however; when the pier expansion is complete, four cruise ships should be able to dock right in town and at the entrance to the new cruise passengers entertainment center. Some highlights in Tortola for passengers to book excursions with include a canopy tour where people can zoom down a zip line. Another vary popular excursion is in Virgin Gorda, a short boat ride to a unique naturally formed bath area with caves to explore. From my short visit to Tortola, I noticed it was among the more clean and well-maintained towns.

Our next port was Antigua, which is in the Leeward Islands. Our ship, the Costa Mediterranea, docked in Antigua, and I was pleased to see several other cruise ships in port including the Thompson Celebration which is United Kingdom-based cruise ship with Thompson Cruises. This ship started out in 1984 as Holland America's Noordam. I walked several miles from the ship into town and noticed quite the contrast between the other ports we visited and the town of Antigua, which happened to be an older more run-down town. There was obviously more poverty in this town, and it is possible there had been one too many hurricanes that caused some devastation. The streets were narrow and very crowded with locals and the thousands of cruise passengers streaming into the city. I walked with my brother, Paul, to the top of the hill where an old church stood with a creepy, run-down graveyard you might expect to see as a typical haunted place. Some gravestones were tilted, or broken, or worn down to where you can barely read the inscriptions. Some gravestones read as far back as early 1800's. There seemed to be a project underway to restore the old church building, however; they have a lot of work to do because the structure looked like it was about to topple over.

On the seventh day of our eleven-night cruise aboard the Costa Mediterranea, we docked in Guadalupe, which is also in the Leeward Islands. This is a very French port where everyone spoke French. Even the layout of the streets and buildings resembled parts of Paris. The Euro was the form of currency in Guadalupe, and they did not accept U.S. dollars. There were plenty of ATM machines around town to acquire the Euro. Again, as a ship spotter, I noticed a very cool looking yacht docked at the end of the pier, it was a Russian

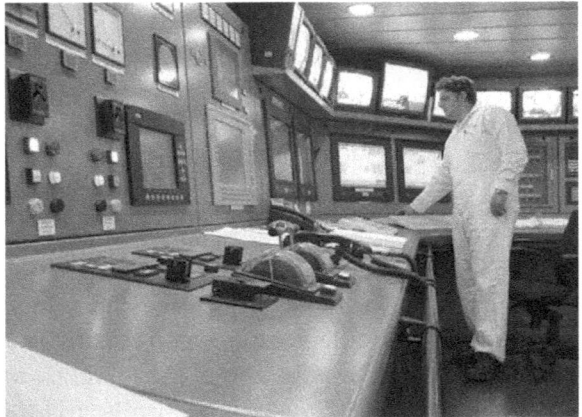
Control room deep inside the Costa Mediterranea

Billionaire's yacht that was in for some refurbishing. I found out this was a $300 million dollar superyacht, and at 400 feet long it's nearly the size of a small cruise ship and can reach speeds of up to 27 Knots. Ok, enough about the yacht and back to Guadalupe. I enjoyed walking through this town and peeking into the many shops. One observation is that you better not have to use the bathroom while exploring Guadalupe, because the only toilets require payment to use. Trying to use a restroom in a shopping market didn't go over too well, as we were turned away. So make sure you have some Euro coins in case you have a need to visit the toilet while in Guadalupe. There were nice open-air markets and excellent opportunities for shopping where you can buy unique spices. Like most big cities there are areas of poverty, and areas that are bit more upscale. Most of downtown Guadalupe, however; tended to lean more towards the poverty and middle-class citizens. I did notice many interesting vehicle brands that I didn't know existed, like SKODA and MEGANE, and I did see some typical French cars like: RENAULT, ALFA ROMEO, CITROEN and PEUGEOT.

Two other ports we visited during this eleven-night cruise include St Maarten, Nassau, Bahamas, and Freeport, Bahamas. I'm not going to write too much about these ports other than I noticed St Maarten is stepping up it's game to be a major cruise port. There were SIX giant cruise ships including the Costa Mediterranea, docked in St Maarten the day we were there. I estimate there could be as many as 19,000 tourists flooding into St Maarten in one day. Our group decided to visit the beach at the end of the runway to the airport, where jets fly within a few feet of beach goers. And when a big jet is about to take off and it revs it's engines, beachgoers will often be caught in the jet blast and sand will get blown all over the place. It's somewhat of a novelty to see this and beachgoers can be seen cheering on the big jets as the take off and land. I also notice that St Maarten has grown immensely since I had last visited the island only a few years ago. My brother, who has never cruised before and has never been to the Caribbean said he was impressed with St Maarten and could see himself vacationing there for a week or two.

Speaking of my brother, Paul, It was such a thrill for me to bring my brother on this cruise with me because it gave me an opportunity to get his perspective on his first-ever cruise vacation. Not only was this Paul's first cruise but it was his first time visiting the Caribbean. It was also a great chance for us to bond as brothers, since we truly don't often spend that much time together. Some of Paul's observations were that he liked the flexibility to relax and do nothing in our stateroom. Paul enjoyed spending time on our verandah watching the ocean and soaking in the sea air. Paul enjoyed the food onboard and the ability to explore multiple ports during one vacation. As much as he enjoyed the cruise, I don't think a cruise would be his first choice for the perfect vacation, but that was his personal feelings. I think Paul would rather go to St Maarten and stay for a week or two rather than embark on another cruise. Who knows one day I might be able to entice him on another cruise.

This was Costa Mediterranea's introduction to this seasonal itinerary, and so there may be a few tweaks here and there that might have to happen to appeal to the North American market. A few suggestions and observations I noticed during this eleven-night journey to the southern Caribbean aboard the Costa Mediterranea are as follows.

- No ice tea or juices were available during meal times or off-hours between meals
- You had to ask for special accommodation from your waiter to have water at meals
- Bacco Deck (boat deck) has no deck chairs for reading while at sea
- Lido Buffet was not organized well
- There were times when no food was available anywhere on the ship between meals
- Boat drill was lengthy
- Announcements were often made in numerous languages

Let me take each of these observations and expound on them a little. First, the fact that there was no ice tea or juices available anywhere on the ship, especially in the Lido buffet area. On every cruise ship I have been on there was always an assortment of juices and ice tea available 24 hours throughout the ship, particularly in the lido area, for that person who happens to be thirsty for something more than just water. It was odd that only water or coffee was available in the lido. One day I took my ice bucket from my stateroom and went to the lido to fill it with hot water, I grabbed some tea bags and sweetener and made my own ice tea in my stateroom. If the Costa Mediterranea is going to cater to the North American market, they must offer ice tea always and without cost. When I asked for ice tea in the dining room, the waiter asked for my sail & sign card, so I stopped him and asked what he needed that for....he said the ice tea was in a can or bottle and costs a few dollars. I cancelled my order for ice tea. At breakfast, lunch & dinner, the typical expectation at any restaurant is to have a nice glass of cold ice water at the table before a meal...not so on the Costa Mediterranea, guests must ask for water and must pay for bottled water, and it's an additional hurtle to ask for ice. I understand some of the cultural differences where in some places in Europe, water is not automatically offered, but this ship will be catering to the North American market so it is essential that water with ice is offered. A favorite past time while cruising at sea, for a hundred years, has been to sit in a deck chair on a deck near the ocean, and enjoy a good book to read, away from the masses by the pool decks. Passengers love to walk the deck, do their laps, stand at the railing and watch the sea go by and even snuggle into a deckchair with maybe a blanket and enjoy the sea air. This is not possible on the Costa Mediterranea because the Bacco Deck or (boat deck) has no deck chairs or chairs of any kind on this deck. When asked about why this is so, the response was because it was under the lifeboats, it was a possible safety issue, however; many ships in the same "Spirit-Class" hulls do indeed have deck chairs in this area.

The Lido buffet area was often crowded and a bit confusing as to where certain entrees were located. The quality of the food was ok in the Lido area, except for the pizza, which is a HUGE surprise considering we were on an Italian cruise ship. The pizza was bland and often doughy. Another observation about the Lido buffet area is watch out for closing time, because in a flash, all food-serving locations in the Lido would shut down quickly, and if you're hungry, you're out of luck, and must wait till your next designated feeding time. Never have I experienced a cruise ship that shut down all access to food so abruptly. Usually there is a grill that is opened longer somewhere on the ship, but not on the Costa Mediterranea. Boat drill lasted a long time, primarily because there were so many languages that had to be considered. On our cruise there were French, Italians, Germans, Dutch and some Scandinavians, as well as a few hundred Americans. So anytime there were announcements, expect the same announcement in at least three or four different languages. It's not a bad thing, you get use to hearing the many different languages, and you might even learn how to speak Italian.

Now for some positive things to say about this cruise aboard the Costa Mediterranea. The ship is well maintained and very clean on the inside and outside. Maritime designer Joseph Farcus, who also designed the interiors for most of the Carnival Cruise Line's ships, designed the interior of the Costa Mediterranea. I have to say that the interior designs were not my favorite and the main lobby was so splashed with many different colors and shapes it made me dizzy. It was a very eclectic and unusual design that I must admit grew on me after about day ten. I did notice on the Tersicore Deck forward was the Piazza Casanova lounge, which had a rather large dance floor and usually a live band playing. So for those who love to dance this lounge is the place to be. There are a few other quaint spots for dancing with a live band, and two excellent piano bars. The main lobby bar, (Atrium Maschera D'argento) has an outstanding singer that burns the keyboards with many favorite pop songs.

Dinning onboard the Costa Mediterranea was excellent with an Italian flare. Emanuele Canepa, the Executive Chef onboard the Costa Mediterranea, says the galley has seven fresh made-from-scratch-on-board pastas and ten dry pastas, so anticipate a glorious gastronomic experience that includes pasta at nearly every meal. It's truly a cultural experience alone to enjoy the expansive menu of wonderful pastas, fish dishes, chicken, pork, beef and vegetables. One absolute must is to experience at least one time during your cruise is to make a reservation in the specialty restaurant on Cleopatra

Deck called Club Madusa. It's in this specialty restaurant where the chefs have more flexibility to be creative and use mostly fresh, made from scratch, ingredients with larger portions and the best cuts of meats. Diners in Club Madusa will enjoy a pianist playing lightly in the background, and an interesting fresco painting on the ceiling dome. The Club Madusa restaurant is connected to the deck below with a signature glass staircase that sticks out over the top of the Atrium with a scary view ten deck below. Most of the "Spirit-class" vessels have this same staircase with glass steps, so beware if you have a fear of heights. My favorite main-course dish throughout this cruise was the sword fish steak served in the main Argentieri Restaurant.

It was fascinating to learn that the Cruise Staff are actually called the "Adult Animators" meaning they encourage the passengers to participate in various activities. The staff also has Youth and Children Animators. This is a term that translates in English to Cruise or Entertainment Staff. The shows in the Osiris Theater were excellent with a wide range of Chinese acrobats to a magician, singers and dancers.

Our Stateroom was 6238 on Narciso Deck, a standard verandah stateroom. The room was compact and maybe even a bit on the small side. Beds were comfortable and the room was quiet. There a couch and a vanity and a flat-screen television hooked into the ship's satellite, so occasionally the TV service was spotty. Movies were broadcast in several languages. The bathroom was compact and the shower had decent water pressure. We absolutely adored our cabin stewardess, she did an incredible job keeping our room clean and organized. The favorite feature in our stateroom was the verandah, where we would spend a lot of time watching the ocean and it was a great spot to watch as the ship arrives and departs a port.

One of my favorite things to do on a cruise is luxuriate in the spa, and the Ischia Spa on the Costa Mediterranea was no exception. I enjoyed the wonderful steam room and sauna. The exercise room had plenty of treadmills and workout equipment to stay fit during your cruise. The spa manager's name is Elvis and he keeps a tight ship with great service. I desperately needed a haircut, so I made an appointment in the Venus Beauty Salon. One thing to take note of when cruising, most ships in the cruise industry are operated by Steiners of London, and they provide an incredible menu of exotic massages and skin treatments. Don't miss out on the opportunity to indulge in a massage or get a skin treatment, a facial, a body-wrap, there are so many great services to try. The products they offer onboard, like Elemis, are excellent and you can even bring your spa experience home with you by ordering your Elemis products online and have them shipped to your home address.

Overall, this eleven-night cruise to the Caribbean aboard the Costa Mediterranea was a hit, especially the itinerary. Expect a cultural experience with many Europeans flying over from Europe to cruise the Caribbean. You'll have to get use to some of the customs and sometime lack of understanding when it comes to standing in lines. Many Europeans don't understand the concept of Quing....it's a matter of survival of the fittest when it comes to lines. My advice is to take a deep breath, relax, and don't let the little cultural idiosyncrasies bother you. The staff onboard were professional, the children will enjoy the entertainment and youth areas, especially the giant twisty-slide on the top of the ship. The Costa Mediterranea will be cruising the Caribbean seasonally through May of 2015.

Above left: Our ship, the Costa Mediterranea at anchor in Samana

Above right: An example of a high-occupancy mass-market cruise ship with hundreds of passengers enjoying a show performed by the wait-staff.

Voyage with an Old Friend – A Greek Cruise

I embarked on my first journey to Greece and Turkey yet the anticipation and thrill of this trip stirred my passion for travel by meeting up with an old friend and reminiscing of fond memories of the past. There were new experiences mixed with an encounter with a ship that I used to work on in 1989 with Royal Caribbean aboard the Song of America. Today with Celestyal Cruises, the same ship from my past is now called the Celestyal Olympia. Celestyal Cruises has truly refurbished and rejuvenated this ship like she was new again. My expectations were that the ship would be tired and run-down after 27 years since I was last onboard, however; I was thrilled to see this ship again and that she has been updated and taken care of so well by her new owners. This vessel has changed hands a few times and has had several names, starting with Song of America, then she was the Thomson Destiny, then the Sunbird, Louis Olympia, and now Celestyal Olympia, a fitting name for this cozy and well-maintained ship. My experience onboard was truly like seeing an old friend again after many years. The Can Can Lounge is now Muses Lounge, freshened-up with a new color scheme and a slightly modified stage. I recall a lip that came out from under the stage to extend out closer to the audience. Of course in her Royal Caribbean days the Song of America had Scandinavian imagery throughout the corridors and stairwells, these have all been changed to show her new Greek heritage. The Oaklahoma Lounge aft, now the Selene Lounge, still has the orange carpet and look, with subtle modifications to relocate the band aft, rather than in the middle of the room. The Viking Crown lounge is now the Thalassa Bar and is still under-used...passengers just don't seem to know how to get to this unique lounge that surrounds the funnel. There are new staterooms that have verandas, which is a nice touch, however; these new staterooms do not distract from her fine lines. Celestyal Olympia is a fitting name for this cozy, comfortable, and well-maintained vessel.

Celestyal Olympia at Sea

Celestyal logo on the side of the ship

Celestyal Cruises has dispatched the Celestyal Olympia on some unique cruise itineraries that reach out to Greek ports that are truly enchanting, with a stop in Kusadasi, Turkey, which mixes it up a bit. For those who prefer to experience a port intensive cruise, Celestyal Cruises offers a great experience with an emphasis on "intensive". The cruise I was on visited two ports a day, which was unlike any cruise I have ever been on. The following are my comments on the ports and excursions I experienced. The first day we departed Athens, Greece or Piraeus. And after cruising for a few hours we arrived in Mykonos, which took me by surprise. Mykonos was a jet-set, upscale, Newport Beach-like port that attracted the very wealthy, and the "high-brow" vacationer. With a guide, we did a walking tour of Mykonos, and saw the famous windmills by the sea, and the white-washed buildings, ending with a fabulous dinner in a local restaurant at sunset, which was spectacular!

Our Next port the next morning was Kusadasi, Turkey, where we explored the ancient city of Ephesis from biblical times. John, from the bible, preached in every corner of Ephesis, which is where the book of Ephesians came from. The ruins of Ephesis was spectacular, particularly the main road in Ephesis, which made it's way down a hill, and to the library and the massive odeon theater which could accommodate up to 20,000 people at one time. Upon our departure of Kusadasi, we cruised to the port of Patmos, Greece, where John was imprisoned for 18 months. Of course there were monasteries and shrines built around the visit of John in Patmos particularly a monastery built around the very spot in a cave where John lived and had his revelation from God. It was a cave, now called, the Holy Grotto of the Revelation, that had several very specific spots where John wrote his portion of the Bible and where he laid his head and even a spot where he pulled himself up from a sitting position. Apparently, when John had his "experience" with God Almighty, there was a split in the rocks above him where there were three cracks in the rock. The three cracks represented God the Father, Jesus, and the Holy Spirit. It was in this spot that John had a vision of God the Father, and the very spot where he wrote his portion of

the Bible. Higher-up on the hill in Patmos, was the Monastery of St. John, that was constructed in 1,000 BC, by a monk named, Christodolous , in homage to Saint John. It was in this hill-top monastery that I had a discussion with a monk about the relics and the root of his faith which was Greek Orthodox. This monk was very knowledgeable about the Greek Orthodox faith and why it is different from the Catholic faith. I was particularly privileged to be taken into a secret chamber where the monk revealed in a glass case, three links of chains that were allegedly used to chain John when he was exiled and taken to the island of Patmos, and in a silver cross, there was a small glass case that enshrined a piece of the cross that Jesus was crucified on. The Catholic and Greek orthodox faith seem to revere ancient relics that are tied to Jesus and his crucifixion. It was an exhausting day experiencing two ports, but our dinner onboard the Celestyal Olympia was exquisite. Every evening that we had dinner onboard the Celestyal Olympia was wonderful with tempting, local, Greek Cuisine. My initial expectations of Greek cuisine, was not favorable, but the options presented on the ship were very tasty! The Celestyal Olympia cruised throughout the evening and the next morning we were in Rhodes, Greece. I was particularly fascinated by the story of the Colossus of Rhodes, which is an ancient wonder of the world. Apparently, the location of this Colossus statue is not so well understood. The original thoughts were that this massive one hundred foot, copper statue was built with his legs above the entrance to the port, so ships had to pass under the statue's legs.

The massive statue also held a pot of fire either in his hand stretched-out, or in his hand above his head. The fire was sort of a light-house effect for ships entering the port.

Our guide seemed to think that the statue was not at the entrance of the port, but rather, in the location of a palace that was destroyed and then re-built, or on the top of a higher hill that had an Apollo temple. Local archeologists seem to think that the giant statue was most-likely in the location of the palace near the port, because legends state that when the earthquake toppled the statue, it fell on many homes or buildings at the base of the statue, so if it toppled from a location over the entrance to the port this would not be possible. Also, our guide said there was a slab of stone under the palace, that could possibly be the stone, which the statue was constructed on top. Speculation of exactly where the giant Colossus of Rhodes stood is not defined, but the historical relevance to the city of Rhodes is another fascinating tale. As a tour-group we had a magnificent dinner in a local restaurant, Nikies Place, and I think I enjoyed the best swordfish steak I have ever encountered in this restaurant. It was in this port that I had the great privilege to visit another ship in the Celestyal fleet of two

Celestyal Crystal sister ship

ships, the Celestyal Crystal. The story of the Celestyal Crystal is interesting as it was cruising the Greek islands this season, then off to be permanently positioned on the Jamaica to Cuba itinerary. After our visit to Rhodes, the Celestyal Olympia

was off to Crete, Greece, the next morning, where we visited more ruins. I was thrilled to be on the bridge of the Celestyal Olympia during our departure from Crete. I was truly fascinated to discover that there was no need, apparently, for a harbor pilot to be present during our departure. I watched as the captain masterfully maneuvered the ship out of the port and out to sea.

After a short visit to Crete, the Celestyal Olympia embarked on it's journey to the mythical, magical destination of Santorini. The ship arrived in the location of Santorini along with two other cruise ships, the Celebrity Reflection and the Seabourn Odyssey. This port is too deep to anchor so the ships simply floated in position during it's visit. Santorini was on my bucket list of places to experience, and it was no surprise that it was a very unique and special place to see. Unfortunately during our visit it was very hazy, so the spectacular views were muted just a bit. I could still see how majestic it would be, regardless of the haze. We did encounter a fabulous

sunset in Santorini and everyone in our group was very pleased with the view. What I found particularly interesting about Santorini was the history with the earthquakes and volcanic eruption that shook the town to it's core in the 1950's. Centuries ago, there was a massive volcanic eruption that shaped the landscape and formed the unique island formations. The volcano is still active and it still produces heat from within, and I was told that there are some fascinating hot-springs on the volcanic island that bathers can experience a very unique detoxifying experience. The city is on the top rim of the island, and the scenery of the ships below is breathtaking. After viewing the beautiful sunset in Santorini, we took a tram to the base of the mountain and then embarked on the tender to the ship.

For me the highlight of this cruise-tour was the ship and the ports. The itinerary was very port intensive, where we nearly had two ports a day throughout the duration of the cruise. The operative word is "intensive", because, as fascinating each port was, it was also exhausting, and the cozy Celestyal Olympia was the perfect host for this compact voyage. I cannot say enough how much I enjoyed the Celestyal Olympia. Not only was it a special ship for me to be reunited with, I was impressed by the Celestyal Cruises brand. The crew was multi-cultural, not specifically Greek. This was a happy ship, as the crew seemed to truly enjoy their job on the ship. The entertainment onboard was uniquely Greek with an interesting show featuring an Actress and Actor singing and acting out a love story with only the sounds of percussion instruments played by only one man. With stage lighting, a little atmosphere fog, dancing and singing, a mythical Greek story was brought to life. The ship was kept in pristine condition. I watched as workers were on their hands and knees sanding the teak decking, which is the same as it was as the Song of America. The ship is under continual refurbishment, and it was evident when you look closely at the railings or the hull, to see many coats of paint that have preserved the original elegance.

The service among the crew was top-notch, and I would compare service onboard to above mass-market standards. I was truly impressed with the Celestyal Cruises brand and think that there is tremendous opportunity for this cruise line to be the best choice for a trustworthy, Greek cruise adventure. Do not hesitate to book passage with Celestyal Cruises, for the most intimate, and culturally-inclusive, Greek cruise experience.

All voyages like this must come to an end, and our journey concluded in Athens, Greece. Celestyal Cruises also has a great city-tour excursion of Athens, which included the magnificent tour of the great Acropolis and the Acropolis museum, which is a must-see when visiting Athens. As expected, with a monumental sight as the Acropolis, there were thousands of tourists there to see the great, ancient, structures.

Your cruise-tour with Celestyal Cruises should begin and end with at least a one-night hotel stay, so that you can acclimate yourself with the time-change from the states. Find a four to seven-night cruise combined with hotel stays before and after your cruise to enjoy the best experience.

Song of America 1989

Celestyal Olympia in 2016

Wondrous Great Lakes Cruising with Victory Cruise Lines

Hugging the boarders of Canada and the United States is a bountiful series of fresh-water lakes that have a rich history in maritime cargo, commerce and the occasional passenger vessel. Ships navigate the many lakes, rivers, locks and a seaway that leads out to the Atlantic. Connecting Michigan with Wisconsin and Hwy 10, is a coal-burning steam ship that has been ferrying cars and people since the 50's. Giant, one thousand foot tankers, can be seen cruising out of Duluth and Detroit to Montreal and beyond. The Saint Lawrence Seaway is the escape-route from the Great Lakes to the open Atlantic Ocean. Comparable with the Norwegian coastal terrain without the mountains and perhaps the rivers, lakes and locks that cross Sweden, the Great Lakes of North America offers a charm and beauty that's unique to this part of the world. Launched in July of 2016, Victory Cruise Lines connects passengers with grace, style, and luxury to fascinating cultures from the Ojibwe people to the Victorian-era Grand Hotel on Mackinac Island, and the industrious port of Windsor and Detroit. Passengers can embark on memorable seasonal voyages throughout the Great Lakes during the summer months and out of Miami to Cuba in the winter.

Built in Jacksonville, Florida in 1999 as the Cape May Light, the three hundred foot long, 210 passenger, Victory I, was designed for coastal cruising. The vessel has had several names over the years including, Sea Voyager and Saint Laurent. In 2010 the ship was given a U.S. registry, and then in

Seascape Tavern Deck Two

2011 her registration was changed to the Bahamas. With 81 crew members, Victory I coddle her passengers with superb service and style that is often found on luxury ships. It doesn't take long for passengers to explore the ship with the Shearwater Dining Room on Deck One, the Compass Lounge and Seascape Tavern, Purser's Office and Salon are on Deck Two. The majority of staterooms are on Decks Three and Four. The Cliff Rock Bar & Grille is also on Deck Four aft. Finally, Deck Five is perfect for reading a good book in a deck chair and watching the Great Lakes scenery float by.

Victory Cruise Lines has developed nearly un-tapped itinerary options by cruising the Great Lakes in the Summer and Miami to Cuba in the Winter. A Great Lakes ten day itinerary includes a departure from Montreal Canada, a day at sea through the Saint Lawrence Seaway, Port Weller, (Niagara Falls), then Windsor Ontario, Lake Huron, Little Current, Sault Ste. Marie, Mackinac Island, cruising Lake Michigan before arriving into Chicago. Each port was carefully crafted to offer the best of the Great Lakes. Each port has it's own unique immersive excursion experience. Our first excursion took us to Niagara Falls, an epic excursion on the Hornblower right into the

wake of the massive waterfalls. Everyone is given a red raincoat for protection from the spray of the waterfalls. After an invigorating visit to Niagara Falls, our Victoria I excursion bus took us to the Chateau Des Charmes winery, where we had a tour of the place before enjoying a delightful lunch. Our visit to Port Weller began with tour buses awaiting us next to the Victory I , to take us to the Henry

Niagra Falls

Ford Museum in Detroit. The Ford museum was packed full of fascinating items from the car JFK was shot in, a full-size DC3 aircraft, a replica of the

Wright Brothers airplane, and the chair that President Lincoln was shot in the Ford Theatre. The massive museum building had hundreds of interesting items from history. Crossing the border of Canada and Michigan was simple. Apparently the tunnel and bridge that cross back and forth from Windsor to Michigan is one of the most busy border crossings in the USA. Even on a Great Lakes Cruise, we enjoy a day at sea cruising Lake Huron. Our next port adventure took us to Little Current, where we visited the Ojibwe Cultural Foundation. Our tour group saw up-close and personal, a traditional Ojibwe dance lead by the beating of a drum. The next port was

Sault Ste. Marie, where we crossed the gangway of the Valley Camp museum ship originally launched in 1917. The Valley Camp is a tanker that served on the Great Lakes for nearly 50 years. Inside the tanker was a collection of fascinating artifacts that told the story of the Great Lakes, including a lifeboat from the Edmond Fitzgerald that was beaten up pretty bad. Finally, the Victory I docked at Mackinac Island, where passengers boarded a horse-powered carriage for a tour of the Island. Our tour concluded with a fabulous lunch in the Grand Hotel. This hotel was constructed in 1887 and was truly like stepping back in time. The Christopher Reeve and Jane Seymour movie, Somewhere in Time was filmed at the hotel in 1980. The Grand Hotel hosted five U.S.

presidents and even Thomas Edison and Mark Twain.

Life onboard the Victory I is relaxing with a slower pace than most cruise ships. Veteran Cruise Director Michael Crowe brings a classic approach to entertaining passengers, with classic games of Bingo, the newlywed, not so newlywed game and trivia. What's particularly interesting about the Newlywed game is that the average age of passengers was about 80, so it was more like the "Not So Newlywed Game". Attendance was excellent for the informative lectures about the era of prohibition where alcohol was banned, and an esteemed geologist talked about the Great Lakes area and a geologic history. When

the Victory I is at sea or passengers return from a world-class excursion, the perfect place for a short nap is in one of the 105 staterooms. The average size of the staterooms are around 160 square feet, but don't let the smaller size distract you from the fact that the beds and linens are extraordinarily comfortable. Staterooms on Deck Four open-up to an outside deck area.

The Shearwater Dining Room on Deck One was a favorite gathering place for passengers because the daily menu was exquisite. The best seats in the restaurant were next to the large picture windows. Waiters made an effort to remember your name and some of your preferences. The true evidence of a luxury cruise can be found in the quality of the menu and the consistently excellent taste of the cuisine by a master chef. Passengers also have the option to dine on deck at the Cliff Rock Bar & Grille. Reservations are suggested because there is limited seating in the outdoor restaurant. The specialty on the menu is the Hot Rock cooking, where diners can cook their own steak or fish on an authentic volcanic lava hot rock.

Small ship luxury cruising has a new ship and a new cruise line for adventurers to consider, the Victory I with Victory Cruise Lines. The entire crew from the Captain to the waiter are seasoned professionals, and many came from working on the bigger cruise ships. Victory I is a "happy" ship which is reflected by the crew, who love their job. Michael Crowe, the Cruise Director, said something worth repeating, "There are good ships and bad ships, but it's the friendships that really count". When booking a Victory Cruise Lines journey, whether cruising the Great Lakes or Cuba, passengers will experience a crew eager to serve with a smile. What makes a Great Lakes cruise "wondrous"… the ship, it's fabulous crew, the fascinating ports and excursions, the all-inclusive element and the delightful cuisine, all found onboard the Victory I.

Full-size DC3 from North Central Airlines

Oiibwe Cultural Foundation

Cuisine was of exceptional quality

One of the many fascinating Locks

The following is an example of the podcasts and interviews that can be found on the Cruising Authority website.

Liberty of the Seas, Virtual Cruise Experience was recorded into five episodes in May and June of 2008. I took my family on a seven day cruise aboard the Liberty of the Seas, and produced a five-episode series of audio interviews and commentary which can still be listened to in our podcast audio library.

In July of 2009, I took my family on an Alaska cruise aboard Regent Seven Seas Mariner, and I recorded three audio episodes and several videos. One epic experience we had was a helicopter ride to the top of a glacier where we experienced a two-mile dog sled run.

Check our audio library for this September 2009 three-part episode recorded during a Yangtze River cruise aboard Viking River Cruises. I must say that this trip to China was among the most memorable and epic adventures my wife and I have had the opportunity to experience.

Starting in October of 2010 is a three-part series of podcasts from our Hurtigruten voyage along the coast of Norway. This was another very unique cruise / travel experience where my wife and I stayed in the most beautiful village called Reine, Lofoten.

January 2008 is an interview with Carol Marlow, President of Cunard Line at the time.

March 2008 is an interview with Bob Dickinson, retired President of Carnival Cruise Lines

April 2008 is an interview with Bruce Nierenberg a long-time cruise industry executive.

January 2009 is an interview with Dan Hanrahan who was President of Celebrity Cruises.

November 2008 is an interview with Vicki Freed and Executive at Royal Caribbean.

April 2009 is an interview with Rick Sasso, President at MSC Cruises.

April 2009 is an interview with Maurice Zarmati, President of Costa Cruises.

January 2008 is an interview with Peter Knego who is a collector of ocean liner art.

January 2008 is an interview with John Maxtone-Graham, ocean liner author & historian.

February 2008 is an interview with Bill Miller, ocean liner historian and author.

December 2008 is an interview with Douglas Ward, author of Berlitz Guide to Cruises.

August 2010 is an interview with Jeraldine Saunders, author creator of The Love Boat.

April 2008 is an interview with Susan Gibbs, Grand Daughter of William Francis Gibbs.

May 2008 is an interview with Joseph Farcus, maritime architect at Carnival Cruise Line.

May 2008 is an interview with actor Gavin MacLeod who played Captain Stubbing.

December 2010 is an interview with Actor Bernie Kopell who played "The Doc".

September 2008 is a podcast about Static Ships.

November 2008 we discuss the SS Norway

May 2009 we hear the actual whistle from the Titanic being blown.

On the Cruising Authority website is an audio library of about 166 audio podcasts from late 2007 to 2016 with numerous interviews and cruise ship reviews. There are also a few episodes that feature cruise-related music. Visit our website and the Cruising Authority library of podcasts and find a topic that interests you.

Final Thoughts and the Conclusion

My life revolves around the cruise industry. There are hundreds of cruise options out there to choose from and everyone has their own reason for choosing a cruise as their vacation. After having been on numerous cruises around the world, I am now seeking to choose far out destinations that I have not experienced yet. On my bucket list is a cruise to Antarctica, however; my wife doesn't find that itinerary particularly desirable because she doesn't like the cold. The Holy Land is also of great interest to me. I'd like to do more river cruises, perhaps to Russia and France. South America would be interesting and it's amazing, but I have never been on a cruise through the Panama Canal. Australia and New Zealand is also on the table, so yes, I have been on a lot of cruises, but the there are still numerous destinations and cruise lines I would love to experience, write about and produce video reviews.

Recently a new cruise line has emerged under the Carnival Corporation banner called Fathom, and this cruise line will be the first major U.S. based cruise line to visit Cuba on a regular basis. I attended a Fathom event in the Dominican Republic and what makes Fathom unique is that they offer what is called Impact Travel excursions for passengers to build water filters, plant trees, help entrepreneurial women at a chocolate factory and help elementary school children to work on their conversational English. Fathom is tapping into the humanitarian concept geared for vacationers to reach out to the needy in third-world countries and make a positive difference in the local communities.

Before they are all gone, I'd like to cruise on some classic ocean liners that are still in service. The Marco Polo is a vessel I'd like to cruise on before she is removed from service. Marco Polo has a classic ocean liner hull and although remodeled, it would be like travelling back in time. I have already lived out most of my wildest dreams by cruising onboard the SS Norway / ex-France, and I had the great opportunity to work aboard the QE2, which was a dream come true. I cruised on some other older ships like the Azure Seas and the Caribe I, which became the Regal Empress. Of course I was able to cross the Atlantic on the Queen Mary 2, a true modern ocean liner.

This past year we lost a great maritime historian and author John Maxtone-Graham. I was a huge fan of his writing and John was very gracious to invite me into his home in New York to interview him. I was able to call John Maxtone-Graham a friend, and his passing leaves a hole in the hearts of many who continue to read his books. There are still a few of his books I need to purchase to complete my collection of his work. I created a website called The Cruise Channel and on that website I had a section called The John Maxtone-Graham Liner & Cruise Historical Society, and I was going to collaborate with John on this project, so now I'm not sure what I'm going to do with that concept of a society of members who love to research and study the history of ocean liners and cruise ships.

Another man I was thrilled to meet was Gavin MacLeod who played Captain Stubbing on The Love Boat television show. I met with Gavin onboard the Queen Mary in Long Beach to interview him about a movie he was in called

The Secrets of Jonathan Sperry. I also interviewed him in his role as the Ambassador of Princess Cruises. Growing up I watched The Love Boat television show, so of course it was an incredible privilege to meet with Gavin and interview him. Unfortunately, he was in a lot of pain at the time from an infection in his back, but he was so gracious and it was obvious he enjoyed talking about The Love Boat days and his role at Princess Cruises. For many Love Boat fans, the very first episode of The Love Boat was filmed in-part on the Queen Mary in Long Beach, so to meet with Gavin and walk with him on the Promenade Deck and reminisce with him about when that first episode was filmed on the Queen Mary. Gavin was in pain, so with my arm around his arm, assisting him in the long walk aft to the Verandah Grill area was a very special moment for me. I so respected this man, not only as an actor, but a man with a strong Christian faith. When we said goodbye, he kissed me on the cheek....a genuine, Godly man that I respect.

I'm trying to wrap this book up, but there is so much more that I'd like to share. There have been so many memorable experiences, and fascinating people I've been able to meet because of Cruising Authority the talk show. I'd like to mention that it has truly been a pleasure to meet other journalists who do kind of the same thing I do. I've met up with Ralph Grizzle a few times, he operates the Avid Cruiser blog. Ralph has quite the gig, he seems to travel mostly on the luxury upscale ships, something that I aspire to. I've cruised with Peter Knego a few times. Peter has a very interesting story....he make pilgrimages to Alang India to visit ships about to be scrapped. Peter then, purchases artwork, paneling, chairs, couches, fixtures and items from these ships to preserve their history and offer these fittings for sale when he gets home in southern California. Peter ships containers from India to his home in California and then keeps these items in storage. You can see a picture of Peter Knego in my article about the Nieuw Amsterdam. Another man I see often on the ships is the Host of

Doug Parker with Cruise Radio

Cruise Radio, Mr. Doug Parker. We have had a blast cruising on the same ships and even going on shore excursions together. Doug is fun to travel with, and I hope we have many more opportunities to cruise together. It's a funny story...I was cruising on the Silver Spirit and after the cruise heading home out of Barcelona, I was going up the escalator and this guy calls out my name and says, "Hey you're Barry Vaudrin". It was Doug Parker finishing up a cruise on a Carnival ship and heading home. Since first meeting Doug in Barcelona, we have cruised Alaska and with Costa and the Poesia. He has a great show too called Cruise Radio at cruiseradio.net.

It is my sincere desire that those who read my book enjoy the stories, the cruise reviews and some of the tips on cruising like a pro. Thank you for purchasing this book! I have poured everything I have into writing this book...it has taken me three years to write it, so I hope it is worth-while for you and that you enjoyed reading it as much as I have enjoyed writing it. Some people that follow my articles, videos and podcasts tell me they live vicariously through my work, and so now readers can take this book on their next cruise and read all about the adventures and cruise stories I have to share. As I say on my shows, I want to wish you Smooth Seas!

Here are two "coupons" that will make this book more affordable to anyone, exclusively for those who purchase this book.

www.ingramcontent.com/pod-product-compliance
Lightning Source LLC
Chambersburg PA
CBHW030415100426
42812CB00028B/2976/J